IN THE TIGER'S SHADOW

The Autobiography of an Ambedkarite

NAMDEO NIMGADE

In The Tiger's Shadow: The Autobiography of an Ambedkarite
Namdeo Nimgade
ISBN 9788189059309

This edition is published in 2024 on the occasion of 20 years of Navayana as part of the EVERBLUE series.

Navayana Publishing Pvt Ltd
155 2nd Floor
Shahpur Jat, New Delhi 110049
navayana.org

Printed by Saksham Enterprises, Delhi
Distributed in South Asia by HarperCollins India
Subscribe to updates at navayana.org/subscribe

Foreword

There are many tigers in Namdeo Nimgade's India. Some spring from dense undergrowth deep in the jungle, leaving few remains for kinfolk to bury. Others attack their neighbors in the village—because the neighbors are "low" caste or untouchable or sympathize with the lowly and the ritually impure. Heroic tigers marched the streets of Nagpur, Bombay and Delhi in the decades before Independence, agitating for freedom from the British, the annihilation of caste, and access to education, jobs, and dignity. Others crouch in the cubicles and hallways of bureaucratic India, then and now, awaiting their political prey—old rivals at the ballot box and their new nemesis, the ferocious activists for a new society in which all citizens of the Republic are created equal.

Nimgade is a tiger for change. Rising from the dust of Sathgaon, a remote village of subsistence farmers, Namdeo tended cattle while children of greater privilege attended school. As a mahar, a member of an untouchable caste of servants, he shared a hut with his family of fifteen and went without food when work was scarce. Only when the bullocks he was tending bolted into nearby fields one day, resulting in a brutal beating from the owner of the fields, did his family allow him to begin his education at age fourteen. Now he faced the rigors that united untouchable students throughout India: commuting miles on foot to a school that would accept him, sitting outside the classroom to avoid contact with the "touchable" boys inside, and suffering life-threatening thrashings from teachers and students when caught breaking the rules of ritual separation.

Bloody but unbowed after one such attack, Namdeo considered his future:

> I washed my hands and mouth in the river and headed home. I did not tell anyone what happened. My clothes hid many of my bruises, and in any case, my parents were used to the idea of caste-based beatings. Inwardly, I began dreaming of excelling in school, improving myself, and bettering my condition.

In the years to come, Nimgade's dream guided him from success to success. Sometimes narrowly passing his examinations when the plight of family members, friends or strangers divided his time, but more often winning the highest academic honors among classmates from the most privileged families in India, Nimgade would ultimately graduate from the Agricultural College in Nagpur, the Indian Agricultural Research Institute in New Delhi, and the University of Wisconsin, where his Ph.D. was heralded as the second such degree earned in the United States by a person of untouchable birth.

But Nimgade's extraordinary pilgrimage 'from dust to destiny,' as he once called it, cannot be credited alone to his grit and determination, or to the sunny optimism and charm that saved him more than once from disaster and despair. Members of Namdeo's family, devoted classmates and neighbors, scholarship officials and the jeweler down the street all helped at critical moments. Yet William Blake's urgent question remains:

> Tiger, tiger, burning bright
> In the forests of the night,
> What immortal hand or eye
> Could frame thy fearful symmetry?
> In what distant deeps or skies
> Burnt the fire of thine eyes
> On what wings dare he aspire?
> What the hand dare seize the fire?

It was Dr Bhimrao Ramji Ambedkar (1891–1956), leader of India's untouchables before and after Independence, that Nimgade credits with his success. And to *dalits*, the "broken people" of India, once condescendingly known as *harijans*, Gandhi's "children of God," *ex-untouchables* (freed in principle by India's new Constitution), and *SC/STs*, the "Scheduled Castes/ Scheduled Tribes" of government records—to all of them, it is Dr Babasaheb ("respected father") Ambedkar who qualifies as Blake's "immortal hand or eye" who traverses "distant deeps and skies," who "burns the fire in their eyes," who lifts them all on wings of desire. In the India of Namdeo Nimgade and more than 170 million dalits today, Dr B.R. Ambedkar is the "Tiger, Tiger Buring Bright."

It was Ambedkar who earned the first Ph.D. degree in the United States (Columbia University, 1927), who challenged caste-bound Hindus to admit dalits to public drinking water sources, to temples that claimed to serve all Hindus, and to educational institutions and government employment that were reserved for the elites. It was Ambedkar who announced in 1935 that he would not die a Hindu, but seek a religion founded on universal human dignity, and it was Ambedkar who was appointed by Jawaharlal Nehru as the first law minister in the Republic of India and as the chairman of the Constitutional Drafting Committee. Finally, it was Ambedkar who published numerous volumes of writings and speeches during his long career as a political leader and public intellectual, and who embraced Buddhism, along with nearly half a million of his followers, in the city of Nagpur on 14 October 1956, only six weeks before his death.

Ambedkar, the blazing tiger of India, makes many appearances in our story, as the organizer of public protests and organizations for the uplift of "backward classes," as the caring mentor for Nimgade and scores of young men and women who came to him for personal advice and encouragement, and as the embodiment of the slogan of the movement for dalit human rights: "Educate, Organize, Agitate!" (*Shika, Sanghatit Vha Sangharsh Kara*).

In the end, Nimgade describes the hundreds of thousands of pilgrims who converge at the *Dikshabhoomi* or conversion ground in Nagpur on 2 October 2006 to celebrate the fiftieth anniversary of the mass Buddhist conversions led by Babasaheb Ambedkar. Landing at the Dr Babasaheb Ambedkar Airport and proceeding to the massive white stupa erected at the place where Ambedkar recited the Three Refuges, the Five Precepts, and the Twenty-two Vows that signified his embrace of the "New Vehicle" (*Navayana*) strain of Buddhism, visitors from around the world joined their dalit Buddhist friends in celebration.

As a member of this joyous assembly, I had the honor of meeting Dr Nimgade and Mrs Hira Nimgade for the first time. With their son, Dr Ashok Nimgade, a physician from Boston who had shared some of the stories in this book with my students at Harvard, we all agreed that fifty years had been good to the ex-untouchables of India, but much remained to be done. Only later did we learn that, as we spoke, a dalit family was raped and murdered, their bodies hacked apart and strewn in a drainage ditch by caste Hindus in Khairlanji, a village not far from Nagpur. These ambedkarites were killed, according to press accounts, because their daughter had dared to get an education and because the family refused to allow caste-Hindu neighbors to trample their crops in a shortcut to the fields beyond. When local police refused to investigate – a widespread problem in India today – activists burned down the police station. Only then did the national and international press report the story.

Few people outside India realize that the caste system still oppresses millions of citizens. According to Human Rights Watch, more than one-sixth of India's population, some 170 million people, continue to be denied full access to economic and educational opportunities. In *Broken People: Caste Violence Against India's "Untouchables,"* (1999), HRW found that

> Dalits are discriminated against, denied access to land, forced to work in degrading conditions, and routinely abused or killed at the hands of the police and higher-caste groups that enjoy the state's protection. Dalit women are frequent victims of sexual assault. In what has been called India's "hidden apartheid," entire villages in many Indian states remain completely segregated by caste. National legislation and constitutional protections serve only to mask the social realities of discrimination and violence faced by those living below the "pollution line."

While the lions of the ancient Buddhist king Ashoka grace the national currency of India, as proposed by Ambedkar at the dawn of the Republic, it is the Royal Bengal tiger that is the national animal of India, Bangladesh, and Nepal. Yet of the nine known sub-species of tiger, three are extinct and the Royal Bengal tiger, the most common surviving variety, numbers fewer than 5,000 animals. As a result of severe habitat loss and the long-term effects of poaching for pelts and body parts, the remaining tigers are designated by conservationists as an endangered species.

While the towering figures of Dr Ambedkar, Dr Nimgade and the many whom they have touched are the heroes of this *Tiger's Tale*, we may hope that the predatory forces and grisly results of India's ancient caste system may be placed on the endangered species list of evil social systems whose time has come and gone forever.

Christopher S. Queen
Harvard University

Preface

Without the years of meticulous concentration and hard work on the part of my wife Hira, who worked with me in writing out the Marathi and Hindi drafts by hand, you would not today be reading my life story in English.

I have traveled to many places, and I have spoken to many people, whether to one person at a time or in speeches to large audiences, about my life experiences and my struggle with untouchability. Wherever I have spoken, I have found that people were touched by my reminiscences. In the words of the medieval Indian sage Guru Nanak, 'Wherever one speaks, and the other listens with understanding, then both the speaker and listener become wiser.' Although I initially questioned what would be worth writing about for a simple man such as myself, many colleagues and well-wishers urged me to write about my experiences. Through the written word, these memories and lessons may perhaps help provide guidance for coming generations.

When writing these words, I could often clearly visualize my past, but not always about what to write. Now I am almost ninety years old. Even if I condense my childhood experiences the challenge is to prevent the book from becoming too large. I remember once asking Dr Ambedkar, my mentor, why he had never written his own autobiography. He replied, 'It is easier for me to write about other topics... it takes a lot of time to write an autobiography!' It is indeed difficult to reconstruct even one's own life, and I have had to work in partnership with my wife. I have written in a straightforward way about the sorrow and happiness, the bitter and the sweet, the comic and the tragic. I hope that the words I have put on paper about friends and relatives who have passed from this world serve as a memorial to them.

As a backdrop to the discrimination and suffering I had to overcome as an untouchable in rural India, let me first outline the religious system that had subjugated me at birth. From ancient times, under the Hindu caste system *(chaturvarna)*—four castes exist: *brahmin* (priests), *kshatriya* (warriors), *vaishya* (traders), and *shudra* (craftspersons and serfs). Each of these castes was supposed to have originated from a different anatomic part of a primordial deity. Those without caste lack any social standing within this system and are known as the untouchables (or more recently, as *dalits)*. The lowest order untouchables are supposed to be born from the feet of the above-mentioned primordial deity—a very degrading origin indeed! We were considered outcastes, untouchable, and even unseeable. Over thousands of years, the traditional orthodox mentality behind the caste system had reduced the dalit people to a state of indignity, injustice, suppression, and slavery. As a result, ignorance, backwardness, poverty, and helplessness were to be our lot in life.

To make things worse, there were a total of some 6,000 subcastes within the major four, ensuring further division between human beings and even among outcastes. I belonged to the *mahar* subcaste, consisting of landless laborers. Even below us were subcastes such as the *mang* (musicians), *chambhars* (cobblers), and *mehtars* (sweepers and scavengers).

Because of poverty and untouchability, I was not able to start attending grade school until age fourteen. But my lot would certainly have been much worse – a life of degradation in the dust of my birth village – had it not been for the inspiration of a remarkable man, Dr Bhimrao Ambedkar, whom we affectionately referred to as Dr Babasaheb Ambedkar, or just Babasaheb (Father Sir). Himself a dalit, Dr Ambedkar rose to become the framer of the Constitution of India—the world's largest democracy. A cornerstone of my memoir, as you will see, is Dr Ambedkar.

I would like to first thank Dr Christopher Queen at Harvard

University, who infused the project with enthusiasm, and also provided invaluable feedback. Dr Queen helped make us conscious of the theme of the tiger that had subconsciously permeated this tale. For his dedication to spreading the word internationally about engaged Buddhism, we are proud to have Dr Queen write the preface.

I am grateful to the English translation team headed by Hira Nimgade, Rekha Doraiswamy, Bhim Nimgade and Ashok Nimgade. Ashok also facilitated the publication of this version. The translation ended up being a transcontinental labor of love, involving numerous long distance calls and travels. What an irony for someone coming from a humble illiterate village background!

Thanks are due also to: Karuna Doraiswamy for identifying editorial gaps; Buddhist scholars Bhagwan Das and Dr Eleanor Zelliot for their encouragement and advice; Dr K.P. Wasnik for translating a chapter, and Bhante Vishwapani of the BBC, for editorial feedback. We are grateful to Vasant and Meenakshi Moon for their steadfast encouragement that I write my story in book form; and to Vasant Khobragade, Ankush Nimgade, and Rambhaj for supporting this project in countless ways, large and small. And finally, thanks to readers of the Marathi and Hindi versions from various castes and creeds who urged this English translation.

And now, let me transport you to my lowly birthplace, in a primitive village named Sathgaon in central India...

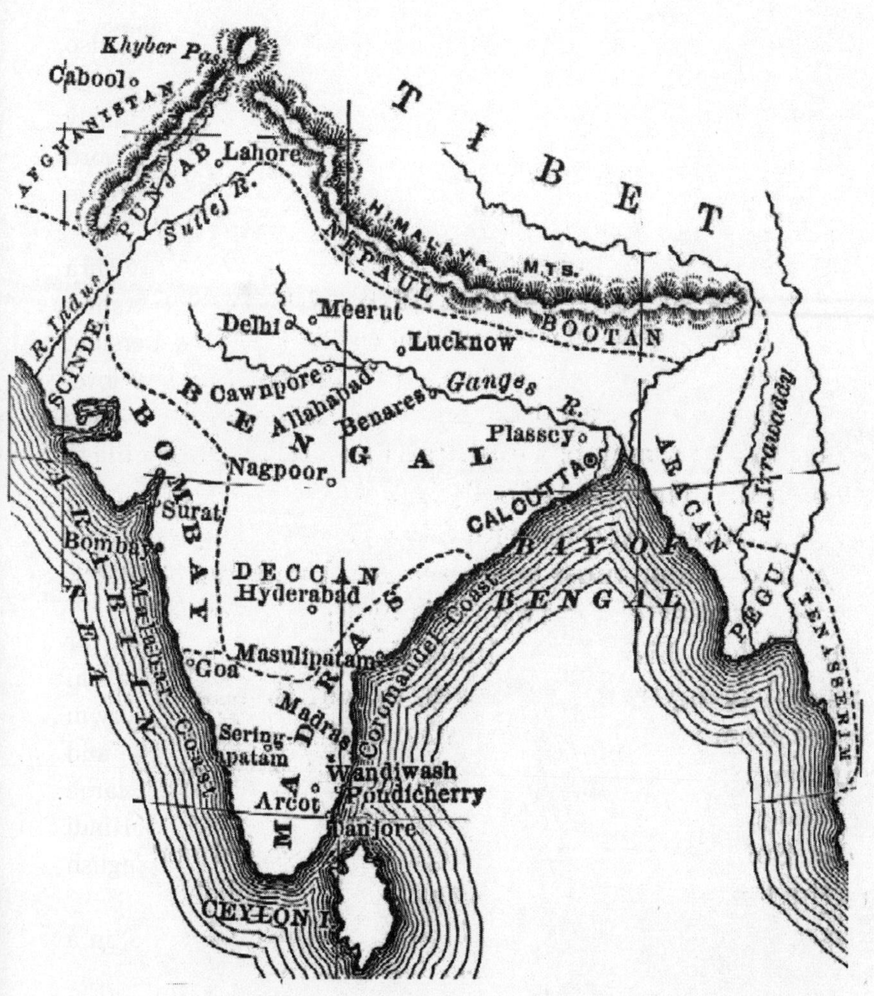

The story begins in central India, in the village of Sathgaon, outside Nagpur. The map shows British India, 1889, courtesy Center for Study of the Life and Work of William Carey, D.D. (1761–1834), William Carey University, Hattiesburg, Mississippi, USA.

PART I

VILLAGE AND JUNGLE

The mystery of the two pillars

When I reach back through the more than eighty years of my life, the earliest memory I can summon is of a dark, earthen hut, lit by a flickering clay lamp. The feeble illumination barely reached to the low ceiling of grass thatch. The lamp sat on a low, earthen platform alongside two mysterious rock columns, which were about a foot high and decorated with flowers and turmeric powder from *puja*. Ash from burned incense sticks lay everywhere and the air was heavy with the scent of camphor.

But within this prayer hut, all was not reverent silence. Several naked children were jumping and scampering over the platform, scattering the ash with their feet, throwing flowers at each other and shrieking with delight at finding this new place to play.

Suddenly, the door was flung open, and a dark figure stood stooped at the small doorway. We froze and he roared, '*Arrey!* What are these pests doing here?' I recognized my grandfather's voice, and his tall frame and his fierce moustache. We scattered to the dark corners of the hut like frightened rabbits. 'I have told you not to play here and make mischief! And you are desecrating the sacred place by touching it with your feet!'

Grandfather came in, sank to his knees and held his ears in a sign of reverence, laying his forehead on the altar. He was a pious man who prayed here frequently, starting right after his early morning ablutions at the river. 'Oh Lord! Please forgive these innocent children. Please keep your benevolent eye always on this family.'

I was about six years old then. But through the decades, the image of the two pillars remains alive in my mind. The mystery behind this – a poignant tale of friendship and loyalty that transcended caste and creed – would be revealed to me later.

Abutting this small prayer hut was a slightly bigger one,

The mysterious two pillars in the prayer hut (photographed in the 1970s).

perhaps about six by ten meters with just one tiny window. This is where my mother gave birth to me and to my seven siblings. About fifteen people in our extended family lived under the same roof. This was in the remote village of Sathgaon in the state of Maharashtra, 500 miles – and a universe away – from what was then Bombay. We were surrounded by a dense jungle with wild and dangerous animals. Around us were also life-giving rivers, but they often dried up in the tropical summers. The landscape could change dramatically, from a rich green during monsoons, to dusty parched land during droughts that deprived us of food and water. And of course, there was no post office, hospital, or paved road, let alone a bus route anywhere near this primitive patch of land.

My unlettered parents could not keep records, but informed me that I was born in the month of *Sawan* during the monsoon, on a Wednesday. I estimate my birth year to be around 1920. Our family name Nimgade probably derives from the neem tree, which is known for its healing properties and health benefits. Many people from our untouchable community bear names referring to trees or plants, such as my brother-in-law, *Khobragade*—which refers to a coconut. There's similarly

Ambagade, referring to mango, *Jamgade* to guava and *Borkar* to berry. Quite likely, these arboreal names derive from the peaceful Buddhist period in Indian history, and are cited as further evidence that many of India's untouchables were previously Buddhist. According to the custom of the day, when the first child is born, village musicians appear to fete the family in return for money and food. But when I was born, we had nothing to give them, and the musicians departed empty-handed.

As the first child, born after a long period of barrenness, I was much loved by everyone in the family. But there was little time or energy for anybody to spend fussing over the new baby. When I was just twelve days old, my mother had to return to laboring in the fields. She barely got enough food to nourish herself, let alone to produce milk to feed a baby. I would cry constantly with hunger.

My mother was always worried about how to keep me alive. Sometimes she would cook just a spoonful of flour in a cup of water for me. There was a female donkey that had just recently given birth, so my mother, seeing this as a godsend, took some of this creature's milk for me. Several kind neighborhood women, upon hearing my cries of hunger, would suckle me along with their own babies. So I felt that I had several mothers in the village, including a donkey, who kept me alive. For many years, whenever I would visit my village, I would thank these women, saying, 'Because you suckled me along with your own children, I was able to live, and I was able to accomplish something with my life.' I would give them gifts of new saris, but in my heart I felt that these articles of clothing could never repay them for the gift of life they had bestowed upon me.

My grandmother Saguna would sometimes advise my mother, 'If you have no milk why do you hold him to your breast? Give him opium so he will sleep and you can work in the fields.' So my mother would give me a little speck of opium (the size of "the eye of a fly") and I would sleep all day. I am thankful that my mother was careful; an overdose could easily have put my earthly existence in jeopardy.

But other accidents could also have ended my life. Once, my father's aunt entered the hut bearing a heavy pot of river water. Coming in from the bright daylight, she could see nothing inside the relatively dark hut, which had just one small window covered with bamboo slats. With her next step, she felt something soft and squirming underfoot. Thinking it was a snake, she shrieked, dropped the pot and fled outside.

But it was me that she had stepped on. Only my screams brought her back into the hut after she realized her mistake. Then she sobbed loudly, afraid that she might have killed me with either her foot or the heavy pot. Hearing the commotion, my mother and neighbors came running. Everyone reproached my mother for letting me sleep unattended on the floor. My mother sank to the ground, weeping, with me in her lap.

Outside the hut was no safer. One day, when I was sleeping alone in the courtyard, a small frisky calf came capering and jumping by and one of its hoofs came down on my stomach. I woke with a loud cry and my mother rushed to my rescue. She lifted me to her breast while shuddering about what could have happened had the calf trampled me.

Death was not easily thwarted, though. When I was about three or four months old, death paid me another visit. This occurred during a seasonal migration that our community of landless laborers took to Varhad, some 100 miles away, in search of farm work. (At Sathgaon, steady labor jobs were only available during the rainy season in the rice fields.) We took one bullock cart, on which we loaded essential belongings, children, and aged relatives. The able-bodied adults walked alongside the cart.

On the way, we stopped by a river at Pandarkawda village, for food and bathing. My mother and I were struck with high fever. While tending to my sick mother, my grandmother Saguna discovered that my body had turned cold and lifeless. Frightened, she screamed for help. People came running. My grandfather Budha, the village healer versed in folk medicine and healing mantras, could not find a pulse in my cold body. Upon confirmation of my death our company began to weep. Because my parents had been childless for a long time, my death hit them very hard. The men dug a burial pit. Just as they came to take my body, my fever-wracked mother sat up and cried out to hold her baby boy for one last time.

She sobbed and caressed me as only a grieving mother could. The ever-practical Saguna then grabbed my body to prevent Mother from being overcome by grief at a time of a dangerously high fever. In doing so, Saguna suddenly noticed my thumb twitching. She called Grandfather Budha to examine me again. He began massaging my palms and soles, and soon my limbs also twitched. The atmosphere of grief immediately changed to a hopeful one. Apparently, I had been unconscious from the fever, and my mother had unwittingly revived me through her repeated caresses—the heat of her fever-ridden body warming me back to life. Once again, I was among the living.

WHEN I WAS just a few years older I started to help my family by caring for the younger siblings while the adults worked the fields. We children had little clothing and often played around the hut naked. Sometimes I was fortunate enough to inherit a worn-out shirt from an uncle. Usually it was long enough to serve as both shirt and trousers!

When my mother returned from the fields in the evenings, I sought her affection, but she had no time to devote to me. Her first duty at home was to fetch water from the river, which she did, despite her great weariness. Then she had to cook dinner on the small wood fire for our large family. I would actually fall asleep while dinner was slowly being cooked and would eat while half asleep. As a child, I did not even know what the word "school" meant. That was our golden childhood, a time of simplicity: no school, no toys, no clothing, and sometimes no food.

Grandfather marries a plant

In rural India, when I grew up, everyone traditionally lived in a joint family headed by the eldest relatives. Thus, my grandparents were central to my life. My grandfather Budha had a majestic voice that radiated health and robustness. He was dark, but with a radiant face. (To clear up potential confusion, Budha was so named because he was born on a Wednesday – *Budhwar* – and he was not named after the Buddha.) His long, thick moustache gave him a commanding appearance. His lifestyle was very simple. He wore a dhoti down to his knees, and a cloth turban wrapped around his head, but with a bare torso. Even in his advanced age, his vigor remained intact, as did all his faculties and teeth. This was actually a matter of consternation for him, because Indians venerate the aged. Once, while on a pilgrimage to the holy Ganga, he tried prying out some teeth as an offering to the sacred river, but he could not succeed and went to his grave with all teeth intact.

We referred to my grandparents Budha and Saguna respectively as *Ajoba* (grandfather) and *Ajibai* (grandmother). It is exceptional that my grandparents actually fell in love with each other and had a so-called "love" marriage—that is, a marriage not arranged by their family. Grandfather Budha's brother Kavdu related the romantic story thus:

> Budha was engaged to marry a woman who, unfortunately, contracted smallpox and died just days before the planned wedding. This shocked Budha so much that despite repeated entreaties from his parents, he refused to consider marriage again. Instead, he started going from village to village as a *hakim* (medicine man). One day, when he was about forty, he went to the nearby village of Harni to treat a young widow named Saguna.

Saguna was about thirty years old and had married into a good family, but within just a few years she had lost both her children and then her husband to various illnesses. She had grown mad with grief and had become physically ill. Her relatives had tried many treatments, but to no avail. Eventually, someone had recommended calling upon the healer, Budha. Over months of treatment, Budha used herbs, powders, and mantras to restore Saguna's health. Saguna's intelligence and fine features gradually resurfaced, and appeared to have made a favorable impression on her healer.

When Budha came to know that Saguna's parents were seeking a new husband for her, he rushed home to seek his parents' counsel. But lightning might just as well have struck the hut. Budha's parents were deadset against any such matrimonial alliance—for a bachelor to marry a widow was considered improper and inauspicious. They promised to search intensively for a suitably young maid. But Budha disliked the idea of marrying someone young and immature.

The next day, Budha returned to Harni and told Saguna's parents of his desire to marry their daughter. Saguna's father was delighted because he admired Budha's intelligence, character, and compassion. To proceed further required appeasing the spirit of Saguna's deceased husband through a *shanti puja* (a prayer of appeasement). The problem of a bachelor marrying a widow remained, but there was a loophole, and the very same day, a mock wedding ceremony was conducted in which Budha "married" a milkweed plant. Whether he subsequently divorced the plant is unclear, but it paved the way for a simple wedding ceremony in which Budha and Saguna became man and wife.

When the newly married couple returned to Budha's village they faced a cold reception. The extended family sharply rebuked Budha for the "improper" marriage and barred him from entering the house. Poor Budha and Saguna then built a small *jhompri* (hut) for themselves a short distance away.

Through hard work, the couple carved out a new existence for themselves. They had a daughter, and this appeased

> Budha's parents somewhat. Then they had a son, named Maratrao, who was to become my father. Maratrao was a handsome child—fine featured like his mother Saguna. Now it was difficult for the paternal grandparents to keep their distance. They accepted the couple and everyone resumed living together.

My grandparents Budha and Saguna were opposite in personality as well as in behavior. Budha, although physically strong at six feet tall, was pious and simple. He never quarreled or cursed. By contrast, Saguna, although beautiful, was sharp and outspoken. When angered, a volcanic Saguna could rattle off colorful words and biting proverbs, much to our amusement. We would hold our stomachs with laughter as we watched even grown men wither under her temper and tongue! Such was her presence that we children felt protected by her side as a lioness's cubs might feel by their mother.

With an iron hand, Saguna maintained discipline and a firm work ethic. She made the entire household, including children, rise before dawn. To this day, I maintain her discipline of rising early. With her various daughters-in-law, Saguna, like many of her peers, was very tough. But she was also fair with them, and in their illnesses she served them with heart and soul as though they were her own children.

Because of poverty and famine, Saguna always scrimped to fill our stomachs and maintain financial discipline. Every little grain of rice still covered in chaff was carefully and lovingly gathered and cleaned by her for future use. She would even salvage this chaff and add it along with wild jungle flowers to the chapatti dough to stretch our meager rations. Saguna discovered that simply boiling dough would make it puff up and appear larger. If we were entirely out of food she would scour the jungle for *wabit* grass, a weed, with which to make bread. During religious festivals, she would declare a fast for the entire family. This not only provided spiritual cleansing but also conserved food.

Saguna and Budha had several more children. Especially in

those days, daughters were judged primarily by looks, and their second daughter Bhagga was considered extremely good-looking. Once, while the family was doing migrant manual labor working near the village of Varhad, they were approached by some foreign missionaries who asked to adopt Maratrao and Bhaga. The missionaries promised that the children would lead an easier life and would be well-educated. Budha and Saguna declined the offer. After the missionaries left, Saguna, true to her character, let loose a stream of invectives. 'We are poor! But we will work hard to raise our children the best way we can—we will never give them away to those white ghosts!'

I still wonder to this day how the lives of my father and Bhaga, who spent all their lives in rural Maharashtra, would have turned out had they lived with the missionaries, and perhaps even have gone abroad. After that, three more boys were born to Budha and Saguna (Patwar, Someshwar, and then Rameshwar).

I was born into a household consisting of my grandparents, parents, and three uncles. Because of the large families, the generation distinctions often blurred: my uncle Rameshwar was only seven or eight years older than me and was more like a big brother. When my brother Ankush was born I was overjoyed to have a younger sibling to play with. I was also blessed with a sister with delicate features, resembling a lovely lotus springing forth from the mud of poverty. In all, I was to have eight siblings, of whom two died from childhood diseases.

When I was about seven, Grandmother Saguna said to me, 'You have become quite a large horse, why don't you now work the fields with your mother?' Shortly thereafter, my own mother also said 'Namdeo, why don't you come with me to work? At least you will get one to two paisa wages and that will help a lot.' So I started laboring at an age where I should have been going to school. My work was to run back and forth with seedlings and small plants for laborers to transplant in the rice paddies.

In the confines of the fields I was shielded from the reality of my lowly birth. Perhaps in that ignorance lay snatches of a golden childhood. Only with time did I realize that life outside our *mahar vasti* (neighborhood) was rather different, and that we were considered unworthy of even being touched by higher caste people. These high-caste people seemed to have farms, houses, fields, food, and good clothing. It would have been inconceivable to me that these well-to-do people, in turn, were being ruled over by yet another group—the British colonialists.

A dandy and Gandhi

One day my maternal uncle Dayaram, from the town of Umrer, visited us and presented me a cap embroidered with golden thread (*zari*). Because nobody else in our neighborhood had such a fine headpiece, it conferred status and a semblance of wealth upon me. Never mind that I had little other clothing! Needless to say, my mother usually kept this cap hidden in a safe place.

The temptation to walk around in the golden cap proved too much for me, however, and one day, I extracted the cap from its hiding place (ours was a small hut, after all). Resplendent in my cap of zari – with no other clothing – I walked to the village marketplace to observe and enjoy the wealth and style of the richer classes. They had bountiful markets and colorful festivals.

Suddenly I heard a commotion. I turned and saw a huge bonfire in the bazaar. Thinking it was a festival, I ventured there. People were burning clothing, ropes from cots, and assorted household items. Some were shouting 'Mahatma Gandhi *ki jay*' and anti-British slogans. Suddenly, I felt my cap being snatched off my head. Shocked and paralyzed, I watched helplessly as the cap flew into the fire. No sooner had I thought of rescuing my cap when the golden threads were already afire. I felt my *man, tan, dhan* (mind, body, wealth) being destroyed by fire. I cursed, fell in the dust, and cried with pain. My voice was drowned out, like a small flute amidst jungle drums.

I rushed home dusty and crying. I had gone to see a spectacle but became one myself. Grandmother Saguna forced the entire story out of me. Then she cursed me in choice, piercing words. I felt like a lamb under a tiger's paw when she roared, 'Which scoundrels burned your cap? Had I been there I would have flung their dhotis into the flames myself. They should set fire to their own homes!'

I approved of my grandmother's curses until they became directed at me. 'Who invited you there?' she shouted at me. 'Who were you trying to impress with that zari topi? 'What good is sudden wealth without reason?' Then she turned on me and began beating and slapping me while I cowered.

My mother showed up carrying firewood. Upon seeing me cry she dropped her load to embrace me. But when Grandmother explained everything, my mother's sympathy quickly dissolved. Her brother, after all, must have worked to save up for the cap. She grabbed a piece of firewood and began beating me with the words, 'I hid the cap for safekeeping. Why did you sneak it out of the house to show off?'

After another session of beatings I slipped away and hid in the prayer hut and cried myself to sleep. I had never been beaten so much before. When Grandfather Budha came to evening prayer, he discovered me asleep there.

The next day we heard that Gandhi had been urging people 'Burn foreign goods: be Indian, buy Indian!' The decades before India's independence from Britain in 1947, after all, were marked by nonviolent protests spearheaded by Gandhi and other primarily upper-caste Hindu and Muslim political leaders. One strategy adopted by Gandhi involved squeezing the British out of Indian markets through economic self-reliance and boycotting of British-made goods, especially textiles woven from Indian cotton in British factories. Upon hearing this I felt mad at Mahatma Gandhi, as though he were a *rakshas* (demon tormentor) in a children's story. His nationwide movement, after all, had ruined my simple childhood pleasure of the golden cap.

Running with the bulls

As I grew older my duties in the fields grew more complex. I now had to help weed, transplant seedlings, and harvest crops. Sometimes I accompanied my uncle on all-night patrols to protect the fields from wild animals and thieves. By now, my years of toil in the fields had strengthened my physique.

My grandfather was a bonded landless laborer working for a high-caste landholder. His various tasks included removing animal waste, cleaning animal stalls, gathering and chopping firewood, and even conveying important messages to neighboring villages because there were no post offices around there. This was the life of servitude bonded laborers could look forward to. When old age made it hard for Budha to perform his duty, I and my two uncles, Rameshwar and Someshwar, helped out. Rameshwar was younger and sturdy, but Someshwar was delicate, so sometimes his burdens fell upon me.

When the master's family celebrated occasions such as weddings or births we became even busier. Even before one task was over, we would be assigned another. During a son's wedding, a whole retinue of relatives would parade gloriously by bullock cart to the bride's village. At such times, we bonded laborers preceded the bullock carts as a processional vanguard.

I still recall once watching the bridegroom resplendent in zari-bordered clothing, gold and silver ornaments and sparkling headgear. His body was anointed with turmeric paste, and in one hand rested a small dagger with a lemon at the point to avert the evil eye. The groom looked quite regal and handsome, and I visualized myself dressed like him. But it was only a dream.

The bridegroom procession on this occasion took an entire day from the groom's village to the bride's. When the procession set off, my two uncles and I ran barefoot in front of the bridegroom's bullock carts. The carts, and even the bullocks, were attractively decorated. Prodded by a sharp stick, the bulls ran quite swiftly.

In contrast, we ran barefoot in torn and tattered clothes. We were drenched with sweat from exertion, but to avoid being trampled, we had to keep running. Now and then, when the bullocks tired and slowed down, we did too, to preserve our precious breath. We could only stop for a few seconds to pick thorns from our feet or to salve cuts with dust. The procession stopped only when a member of the marriage party was hungry or had to go to the bathroom, or if the bullocks had to be rested or watered. These blessed stops were usually near a pond, river, or well. At these times we also stopped, drank water, and rested under trees to vanquish our fatigue.

It was because of the curse of untouchability that we had to compete with animals. This was but one of several inhumane and very painful but somehow "necessary" social rituals devolving from *chaturvarna,* the Hindu code that created the caste system. For this duty we were never compensated, but at the end of the ordeal were only given leftover sweets and food. After the marriage party and their guests had finished dining, we were called to eat by the village *kotwal* (a fellow untouchable working as a bonded laborer with the bride's party). The kotwal had to shake us awake, so deep was our fatigue. The food served to us was never returned to the kitchen, as it was considered polluted after we had touched it.

But whether we ate or not was immaterial. The hard labor wore us out so completely that we could not remember where we were or why. Fatigue prevented us from enjoying our dinner. We sleepily packaged the leftovers in our clothing for our family back home. The only place we untouchables could sleep was near garbage heaps or by the livestock. With no provided bedding, we had to sleep on the ground and imagine the dark sky, moon and stars as our blanket.

The next morning, our task accomplished, my uncles and I set out for home. I still recall with fondness how on our march we stopped at the banks of a wide river. The soft rays of the rising sun and the brisk morning air wiped away all traces of exhaustion. We hung our food bundles on a tree branch and began to swim and engage in playful wrestling matches. In those days, I wrestled almost every evening to the point where I would have no appetite unless I had worked up a good sweat.

Refreshed, I eyed the food bundles. Temptation got the better of me, and I asked, my eyes still on the food, 'What do you think about...?' My uncles nodded, 'Oh yes, why take last night's stale food home?' We untied the bundles and ate to our hearts' content. We were fully awake and could finally appreciate the expensive delicacies. For a short while, between the sky and water, we were free and happy.

The bullock race

In winters, farmers did not have much to do except watch the crops grow. A cool wind would blow, making the crops sway like a blanket of green. A feeling of contentment hung in the air. With some extra time on hand, we could engage in various diversions. My favorite diversion involved wrestling. I would watch the older boys and young men wrestle in a corner of the village. These so-called *pahalwans* were far more liberal in their views regarding caste because they respected a good match more than anything, and that meant having to step outside the caste barrier. I watched their exercises and would mimic them doing exercises such as *surya namaskars,* sun-salutations that warmed up the body, and *uthan–baithak,* squats that strengthened the limbs. The younger boys and I would then wrestle among ourselves.

Winter was also the time of the annual racing of the bullocks. The *patt* took place the day after *Teel Sankran* (a mid-January Maharashtrian festival). One year Nana Sahib Naik, a wealthy landlord with property in many villages came to Sathgaon to see his favorite pair of bullocks race. In our village of Sathgaon alone he owned much land and had several accountants just to administer his estate.

Nana Sahib Naik's servants prepared for the races by bathing his bullocks at the river and feeding them choice foods such as residue of sesame seeds, chappati dough, and fresh grass. Many people from neighboring villages congregated early one morning to watch the exciting races. Once Nana Sahib Naik, the village chief, and other important villagers had assembled, the races began. First the minor bullocks were raced. As the morning progressed and better bulls were brought into play the enthusiasm of the crowd grew.

For the final race, when Nana Sahib Naik's bullocks' turn came, the Sathgaon villagers could hardly contain their excitement. Because the contesting teams were well matched, the outcome was entirely uncertain. Whenever Naik's bullocks pulled ahead, a cheer went up. When the opponent's pair pulled ahead there was a collective groan. Suddenly, with the finish line in sight, the Naik's pair surged ahead to win by a hair. The people of Sathgaon shouted praises to Naik's bullocks and drivers. The bullocks were exhausted, with flaring nostrils, red eyes, and shuddering bodies. The driver was also tired, but somehow drove the bullocks by Naik Sahib and the village chief to accept the crowd's adulation.

Suddenly one of the bullocks foamed at the mouth and dropped to the ground. The driver immediately took off the harness and started to fan the animal. Someone else splashed water on the bullock's face, but his eyes widened, his ears flapped, and his tongue protruded. Then his four legs slid and splayed on the ground, his body loosened up, and he died on the spot. Everyone was shocked and saddened. Some people started chattering about how the evil eye had befallen the bullock because of too much praise; others blamed it on a magic spell or a mantra from an evil wisher.

For a villager, the loss of a bull is cause for deep sorrow. A bull is essential to village life—it serves not only as a helper but also as a companion. Nana Sahib Naik himself appeared shaken and stunned as he looked at his beloved bull.

Finally, someone asked him about what to do with the dead bull. He replied, 'Follow the usual custom of your village.' Then the accountant suggested a burial. My grandfather's younger brother Kavduji, however, stepped forward, meekly lowered his head, and touching his forehead with a hand said, 'I bow to you who are father to me. The custom here is for the untouchables to dispose of the body, giving the skin to the kotwal and distributing the meat among the mahars.' Nana Sahib assented.

So the mahars then dragged the bull home using ropes tied to sticks. We were primarily vegetarians but savored meat, which was quite expensive, on festive occasions, and we rarely had access to meat so fresh. The bull clearly had been very healthy and had likely died of heart failure due to over-exertion. My grandmother Saguna also went to request some of the digestive contents for use in making an eczema ointment. (She would mix and roast this together with old leather fragments, oil, and leaves of neem and peepul trees.)

So there was much feasting in every mahar household that day. The remaining meat was then sliced thin, doused with salt, and left in the harsh sunlight to dry and cure for later use. This was called *khandraya* or *chanya*. In those days, khandraya held the same status as gold and silver in mahar families and even formed part of dowries. In hard times it staved off hunger or could be traded for other essentials.

Today's educated people may be disgusted and find it unimagineable that such things had occurred, but we were constantly hungry. We often had to subsist on stale leftovers from our higher-caste masters. On top of that we labored endless hours on empty stomachs. I recall the Sanskrit saying, *Bhubhuk sheetaha naraha keem na karoti papam* (the starving are capable of committing almost any sin for food). There is even an ancient story from the Puranas of a well-known ascetic, Vishwamitra, who during a famine stole a leg of a dog at the house of an undertaker. Such is the power of starvation.

My ancestor fights a tiger

When I was a teenager I often accompanied my uncles into the Marupar Jungle to collect wood in bullock carts, for both household use and for sale in the market. The jungle held many dangers, and thinking about it still gives me goosebumps. Being barefoot we had to be especially careful near logs, which harbored poisonous snakes, scorpions, *kan khajure* (wormlike creatures that sometimes crawled into ears of the unwary), and poisonous insects.

Chopping wood would cause us to perspire greatly and become thirsty. But it was difficult to search for water in the jungle since we could fall prey to bears, tigers or cheetahs at the few jungle waterholes. It is no wonder that back in the fields, if we saw a bullock urinating, we would sometimes run to catch the precious liquid in hollowed-out dry gourds to drink. (While we drank bullock urine under duress, brahmin priests drank cow urine on auspicious occasions or for purification!) During severe droughts, however, we villagers sometimes did venture into the jungle to fetch water, which we carried out in gourds.

During monsoons, there was suddenly an overabundance of water. We took advantage of this by growing rice. Our village of Sathgaon had rice paddies right behind our huts. To keep the moisture inside the fields, we had to build a two-foot mud wall around the fields. Unfortunately, these walls also provided nesting sites for snakes, and the monsoon water would often drive the snakes out of their holes. One evening Grandmother Saguna saw a nice long rope lying in the yard, and thinking to save this useful item she picked it up and starting coiling it up. Suddenly, the rope slithered out of her hand. She realized that it was a snake!

One night my uncle Patwar arose to relieve his bladder. In the yard he thought he saw a goat kid wandering loose and sleepily secured it. The next morning when Grandmother Saguna awoke, she beheld in the yard a tiger cub tied to the courtyard pole. This amazed the entire village. Later on, my uncle and Grandfather Budha set the tiger cub free in the forest.

Every evening my grandfather Budha would entertain us children with such stories about wild animals and the jungle. Although illiterate, Budha, and later my own father, could tell marvelous tales they learned from wandering holy men. Grandfather Budha would vary the pitch of his voice anywhere from a majestic, deep regal tone to a feeble bleating.

I recall one winter night when Grandfather Budha sat telling stories with a rough blanket wrapped around him. His story of the evening had reached a climax, when suddenly a mouse came running out of nowhere into his blanket. Pursuing it was a long snake, which quickly slithered into Budha's blanket. Frightened, we ran away, but Grandfather Budha calmly stood up and shook out the blanket and the snake slid away.

In time, through Budha's storytelling, I was to discover the mystery behind the twin columns in the prayer hut. It involved a fight between his grandfather's grandfather Ganba and a tiger. Budha's storytelling was so powerful that we could see the story unfolding before our very eyes. Even without ever having met Ganba, we could sense why he was renowned for his strength of body as well as of character.

This is Grandfather Budha's retelling of the story:

> It was summer. Ganba returned home from the fields and washed off the dirt from his limbs. Upon entering the hut his mother told him that her legs had been aching all day. She had tried several folk remedies involving warm oils and massages. There was only one remedy left now for her. In her words: 'I could apply the heated juice of the beebas fruit around my legs to cure me.'
>
> Ganba the dutiful son said, 'If you want, I will go right now to get you the fruit so you can sleep peacefully tonight.'
>
> Both his mother and wife protested, 'Do not go now, it will be dark soon. Go early tomorrow morning.' Ganba replied,

'It is the full moon in the *chaitra* month (around April), it will not get dark!' He picked up his large lathee and set off.

In the jungle dusk, Ganba soon saw a group of beeba trees. He beat their fruit down with the lathee and collected it in his clothing folds, happy about being able to help his mother. But destiny had something else in store for him. The cool shade of the trees had given shelter to a slumbering tiger. The lathee hitting the trees apparently disturbed the tiger, which emerged and roared with rage. Ganba knew at once he should have brought an axe with him. The tiger's jaws stretched open and its tail moved. It stared at Ganba with red eyes and bared its teeth. It roared more violently and advanced.

Ganba decided he could not just turn his back and flee because the tiger would surely jump on him and end his life immediately. So he decided to confront the tiger.

The tiger sprang, but Ganba darted sideways. The tiger landed, crouched and sprang again. Once more, Ganba dodged aside and then used his bamboo stick to strike the tiger. The infuriated tiger jumped again. Ganba kept beating the tiger at every opportunity available. The fight went on, but it was only a matter of time before the tiger would land upon Ganba, tearing at him with mighty claws.

Still Ganba kept up his defense with the lathee. At last, the lathee broke into two. Now Ganba was forced into hand combat. Like a bleeding wrestler he weakened before the strength of the tiger. The tiger kept attacking with his claws and had dealt him many blows, tearing flesh from his torso. Though Ganba was young, strong, and a good fighter, how could he survive weaponless? But he did his best with all his remaining strength to push the tiger away. Who knew how long he and the tiger were locked in mortal combat? Ganba's lathee had bruised and damaged the tiger's body in many places, while his own body was torn and bleeding, his shirt and dhoti red with blood.

Meanwhile, in the village Ganba's wife and mother had despaired of waiting in the hut and now came to the small path leading into the jungle. As it got darker, their patience frayed and they started to cry.

Elsewhere in the village a very close friend of Ganba named Paika was returning from the field. Although Paika was upper-caste their friendship transcended such barriers. Ganba and Paika were fast friends and used to meet every day without fail after work, though the practice of caste segregation did not allow them to eat together.

After that hot day in the field Paika had just unyoked and fed his oxen and bathed himself in cold water. Now he rested in the shade of a neem tree, smoking a chillum. He started to doze off in the cool evening breeze when he suddenly cried out loudly, 'Oh, my friend Ganba... where are you? I am coming to help. Don't lose your courage!' His wife ran out of the hut puzzled. 'Did you have a bad dream?' she asked. Paika jumped up and replied, 'I think Ganba is in distress and is calling me... I must go to him now.' His wife said, 'The vegetables and bhakar are almost ready. Eat first.' But Paika said, 'No, I must go now, Ganba's anguish rings in my ears.'

So he set off for Ganba's hut, and called, 'Ganba, come out soon, I must talk to you right away.' But instead of Ganba, his wife and mother came out, crying and told him, 'Ganba is still missing in the jungle.' Paika then told them of his urgent feeling of being called by Ganba for help. They all cried upon hearing this. Other villagers returning from the fields now gathered around them. Paika told everyone, 'Gather together with your lathees, axes, spears, and torches. I will summon other neighbors and let us set off together.' Soon a dozen young men of all castes bearing flaming torches followed him into the jungle. After some distance, they came upon the fateful beeba trees.

Their eyes widened at the sight of the jungle floor. Footprints and claw prints were everywhere. The mud was crushed and disarrayed with the blood and sweat of battle, and the air was thick with the smell of it. Brave Ganba had fought until his last breath. His lathee was shattered and his flesh hung from his body. Spread next to him was the lifeless tiger.

Ganba's relatives shrieked. Paika's heart was leaden. 'We could have gone to the jungle together so you would not have died this way!' he wailed. In his agony and sadness Paika fainted. The higher castes picked Paika up and took him away. The mahars took Ganba's wounded body back to the village on a platform of tree branches. Ganba's family's sorrow knew no limits. The news of Ganba spread like wildfire through the neighboring villages. The entire village, including all castes, came to witness the funeral procession of the honorable and brave man who had fought the tiger and killed it before dying himself.

But the story does not end here. The next day there were cries of grief from Paika's hut. The villagers ran there to see what happened. It turned out that the convalescing Paika had screamed out the name of Ganba, but to no avail. Paika died then with his friend's name on his lips. Although Ganba and Paika came from different castes, the astonished villagers muttered, 'This is true friendship! One friend missed the other so much that he also died. In a previous life, they must have been true brothers!'

About a fortnight later at Ganba's house the greiving household held the 13th day puja. In the courtyard, some five to ten yards from the hut two red chilli-like plants appeared to have sprung up from the barren ground and bloomed. The villagers were amazed by this miracle, and called the shorter one Ganba and the taller one Paika. The two plants grew well but never bloomed. And never did they yield branches, leaves, or flowers. With the passage of time, the base of each plant eventually developed into a column. Worshippers started coming from neighboring villages, sometimes bearing sacrifices. We built our family prayer hut around these two columns. This region became known to this day as Waghoba (region of the tiger). Some villagers said that the spirit of the tiger must definitely wander that area on the nights of *amavsaya* (new moon) and *purnima* (full moon). Being so close to the jungle, it would be no surprise to have a tiger visit there from time to time.

Our spines tingled as Grandfather Budha's story winded down. As I listened, I would dream of being a fighter one day.

So that is the story of the two columns in the prayer hut. Today we fear even a little mouse—something that makes me cringe with shame! But I am happy, nonetheless, to count myself among the descendants of that adventurous, fearless Ganba, who lost his own life in service of his mother while vanquishing a fierce tiger.

Late to school

I started working in the fields at about age seven, and some three or four years later, I was placed in charge of grazing cattle belonging to wealthier farmers. A farmer named Batuna retained me for grazing his cattle. He paid me ten *seers* (about six kilograms) of *jawar* (sorgum) grain per month. I worked very hard and sincerely, eventually earned a raise of two more seers of jawar, and was more enthusiastic than ever.

One day, after bathing a particularly large and spirited pair of racing bullocks in the river I led them to my master's fields. For some reason, the neighbor's bullocks got excited upon seeing my wards. I did my best to control my bullocks but to no avail. The bullocks stampeded, and all I could do was slip and slide behind them. The neighbor's bullocks by now had strayed into the fields of yet another farmer, and mine could not resist the fascination and followed them.

Unfortunately, the master of that field showed up. This farmer did not get along with my master, so he became crazed with anger. He plucked a huge jawar plant, which is similar to sugarcane, and started beating me. Usually, members of a high caste would avoid any form of contact with us, but now, even my untouchabliity did not shield me. My torso became bruised and swollen with his blows. I screamed with pain and wet my small dhoti.

'Will your master repay my losses?' he shouted repeatedly. The blows stopped, only to be replaced by kicks, further breaking the caste barrier. The kicks on top of my bruises hurt badly, and I almost fainted with pain.

My mother, who was working in the next field, heard the commotion and came running. She cried even more than I. She took my head in her lap and caressed me. Her tears soothed my burning pain. She sobbed, 'Son, your low birth has led to such troubles. You have been treated worse than an animal!'

THE HUMILIATING beating proved a blessing in disguise. It made my parents seriously consider sending me to school. Although Sathgaon was a fairly large village, it was difficult to reach, being surrounded by rivers on three sides. The nearest school was three miles away at Kolari village. It was not uncommon for several villages to share a public school, which was funded by the government. After much thought, my father took me to Kolari to admit me to their school. Thus, thanks to this beating, I could eventually be educated and write these words.

I began my education in July 1934, starting with a brief interview with the headmaster in his mud-thatched office. For the sake of school records, the headmaster estimated my birth year to be 1925, about five years later than my own estimate. This small act turned out to be a boon, since later it allowed me more years in which I could work as a scientist before reaching mandatory retirement. I was likely about fourteen when I started school. The age range of the other boys, too, varied considerably, given our impoverished setting.

The headmaster admitted me under the strict condition that I, being untouchable, must never enter the schoolhouse. Instead, I would have to stand outside with a handful of other untouchables on the hot verandah and listen to lessons through a window. There were several windows, each about two by three feet. Fortunately, the schoolroom was small and my vision sharp enough for me to catch most of the lessons.

Our school consisted of a long, wide hall with mud walls and a leaky red-tiled roof. Four different classes, simultaneously headed by two different teachers, were held in this hall; each class facing a different direction. Some fifty to sixty boys and one girl attended this elementary school. For us untouchable children it was a difficult proposition to stand for hours at an end in the heat. Now and then the teachers allowed us to sit down by the door, but this proved impractical, as we would have to move every time someone went through. While the upper-caste children could use the school well for drinking water, we untouchables had to go to the untouchable vasti, which was quite far away.

Out of the seven or eight children from Sathgaon attending this school, I was the only low-caste student. Initially, we all walked to school together, although I had to keep my distance from them. Sometimes, if I accidentally touched their tiffin box, they would consider the lunch container polluted and throw it away. Rather than let food go to waste, I would then pick it up and eat it—their food was so much richer and delicious than anything my family had the time or luxury to prepare. I now became greedy and started bumping into my classmates by 'accident.' Fairly soon, they caught on and no longer allowed me to accompany them to school.

In time, three other untouchable children from my village also joined the school. Being of a sociable nature, I enjoyed the companionship, especially as we walked together to school. The four of us would eat mangoes, berries, and other fruits that we dislodged from trees with well-aimed rocks. When we drank water from the creeks and rivers we would sometimes discover fish and crabs. We would forget about school and roast our catches over a crude fire. After that, if we remembered school, we would run for it.

Sometimes, a cloudburst or sudden storm would catch me by surprise. With no question of owning an expensive umbrella, I would clasp the precious bag of books and my slate to my chest and crouch as I walked. In the rainy season, when crossing a swollen river, I would wrap the bag with my shirt and carry it on my head. On such days I would remain in wet clothes all day at school. Occasionally, when the river flooded dangerously, I would sleep overnight in the untouchable neighborhood with other untouchable classmates. We were treated like family members.

We faced other annoyances and perils in the monsoon season.

Our bare feet and legs would sometimes get stuck in the mud, and if we stepped on thorns or nails we would have to simply pull them out and walk on in pain. Our path took us through a jungle where our bigger concerns were running into wolves or snakes. But perhaps the biggest hazard – at least for the upper-caste children – was the need to maintain caste distinctions. This implied that we could only drink water downstream from the higher castes, and we could not even climb the same trees the upper-caste children climbed!

Initially, the school lessons were easy. But after first grade, my three untouchable compatriots started making excuses to avoid attending school. After a few months of scanty attendance, the headmaster struck their names off the school rolls, leaving only me to represent our community.

I missed the pleasure of their company, and soon I, too, started complaining to my mother just before schooltime about a headache here, a foot pain there, or the ever popular "stomach ache." Then I would cry out things like, 'But Mother, I am afraid of ghosts and snakes in the jungle.' She, seeing right through me, would reply, 'The other community students appeared to have no problem with these things, so do not lie.' She would then use a cane to propel me up the path leading to school.

What motivated my mother was the severe beating and humiliation I endured in the fields that fateful day. She also knew the value of education, because her uncle had gained great respect in his community through being able to read and write as well as be a *jyotishi* (astrologer). My grandmother Saguna, on the other hand, would actually say, 'Why are you pestering my grandson to study? Wasn't it good enough when he earned twelve seers of jawari for working the fields?' In retrospect, I understand now with what tact and diplomacy my mother had to balance the economic needs of our family with her vision of my education.

I did my homework each night in our hut with my slate and chalk by the light of a lamp. Whatever our teacher taught, I learned well, earning the highest marks. But this only seemed to anger my teacher, and he would occasionally throw his stick at me. Then he would pick up the stick, sprinkle it with water to purify it after it had touched me, and shout to the other higher-caste students, 'You fools! You can't even learn as well as this boy standing outside!'

But it was in the second grade that one incident sharply brought home the meaning of untouchability to me. One hot afternoon, everyone had gone outside the school building to eat under the tree or play. Being the only untouchable I was eating alone. An idle mind, as they say, is a devil's workshop. I began to think, why shouldn't I enter the deserted building to see how Guru-ji works?

I quietly snuck in. In contrast to the glaring sun outside, it seemed invitingly dark and cool. No one was in sight. I sighed with relief. With my heart pounding, I crept towards the teacher's chair. Then I saw the blackboard, which was mounted on a tripod, and could not resist the idea of writing upon it. I snuck to the board.

In my excitement, however, my foot caught on one of the blackboard legs, and it collapsed with an ear-shattering clatter. I threw down the chalk and turned to flee.

A voice suddenly screamed from the blackboard, 'Oh I'm dying! Save me!'

I froze. We villagers, after all, believed in all sorts of ghosts and magic.

'Help! Quick! I'm dying!' screamed the blackboard again.

By now, the students and teachers had swarmed inside. From behind the blackboard appeared a boy named Sadhuwarthi, the son of a washerman. He had been sitting in a corner behind the blackboard eating his lunch. Not only had I sinned by sneaking into the school, but I had also indirectly polluted an upper-caste boy through the blackboard. Sadhuwarthi was wailing loudly now.

With everyone's angry glares upon me, I wished Mother Earth would split apart and swallow me.

Then the teacher picked up his stick and struck me. Usually, he would just beat me from a distance, but today he ignored that distance. It was as if nothing else existed for him except his stick and my body. He cursed me and my caste. 'You idiots, why are you learning? And as if it isn't enough, how dare you enter the schoolhouse!' With full strength he showered me with blows. Then he beat my feet—'The legs you entered our school with!' All the students watched excitedly as I fell to the ground.

When the teacher tired, Sadhuwarthi, now regarded as the hero in this episode, took over. He beat and kicked me – the symbol of crime and villainy – with full fury. Inspired by his curses, a few other classmates joined in. Now they had a chance to take out on me the scoldings they suffered from the teacher when I outperformed them. I faced a rain of slaps, cuffs, and kicks in what became a free for all.

Ultimately, the students and teachers beat me to their satisfaction and proceeded to the well to purify themselves from my touch with water. Then they paraded in wet clothes to the Hanuman temple to pray. With difficulty, I dragged myself outside. I did not have the energy to stand outside the window to hear more lessons, let alone face the angry gazes. My body burned from the beating, and my soul was full of sorrow from the taunts as I crawled homeward.

'Oh, God!' I cried. 'Before ever starting school, I was beaten severely; now I am learning but I am still getting beaten!' Then, an inner voice calmed me down: 'You received today's beating because you broke the rules. This would not have happened had you not entered the schoolhouse.' I washed my hands and mouth in the river and headed home. I did not tell anyone what happened. My clothes hid many of my bruises, and in any case, my parents were used to the idea of caste-based beatings. Inwardly, I began dreaming of excelling in school, improving myself, and bettering my condition.

Going back to school was a difficult proposition. I maintained my distance at the window for the next few days and avoided the glances of the upper-caste boys. It was inconceivable to me then that society would ever change.

My father the reformer

My father, Maratrao, resembled Grandfather Budha in many ways. He was handsome, almost six feet tall, and well built. He had fine manners and a gentle, compassionate disposition. He had a pleasing voice, far softer than Budha's booming one. My father dressed simply yet elegantly—always in a clean white dhoti down to his ankles, with a white shirt and a white cap. At home all the elders called him Bapu.

My father enjoyed working in the fields, digging paddies, making paddy-mud walls. Despite periods of great impoverishment, unlike his forebearers, he avoided entering into bonded labor with anyone. Cosmopolitan in outlook, he often visited the larger town of Umrer, where he had several relatives including his in-laws. A nice relative named Pandurang (the husband of Budha's sister Pisa) taught him how to write the Marathi alphabet, often guiding his hand. In this manner he learned the rudiments of reading and writing.

My mother's uncle taught my father to read horoscopes, and little by little he began to excel in the craft. The villagers of Sathgaon began consulting him before arranging marriages, naming babies, selecting auspicious times for marriages, and for identifying birth stars and astrological signs. People's faith in and respect for him grew over time. My father never told white lies just to increase his fee. His honesty earned him the title *Sadhu-boa* (saintly one), in the village.

Because ordinary village work was not enough to sustain the family, my father decided to start some small trades with his relatives in Umrer. Because of his honesty, several people wanted him as a partner. Sometimes he would do contract farm work on a mango orchard or on a plot in a chili field. He started to earn more money and our family's conditions improved. We certainly ate better.

In our corner of the village, a kotwal was selling some land and my father bought it for 60 rupees, on a five-year contract, and we no longer had to work on other farmer's fields. We bought all necessities for running a field—oxen, carts, ploughs, etc. In anticipation of his three brothers' marriages, in 1932, my father also increased the size of our hut. This expansion involved digging the ground near the hut, and then, my father's curiosity got the better of him. With the help of laborers he began digging in an exploratory fashion around the two round columns in the puja hut. The columns seemed to extend downward into the ground. They dug some fifteen to twenty feet, but there were no signs of the columns' roots. They just kept going further and further down. Finally, they gave up.

We also purchased furnishings for the enlarged hut including cots, benches, bolsters, and brass utensils. The hut sported several windows, each about one foot by one foot with bamboo lattices. During heavy rains, some water could still splash through the windows or leak through the roof, but we were content with the new dwelling. In our part of the village, our house was the largest, and people referred to it as "the bungalow." All three of my uncles got married in the house, and our joint family grew.

My father decided to stop sacrificing goats and chickens in front of the two columns because he was uncomfortable with this tradition. He would, instead, do puja with turmeric powder, incense, flowers, and camphor lumps. He would break coconuts and distribute them as prayer offerings.

I recall another incident from when I was about nine or ten that illustrated my father's reform-mindedness. In a nearby village, my grandfather had cured a kotwal of a serious illness. In gratitude, the kotwal invited us to a puja in honor of the Ganba and Paika columns followed by a feast. I was surprised to notice that two batches of food were being prepared, one for the kotwal's group, and one for us mahars. Apparently, even though we were all untouchables, we had to follow sub-caste distinctions. My uncles and I ate very well; it was not often that we got such plentiful, delicious food. My father, however, was deeply pained by the social segregation and could barely eat anything.

Even within untouchable communities there were subcastes with strong distinctions among them. The mahars, for instance, considered themselves higher born than the mang—the musician community. The mangs played instruments at festivities, and their women served as midwives. Mahars, therefore, would not use the traditional *'Ram Ram'* greetings with the mangs. My father, however, was forward-thinking about these matters, and would greet mang people with respect. I, too, broke the caste barrier by drinking water from mang households.

This meant going against the principles of close family members. One day, when I was a little bit older and was alone in Umrer, I had invited one of my friends for lunch. He happened to be from the *bhangi (mehtar* or sweeper) caste, which was considered lower than the mahar. Just then, Grandmother Saguna appeared home from a trip back home to Sathgaon earlier

My parents in the 1940s. The photograph is deceptive. They were a study in physical contrast—he was over six feet tall with broad shoulders, and she was about a foot shorter and perhaps half his weight.

than I expected, leaving me in a bind. I could not be discourteous and refuse to feed my friend, and yet I was afraid of the wrath of my grandmother, who disapproved of our consorting the lower sub-castes.

But Saguna washed her face and hands and laid down for a rest after her journey. This was my opportunity; I quickly sprang into action to feed my friend. Just as I was serving Ankush and my friend second helpings, Saguna woke up. I choked with fear. She stared at my friend but said nothing. We quickly finished up and I went outside to see my friend off.

When I went back inside the house, she fumed like a firecracker fuse and then exploded. 'Just because I went back to Sathgaon, you felt you had free reign to do whatever you want! We don't even have enough to feed ourselves. Why must you feed others?'

I listened quietly. To be honest, everything she said was true. After a pause, she asked, 'He seemed like the son of a mehtar. Was he?"

Sensing her uncertainty about his caste, I could not resist opposing her prejudices. 'What happens if we feed the son of a sweeper?' I asked. 'Has anything been harmed or changed because he was here?'

This was like throwing petrol on a fire. 'What is this? The child born yesterday is teaching me what to do? Just because you've gone to school a little, you think you are wise?' There was little I could do but wait until she tired of shouting.

And yet, despite having a conservative mother, my father was always thinking of how to improve the status and life of women. He was moved by seeing the hardships women endured in walking miles to fetch river water. With the help of his father, Budha, he rallied our immediate neighborhood to dig a well nearby. He suggested that depending on their means, families should donate either money or physical labor towards this project. Everyone, and especially the women, appreciated the idea, and to this day, this well continues to serve the community.

During the monsoon, when fieldwork was impossible, Father also introduced a new, edifiying custom in the village. He started inviting a guru named Eknath Maharaj from Bothli village to recite holy verses. (People referred to him as *Maharaj* because he was a ruler of the spiritual realm.) Eknath Maharaj was a pious, learned, and kindhearted person with a deep knowledge of the Puranas. There is a strong belief throughout much of India that just listening to the religious stories of the Puranas will cleanse the soul. Until then, no one in our section of the village had the opportunity to hear epic stories such as the Ramayana and Mahabharata. Therefore, on nights when Eknath Maharaj spoke, some two dozen men and women crammed in tightly on our hut floor, some overflowing onto the veranda.

Marriage at age twelve?

In those days, people had strong religious faith and believed that pilgrimages to holy places obtained religious merit. Therefore, even before our financial circumstances improved, Grandfather Budha and Eknath Maharaj once took off on a pilgrimage to the holy site of Ramtek with two handicapped boys from our neighborhood. Taking along crippled or handicapped people to places of worship was considered worthy of *punya* or blessing from God, and each carried a boy on their shoulders. The trip started with a fifty-mile train journey to the nearest big city of Nagpur, which back then, due to frequent stops and delays, could take some four to five hours. Then the pilgrims walked some thirty miles to Ramtek.

By then, Eknath Maharaj, who was more slender than Budha, was already experiencing difficulty carrying the crippled boy on his shoulders, and the group abandoned ambitions of traveling to their ultimate destination of Benares, along the holy Ganges river, a few hundred miles away.

Ramtek was famous regionally for its temple dedicated to the Hindu deity Ram. At Ramtek, the party proceeded to the namesake pond for a ritual cleansing bath. Although the temple was not open to untouchables, my grandfather and his group could at least face the Ram mandir and do puja.

Afterwards, Grandfather Budha cooked lentils and rice on a fire using large "flame of the forest" leaves that Eknath Maharaj had foraged as makeshift plates. They had cooked extra food to help feed other hungry pilgrims—an act that yields further spiritual merit.

In the time it took to cook the meal, a very poor man in tattered clothes arrived. He was flanked by two pretty little girls, each holding on to his fingers. They were gaunt with thirst and hunger.

Grandfather Budha saw their condition and invited them to eat, and the three guests ate ravenously. The man said that his wife had died recently and he was having great difficulty taking care of his daughters. Then he lapsed into an awkward silence. Occasionally he would open his mouth but then change his mind and remain silent. Finally, Grandfather Budha urged him to speak his mind.

'I am very poor and barely get work,' the man admitted with a heavy heart. 'So we are often hungry. I can no longer bear to see my daughters go hungry. So finally I have decided I will sell them.'

These words dumbfounded Grandfather Budha and Eknath Maharaj. They looked at each other in disbelief and a silence set in. Finally, Grandfather Budha broke the awkward silence by asking, 'How much are you trying to sell them for?'

The father replied with a tone of defeat, 'I would like to get twenty rupees for them.' That was a lot of money back then—enough to buy a hundred adult trainfares from Nagpur to Ramtek.

Budha began to think that if he did not buy them, the two girls might suffer a terrible fate by ending up with people of questionable morals. With proper food, care, and upbringing, the girls could bloom into lovely young ladies. Perhaps the older girl might make a good match for me and the younger one could prove suitable for my brother Ankush. Child marriage arranged by the family, after all, was quite common, although the bride and groom would not really live together until they reached their teenage years. Now that the travelers were curtailing the pilgrimage they had some money to spare. Budha decided on the spot to purchase the girls himself.

He told the man, 'I have only fourteen rupees left with me.' They began negotiating. The father finally came down to sixteen rupees and held firm here. But Grandfather Budha could only afford fourteen rupees. Eknath Maharaj had no funds of his own—in fact, he was traveling gratis as Budha's guru. Ultimately, this transaction could not be completed. But for the lack of two rupees I might have been married off!

Once back in our home village of Sathgaon, when Grandfather Budha briefed everyone about the journey, all our family members were shocked by the story of the man selling his daughters. Everyone, that is, except for the ever-practical Grandmother Saguna. She said, 'Such pretty girls for so little! Had I been there, I would have offered fifteen rupees.'

'You have no business sense at all!' she yelled at Budha. 'Don't you know how expensive it is to search for suitable girls, buy them clothing and jewelry, and arrange for a *barat* (marriage procession)? And these girls could have helped with household work before becoming of marriageable age for Namdeo and Ankush. You could easily have made financial sacrifices to meet his price by returning on foot instead of by train and eating just plain *channa murmura* (roasted grains, groundnuts, and puffed rice).' Further commenting on the stupidity of men, she added, 'And the father of the girls—what a strange and stupid man he is! He set out to sell his two daughters but got stuck on two rupees—as if the two rupees would have made him a rich man! What an idiot!'

Whatever happened, I am so grateful for the lack of those two rupees. Through this twist of fortune, my brother and I were able to escape marriage at the age of twelve. We would have been commited to a lifetime of working the village fields, quite likely with many mouths to feed, since people believed that an abundance of children was a gift from God.

Now that I am a father and grandfather myself, I can imagine the mental agony that the father underwent trying to sell his daughters. It must have hardened his heart like stone to undergo such an ordeal. But at the moment of decision, the love and caring in his heart must have surfaced. No wonder he could not somehow proceed with the transaction. And for how long would the extra two rupees have fed him?

We learn of Dr Ambedkar

'Hey stupid!' Sakhya the village tailor yelled at me. 'Can't you see that our yard has just been purified with cowdung water?'

In the village we untouchables lived apart from the others according to the old saying, *Mahar anhi gaon che bahar* (Mahars should remain outside the village). We could not even enter the yards of high-caste houses—especially not in the morning, after they purified their yards with a sprinkling of *gobar* (cowdung) in water. In those days, even tailors would not touch us for measurements. To figure out the right size, they would measure a higher-caste boy of the same size, or just estimate our measurements by eye. But such was my excitement about possessing my first new shirt that I entered the yard of the tailor by mistake.

Because of the menace in the tailor's expression, I ran away frightened. But, fortunately, a wrestler of enlightened views, named Mahadev, had just rounded the corner and was within earshot. He yelled back fiercely to Sakhya the tailor, 'Why shout at this innocent boy? You hypocrite! What happens to your views on purity when you spend nights with that *baya maharin* (female untouchable)?'

Sakhya quietly dropped his head and returned to work. Later, at a more mature age, I learned that he had been having an affair with a mahar woman who was estranged from her own husband.

Not long after this, when I was about ten years old, another humiliating incident occurred. Eknath Maharaj had been reading from the *Gayatri Purana* that anyone – not just the upper castes – could wear a sacred thread and adorn themselves with sandalwood. Suddenly, several mahar youths started sporting sacred threads around their waists and necks, and sandalwood paste on their foreheads to show the higher castes that we were not inferior to them. I tagged along among the older boys in wearing the thread and paste. This sudden change, however, was more than the high-caste youths could tolerate.

One day while we were playing, some of them came over and started harassing us into removing the thread and sandalwood. Most of the mahar boys retreated quietly to avoid confrontation with the higher-caste youths, whose families were often a major source of employment for mahars. I lacked the judgment to retreat, and a strong nineteen-year-old named Kisan Lohar, son of the village ironsmith, caught me and wiped the sandalwood paste off my forehead with the sole of his shoe. His face glowed with victory, and my forehead stung. My mind burned intensely with thoughts of revenge.

Some days later, I saw Kisan's mother going to the fields with a pitcher in her hand. I quietly followed her, hiding behind a tree. Then I tossed some small pebbles at her, startling the poor woman. Then I disclosed myself and announced, 'Your son wiped the sandalwood paste off my forehead with his shoe! For this insult I am taking my revenge on you!'

She said, 'Poor child, you are such an innocent boy, you do not seem to know whom to take revenge on. If you tell anyone what you have done today I will get in trouble with my caste and my people will make fun of me.'

Hearing this, I took pity on her and immediately left. I felt ashamed of having picked on the mother for the faults of the son.

IN THE LARGER world outside my village, unbeknownst to me, a maelstrom was brewing. Centuries of caste-based discrimination were coming to a boil. In these turbulent times one name started cropping up more and more—the name of Dr Bhimrao Ambedkar, who was emerging as a dominant force for social reform in India. My father first started hearing about Dr Ambedkar in 1930 in the course of his work in the larger town of Umrer. Dr Ambedkar had through brilliance and sheer effort gained a string of higher degrees from England and the United

States, and had dedicated his life to improving the lot of his countrymen, especially the downtrodden castes. In 1930–32, Dr Ambedkar captured the world's attention at the Round Table Conferences in London, which featured luminaries from the Indian subcontinent such as Gandhi, Jinnah, and Nehru. Unlike Gandhi, who had to go to South Africa to experience injustice in the form of apartheid, Ambedkar suffered caste discrimination from birth and thus would gain a groundswell of support from India's untouchables.

During Diwali in 1936, my father invited all untouchable people from Sathgaon, including housewives, elders, and even children to the first ever conference for the local downtrodden people. My father kept me near him and asked me to write down his thoughts during the meeting. Finally, my father told me to read this to everyone.

I stood up to speak. This was my first time speaking in front of a crowd. My hands and feet trembled and my heart pounded. I had no inkling that someday I might feel comfortable speaking in front of hundreds or even thousands of people. But that night, with my father's and Grandfather Budha's encouragement, I managed somehow to read aloud these words:

> A highly educated and intelligent member of our community named Dr Babasaheb Ambedkar has crossed the seas and come back to us as a barrister from the land of white people. He says that we are equal to the higher-caste people. We have rights to drinking water and doing pujas in temples. We must improve ourselves and be proud. We must take several steps to improve our lot. We must stop begging for leftover food and sweets from higher caste festivals. We must stop eating the meat of dead animals. We must start educating our children. We must not maintain caste barriers among ourselves. We must all unite for our progress and wellbeing!

Then Grandfather Budha called out to the gathered crowd, 'Listen folks, please act according to what my grandson Namdeo has just read to you. Send your children to school so that they can read and write just like he does.'

But the village was not yet ready for all these changes. For almost a year, my father and I received the penalty of ostracism even from our own subcaste for breaking caste barriers. Nobody visited our house, and we certainly were not allowed into anyone else's house. Ultimately, as a condition for re-entering the mahar community, we were asked to host the entire vilage to a feast of goat meat. My father and grandfather declined this "honor."

Some time later, my father's uncle Kawdu had arranged the marriage of his daughter. Community members said they would not attend if my father or I or anyone from our nuclear family were present. We stuck to our principles and did not attend.

Tattoed

'You incapable idiot!' The scream rang in my ear. But this time it was my mother's voice.

I had been working in the fields during school holidays, earning two paisa a day. Because our financial situation had improved slightly, thanks to my father's work in the town of Umrer, I could start saving for myself. One day, in a village yard I noticed a few boys playing a gambling game using river shells. My childhood games thus far had been innocent ones such as *dab dubla,* which entailed several children climbing a tree and tagging a boy on the ground. But now, tempted by some of the boys' piles of winnings, I soon joined in the game. My inexperience was readily apparent, and in no time I lost my entire savings of 14 paisa.

At this point my mother appeared, having just been tipped off by a neighbor. After a lungful of yelling she whacked me with her bamboo bellow. 'Gambling like a rich man with money to squander!' A lecture followed, punctuated by more whacks. 'Did you forget Guru Eknath Maharaj's story about how in the Mahabharata epic the Pandava brothers lost everything they owned including their wife with a roll of the dice? These boys play every day because they do not get to attend school.'

Next, mother turned to the other boys. 'Wastrels!' she yelled. 'How dare you take advantage of an innocent boy? You have taken his money by deceit, return it right now!'

After that I never gambled but kept my mind on studies instead. But our small village school posed its usual challenges involving prejudiced teachers. My younger brother Ankush had now started attending school with me, also standing outside the window. One day, when I was in third grade our master presented the students with a difficult mathematical problem. Only two, Mire Patil and I, could solve it. Mire's father was chieftain of the

Kolhari village and thus his family enjoyed great status. Mire had recently been married at this tender age to a girl from my village of Sathgaon, and to this day I recall the delicious feast his family had fed our entire village. We natives of Sathgaon felt pride that such a clever boy of high standing should have married a girl from our humble village.

To reward Mire (I, of course, could not be rewarded), the teacher allowed him to give each classmate a slap on the face. This may strike readers as a curious reward, but it temporarily brought Mire's status on par with that of an instructor in the age of corporal punishment. Later, during the lunch break, Mire Patil happened to walk past us. 'Congratulations!' my brother Ankush said sincerely, 'you are very intelligent and capable.' Forgetting himself momentarily, Ankush patted Mire's back.

Unfortunately, just then our teacher happened to pass by. 'Untouchable curs!' he yelled. 'Day by day you are getting more insolent! How dare you touch the back of the chief's son! If the chief finds out, he will fire me and skin you alive! Is this your father's school that you can do whatever you want?' He set upon Ankush and even me with a rain of slaps, blows, and curses. Then he retreated to the well to purify himself.

Seeing the teacher in such a rage Ankush became very frightened. I was a veteran of such beatings, but this was his first time. At home, Ankush told my father, 'I'm not returning to school again!' My father could not dissuade Ankush. After much thought, my father finally decided to transfer both of us to school in the bigger town of Umrer, where he thought more cosmopolitan views might prevail.

THE TOWN OF UMRER was only twenty miles from Sathgaon, but it seemed like a city to me. In a way, Umrer was not new to me since it was my mother's hometown, and several relatives of my aunt Bhaga also lived here. I remember going with my father to Umrer where I often stayed with mother's cousin Kalabai, who doted upon me because she had no children of her own.

At Kalabai's urging, I once had my full name tattooed on my

arm by a traveling tattoo artist, a woman of the tribal gond community. Back then, people believed that tattoos were the only thing one could take to the next world after death. The gondin was illiterate, so my uncle had to show her how to write the name, therefore it came across a little crooked. Instead of money, my aunt paid the gondin two handfuls of dry chilies. Later in Sathgaon, a distant relative of my mother's came through town on a pilgrimage to *Dattatraya,* a deity with three heads. He tattooed on my hand pictures of Krishna, Ram, and a floral motif accompanied by the sacred word *Om.* All these tattoos still remain on my arms, although blurred with time.

Not wanting to burden any of our relatives in Umrer with the care of my brother Ankush and myself, for forty rupees my father purchased some land in Umrer. Here, with the help of my three uncles, we constructed a hut. In July 1936, when the academic term started, we Nimgade schoolchildren moved here, with Grandmother Saguna to serve as our guardian. The rest of the family remained at the village, tending the fields.

Another aspect of my father's forward thinking was now revealed. He enrolled my sister Rukmini in school as well, making her the first untouchable girl in several surrounding villages to attend school. In Umrer, I started third grade at the Jogithana Primary Scool, while Ankush and Rukmini began first grade at a missionary school. Either my father or my uncles would frequently visit us, bringing grains from our village with which to feed us.

Once my father came to Umrer just before the festival of Dussehra. My uncle, Motiram said, 'Since we are so closeby, why don't we go to Nagpur to see Dussehra?' The biggest thrill of Dussehra was when Raghuji Raja Bhosle used to parade from his palace on his elephant by the crowds that chanted, *'Jai, jai, Maharaj* (Victory to your Highness)!' Every year he would visit and show his prowess by sacrificing a buffalo with just a single blow of his sword. The people, in turn, would respectfully offer him leaves from the *shammi* tree. This ritual was called "offering gold." This symbolism harked back to the protagonists of the

My parents with my sister Rukmini. I am in the background.

Mahabharata, who hid their weapons under the leaves of the shammi tree when they were forced into exile. Upon seeing the multitudes offering gold to the Maharaja, Baburao Meshram, at whose house we stayed, said, 'Why don't we also offer gold?'

My father and Motiram were hesitant due to our untouchable status. But Baburao added, 'Who will recognize us here? When would we ever meet the king?'

Finally, my father and Motiram assented. We proceeded cautiously forward in the line. The King sat proudly on his jeweled throne. He wore a silk turban, a necklace of pearls, resplendent leggings, and a kurta embroidered with zari. His thick, dark mustache, sideburns, and the sandalwood paste and red tilak on his forehead added to his aura of a fierce and magnificent tiger. Once near his feet we offered the gold, and retreated.

Then, we noticed a weaver from Umrer standing nearby. We trembled with fear. If he yelled out that there were untouchables here, would an angered Raja behead us all? The Raja had a reputation for being fearless and for having fought with many

Englishmen. I perspired with fright. I almost felt the Raja's sword upon my neck.

Fortunately, the koshti gentleman, seeing my father's elegant and peaceful face, did not betray our presence. I realized later that my father's dignity, good bearing and manner, upright behavior, and serious character earned him much respect and credit. Upon first encountering him, few would have thought that he was an untouchable.

IN CONTRAST TO my father, my village language was considered primitive and crude, and the town boys would often laugh at my expense. In time, however, after paying close attention to the other students, my speech slowly improved.

Because Umrer was a larger town, we were allowed inside the classroom. I thought happily that my untouchable days were over. Unfortunately, this was not the case. One day I was quite thirsty and started drinking some of the water reserved for all the students.

A Muslim teacher named Kame Guruji noticed this. He quickly came over and hit me with a stick. 'Ignorant fool!' he yelled, and scolded me in a mixture of Marathi and Hindi. 'Who do you think you are?' I stared at him dumbfounded. He hit me again, 'Don't you understand what I just said? How can you make potatoes out of onions?' I did not know what potatoes and onions had to do with water. In Sathgaon, we never had potatoes, and these were imported from distant towns only for special occasions such as weddings. Later, I learned that onions were considered very inferior to potatoes. But now, onions are five times as expensive as potatoes. The soul of Kame Guruji must rest uneasy.

That day I did not get to drink water, but instead endured a diet of blows and scathing insults from him. I then realized that even Muslims could practice untouchability. The strange truth dawned on me that higher castes felt closer to those of other faiths than to a low-ranking Hindu like me.

Our headmaster, Pathak Guruji, was much more fair and caring, but even he observed the caste line. I remember one incident over the Diwali holidays, when some fellow students and I walked by our headmaster's home, and we stopped to pay our respects. He was startled to see us, and seated us on the verandah. He had his sons serve us some of the festival's delicacies. But instead of providing us plates or glasses they put our food on pieces of paper and poured drinking water from above into our cupped hands. This made us sad.

One day our teacher did not come to school, and our class monitor, a rather arrogant and sharp-tongued boy named Chimurkar, took over. He came from the koshti caste. Chimurkar's first act was to approach me saying, '*Dhedya* (derogatory term for untouchable), you can't sit here. Get up!'

'Why can't I sit here?' I asked innocently.

Chimurkar grew mad. '*Abbay Dhedya*!' he yelled, 'get up and leave!'

I held my ground. Angrily, Chimurkar unfolded his dhoti and started urinating on me. I fled. But in my rush to avoid the downpour, my foot hit his slate and it broke. His anger exploded. He marched to the headmaster, who arrived and started beating me.

'I didn't do anything,' I cried, 'but Chimurkar urinated on me.'

Everyone laughed, including other teachers drawn by the commotion. But their laughter was directed at me. I thought silently, 'This humiliating, degrading life has also followed me to this larger town. Untouchability will dog me the rest of my life!'

I realize now, that I was probably beaten more than my forbearers were. My interest in education, after all, drew me in closer contact to other castes than would have been the case a generation or two before me. These beatings were my price for an education.

ALTHOUGH MY UNCLES and father came to Umrer with food grains, sometimes it was not enough for us, or other times it came too late. Therefore, when I was in fourth grade, I would go with Grandmother Saguna to nearby fields to cut grass to earn some money. Then we would sell it in the market. One day, I delivered a grass bundle to a house. In the front yard, I spied a pretty girl of about ten years with long hair, wearing a long, traditional skirt, reading a book. I recognized her as a fellow student. She came from the high-caste Hindi-speaking Lodhi community. I removed the bundle of grass from my head and innocently pointed to her book, touching it. I asked, 'What are you reading?'

She screamed, 'Oh Dhedya, how dare you touch our holy Tulsi's Ramanyan!?'

I was taken aback, that only touching a book would offend her so much. Her mother came out with the money and flung it at me, saying, 'You low-caste brat! How dare you touch our Ramayan?'

I left aggrieved, wondering what in the Tulsi Ramayan had to be protected from my touch. I thought I must read it when I grow up. Later on, when I did read the Tulsi Ramayan, I learned that it contained detailed explanations of the caste system. It heaped praise upon brahmins, but scorn upon untouchables and women with derogatory remarks such as: '*Dhol, gawar, shudra, pashu, aur nari, yeh sabba tadna ke adhikari*' (Drums, uneducated, illiterate, untouchable, animals, and women—these are all objects worthy of beating.)

Each successive humiliation, however, strengthened my resolve to fight untouchability and injustice. But the stranglehold of casteism over society appeared so strong back then that young people like me felt helpless. A famous mahar social leader, Kisan Fagoji Bansode, exclaimed, '*Hai Prabhu, mala pashu kar kimwha pakshi pan mala mahar nako kar*!' (Dear God, make me a beast or make me a bird; but do not make me an untouchable!) Another poet of the mang subcaste, Anna Bhau Sathe, further hectored us, "*Mala sanghoni gela Bhimrao, Duniya badal maruni ghava* (To change the world you have to change it with a bold stroke).'

AFTER A PERIOD of financial improvement, however, our family's fortune changed. In Umrer, the mango crop was lost to hail storms, and the chili crop was diseased. Even though our wheat crop did well, the prices plummeted because of the Independence movement. In Sathgaon, the land we rented for farming for five years had mixed results depending on the vagaries of the monsoon. Slowly, our economic condition deteriorated and we approached poverty again.

My father became greatly concerned about money, and he came to Umrer to explore new financial avenues. Even in the large town of Umrer my father was known by the informal title of *Sadhu-boa* because of his saintly characteristics—modesty, humbleness, and honesty. Even here, his reputation in interpreting the *panchang* (the Hindu calendar/almanac) and reading zodiac signs had started to grow. One day, deep in thought, he ran across an acquaintance of his, a goldsmith named Vithobha Savji Khanorkar. My father's sterling character and fine manners had already made a deep impression on Savji. Seeing my father, Savji said 'Sadhu-boa, you seem very worried. Is all going well?'

My father was hesitant to speak, but Vithobha Savji persisted in his enquiries and discovered the financial losses my family had been suffering. Savji, being a good judge of character, immediately offered my father a job in his goldsmith store, for eighteen rupees a month.

My father had a very positive influence on Vithobha Savji's jewelry business. Being somewhat literate, he could explain the pricing and accounting to illiterate villagers. His character and charisma won their trust and hearts, creating many lifelong customers for the Savji family. Other employees and accountants, all from higher castes, started greeting my father as Sadhu-boa. Vithobha Savji even began regarding him as family, and even the younger Savji brother, Shrihari, greeted him with the respect accorded to an older sibling.

IN 1938, I PASSED my primary school education up to fourth grade. I stood first among all of Umrer's seven primary schools. Therefore, the school system forgave my school fees, and also provided me the rare chance to study English.

My curiosity about English was piqued by an encounter in the Umrer bazaar. My father and I were wandering through the bazaar when a tall Englishman in a khaki hat beckoned us and served us a steaming drink in a small china cup. The drink was sweet and strange. It turned out to be tea! I was witnessing the introduction by the English of this brew into the Indian heartland. His translator gave us brewing instructions, and he offered us a small packet of tea leaves with a free teacup. In just a few years, tea would become a staple of village and town life, displacing our tradition infusion of *ambil,* made from sorghum flour.

Another day I saw another white gentleman in a small bazaar crowd handing out small wrapped packets inscribed with the word "Lux." Back then, British salesmen often learned rudiments of our native Indian languages. He gave me one, too, informing me in Marathi, 'When you bathe, rub this on your skin and then rinse it off.'

I now had a chance to use what our English teacher had taught us, 'Thank you, European!' I said happily. He was so pleased with my limited English-speaking skills he gave me another packet of soap.

Because my schoolwork increased I no longer had the time to collect and sell grass and firewood. Instead, I used some higher income skills that I had learned from observing craftsmen. Now, to earn money on the side, I went door to door in neighboring villages using a hammer and a large nail to resurface dulled household grinding stones and flour mills. I would similarly etch names of owners on their brass and copper utensils. This proved to me concretely the value of literacy.

Because Mondays at our school were half-days, I would also work on these afternoons at the Umrer bazaar, selling matches and sewing needles and threads from a large box slung around my neck. Through this type of work I learned how to socialize with a wide variety of people. One day the nice goldsmith Vithobha Savji spied me at the marketplace and asked, 'Oh Namdeo, how much do you earn from selling these wares?'

'Four to eight annas a day,' I replied modestly.

He said, 'If you sit in one corner of my store and sell gold beads, necklaces, nose rings, and silver trinkets, I will give you eight annas a day.' I happily took the offer, because it would free me from carrying the box around my neck. Thus, I came to sell jewelry alongside my father.

In 1942 I passed fourth grade English, thus ending middle school. I had a keen interest in studying further, but we had trouble even feeding ourselves, and money for education was out of the question. Scholarships were not available then for untouchable students. Fortunately, Umrer had two high schools that took pride in competing for the best students. News of my high marks in middle school had spread, and one of the high school headmasters himself visited my middle school to corroborate my records and then offer me admission to his school with a full tuition waiver. In this manner, I was able to continue my schooling.

GRANDMOTHER SAGUNA was very old by now, my sister Rukmini was not in good health, and my brother Ankush was still young; so all the heavy household chores fell to me—bringing water from the well, grinding grain into flour, separating the rice from the chaff, and so on. I had no time to study during the day. At night, I would study by the light of an oil lamp. Saguna would grumble the Marathi proverb about misspent time: '*Divasa disachi ashetasi, Raat chi kapoos nisi*,' meaning, 'Waste the daylight hours wandering, pick cotton in the fields all night.' Not understanding the process of studying, she would also berate me, 'Why don't you study at school? Why waste our precious lamp oil at night?'

The Umrer area was famous for its chili crop, and farm laborers could make good wages harvesting chilies. My grandmother Saguna would come to school and take me out to go chili harvesting. This happened again and again until the headmaster told her, 'Your grandson is very intelligent and a promising student. Please do not call him to the fields in the middle of the school day. Let him study and finish school peacefully.' After this she would not interrupt my school days any more, but on holidays she would take me with her to work in the fields from sunrise to sunset. One of my strangest tasks had nothing to do with selling or farming.

It all started when my elder aunt Sita was given in marriage to a man from Kargaon village. Her husband, known to me as Kisan Mama, was an actor and singer who participated in *tamashas,* a bawdy form of village stage entertainment. He would have been happy entertaining in this venue had my grandfather Budha not put his foot down. Budha went so far as abducting his own daughter Sita until Kisan Mama eschewed tamashas and in favor of real work. Kisan Mama had no choice, and he and Sita both started doing physical labor until their economic situation improved.

Then Kisan Mama contracted conjunctivitis. The husband of a cousin of mine, who sold various country remedies and nostrums claimed to have an excellent eye medicine with him. When he applied the medicine, Kisan Mama shrieked as it burned his eyes. But the burning stopped after a while, and we waited for the good effects of the medicine to manifest. But no, the medicine proved toxic, and as the days passed, Kisan Mama's sight grew dimmer. He wept and roundly cursed the relative, but by that time the fellow had returned to his own village. Kisan Mama went completely blind, and he could not work. They went to live with Sita's sister, my aunt Bhaga, in Umrer, but things did not improve. Finally, my father bought a small piece of land next to ours and built a hut for them there.

Then Saguna, who worried about them deeply, had an idea. Since Kisan sang well, perhaps he could play the *ektari* (a one-stringed instrument) and go from house to house, singing devotional songs, abhangs, and bhajans. Being very religious minded, people would give alms to earn religious merit. Because Kisan's repertoire of bawdy songs and love ballads would no longer do, Saguna called on Eknath Maharaj to teach him devotional songs fitting his new career.

But then, who would hold Kisan's hand and take him on his rounds? His own children were small and new to Umrer. Suddenly, Saguna thought of me. I never even dreamed that in addition to studies and work in the fields, I would be also be called upon for leading a blind musician. I was in fourth grade at this time. I kept saying my studies would suffer, but Grandmother Saguna persisted. 'As if you'd become a big land accountant with all this studying,' she said scornfully, and continued to harangue me in this vein. She suddenly softened her tone and explained her daughter Sita's misfortune. 'Why can't you help her family in this way? What is to be embarrassed about this? It's not theft or gambling. This is very meritorious work that will reap you many blessings.'

To say no to Saguna would have unleashed a volcano of curses and colorful village epithets—far more unpleasantness than I could bear. I gave in. So, in the mornings and after school, and on holidays, I started taking Kisan Mama to different neighborhoods and localities in Umrer. As we walked, I would scan all directions for any sign of one of my classmates or friends. Upon seeing one, I would immediately guide Kisan Mama in a different direction.

Hearing his melodious and sweet voice singing bhajans, people would fill his sack with rice, wheat, flour, and sometimes money. As I led him by his walking stick, I would ponder the extreme change in his circumstances—from a carefree man acting in bawdy tamashas to a blind man led by a reluctant boy from house to house, singing devotional songs for alms.

I did once have a moment of amusement during dinner when Kisan Mama spat out his food, muttering, 'I don't know why this piece of eggplant is jumping in my mouth.' We soon spied a baby frog hopping away from the pile of food he had spat out! We laughed, but Kisan Mama was not amused. A more lasting benefit I gained from this responsibility was learning all his bhajans and abhangs by heart. Even today they come readily to mind during writing or speeches.

Some time later, relatives took Kisan Mama to the big city of

Nagpur to have an eye operation. He was then able to see with the help of spectacles, after which he could make his musical rounds from house to house himself, and I was freed from my obligation.

Dreams of food, air, and water

'Hey Namdeo, what are you doing eating alone? There is a big wedding today. Come with me—I'll show you what a real feast is like!'

My cousin Phajit was shouting from the doorstep. It was during our school holidays for a festival celebration. I was alone in Umrer while everyone else had returned home to Sathgaon. After laboring all day to earn money, I returned home hungry and started gathering wood to make a cooking fire.

I replied, 'Phajit, I am not even invited to the wedding, so how can I come?'

'Invitation? Oh Namdeo, you don't know anything! Look—there's no need for an invitation; just come with me!

Grandmother Saguna did not at all like the idea of my socializing with friends. She would say, '*Ghari nahin dana, pan patil boan mana,*' meaning, 'Not a morsel to eat at home, but you wander like a landlord.' Sometimes there truly was nothing to eat at home. At such times Saguna resorted to her old trick of making us roti out of rice chaff or weed seeds. If there was nothing to eat the roti with, we would just have it with water. The youngsters Ankush and Rukmini would rebel at this notion, until hunger got the better of them. But in this manner, Grandmother Saguna ensured that our self-respect was intact: we never sought alms from higher-caste people after feasts and festivals.

And now was I being tempted to deviate from her principles?

But Phajit practically forced me along with him. I acquiesced, thinking he would know the ways of this town much better than I would. As we walked together he told me that this was the wedding of the daughter of the prominent and rich merchant Neelkanth Rao Mutthe, of the weaver community.

We were in time to see the groom's procession arrive in great style, in carts drawn by finely decorated bullocks accompanied by a small army of musicians. I had never seen such elegance back in my village, and it left me speechless. After elaborate wedding ceremonies, the groom's party proceeded to a fine tent to enjoy splendid and varied dishes were served on *patals* (festive plates made of leaves). These people must be very fond of delicious and rich foods, I thought, as the aromas wafted toward us. I said, 'Phajit, I don't feel comfortable standing outside watching them. Let us go home and eat. I worked all day in the fields and I am very hungry.'

'Don't rush off,' Phajit said. 'Wait and see. The koshti community has a custom that once all the guests have finished their meal and can eat no more, the whole feast is served again onto their plates.'

I was astonished. 'Why would they do such a thing?'

'It increases their status in society; it means that they are so well-off that they can afford to serve another whole feast. And then, Namdeo, we get our chance!'

'What do you mean, Phajit?' I thought it impossible that such rich and elegant people would give us untouchable kids any kind of invitation. Several other ragged children were also crowding around with us, many entirely naked.

'Oh, Namdeo, I told you that there's no need of any invitation! Look—look now, here's our chance!'

The servants now took the used patals with all the delicious food from the second serving and tossed them on the ground outside the tent. Now the waiting children rushed forward, and Phajit pulled me along with him. But the stray dogs of the neighborhood, which had been circling in the gathering darkness, jumped in, barking and growling to also assert their rights. With kicks, shouts, and a volley of sticks and stones, they were driven off a few yards, and some patals were thrown their way to appease them.

Then the starved children reached for the discarded patals and wolfed down the food. Phajit and I joined in, but I felt strange. The food was very delicious, so different from the meager fare I was used to, but it brought me no pleasure; instead I felt revulsion deep inside me. In my early childhood we would ask higher-caste people for food after festivals, but it was never previously tasted or discarded remainders—it was always fresh and clean.

I determined never to do this again with Phajit. I would have enjoyed eating my own simple food, some roti and chutney, at home with peace and dignity, much more than scrambling with the stray dogs to eat this discarded wedding feast.

IN UMRER THERE was no well in the neighborhood where the mahars lived. Although there was a reservoir pond nearby, we were not allowed to use it. We had to travel four furlongs (half a mile) to get water from a well established by a woman named Sita. She was a beggar who had managed to save up a sizeable sum of money. When she was dying, she asked the villagers to put her savings to good work, and so they built a well and a small *dharamsala*, a rest house for pilgrims.

In 1941, I was in eighth grade and my annual exams were nearing, so I had to study intensively. To bring water from such a long distance was a time-consuming burden. Also, because of a drought, the water level was low in the well, and it would take an even longer time to fill the earthen water vessel. I now decided to save time by surreptitiously filling the vessel from the pond under cover of darkness. This went successfully for several nights, but one night the reservoir caretaker caught me. He slapped and cursed me. 'You dirty untouchable! We have contracted for this pond with our money, and you are stealing our water! If the pond dries up we'll lose our water chestnut crop!' He grabbed my vessel and shattered it on the ground.

I was humiliated and hurt. I had seen cats, dogs, and donkeys drinking from the pond. Cows and water buffaloes would drink their fill, and even bathe and frolic in the water. But if I, an untouchable boy, tried to take one or two vessels full of water, I was beaten and cursed. Were we untouchables considered lower than animals? I told some of my friends about this, but they could not relate to my troubles because fetching water is traditionally women's work in India. Instead, some of them laughed at me for doing this type women's work. Other friends teased me for being surrounded by womenfolk at the well, likening me to the romantic god Krishna playing with village girls.

That same summer, a college student named Dongre returned home to Umrer to visit his parents. I told him about my troubles at the reservoir. He wondered about why we could not use the many government wells in Umrer. He was a captain in the Samata Sainik Dal, a self-help organization for untouchables established by Dr Ambedkar. When Dongre returned to Nagpur he presented this situation to the Samata Sainik Dal leaders. They decided to organize a *satyagraha*, a peaceful demonstration, on the day of the Dussehra Festival in October 1941 to assert our rights to draw water from the government well. We canvassed in the Umrer area and adjoining villages to gain support for our satyagraha.

At that time Umrer district was quite ripe for change, boasting the famous social reform worker Dashrath Patil. The Dussehra satyagraha drew many leaders from Umrer and surrounding areas and provided much encouragement for social reform to the mahars of Umrer. All the participants gathered in Ambedkar Chowk (then Bagarganj Chowk) chanting, '*Babasaheb Ambedkar ki jai* (victory to Babasaheb Ambedkar)!' as we walked.

In a speech, Sadanand Dongre formally proposed that we be granted access to government wells, and I seconded his proposal. Then, wearing their uniforms of khaki pants and red shirts and carrying empty buckets, the Samata Sainik Dal leaders marched us towards the government well. The police appeared to prevent any riots. Over two-thirds of Umrer's population of 22,000 were koshti, and this community was normally not one to retreat from a fight. But when they saw the resolution and confidence of such a big procession they could only watch helplessly. They had heard that in the big city of Nagpur fierce riots had broken out among caste Hindus and mahars. On that basis, they held back, whispering among themselves, '*Na Baba*, the mahars don't just kill, they disembowel people as well.' So no one confronted us. Uninterrupted, we drew water from the government well, thus asserting our rights.

This was only the second satyagraha in our community for the purpose of securing water rights, and it came some fifteen years after Dr Ambedkar's famous 1927 protest for water in the town of Mahad. For a few days after this new victory, we mahar youth made it a point to never travel alone for the sake of safety. A benefit of this was that we became closer and more united, and our Umrer neighborhood gained some fame. Just as a small seed brings forth a large tree, the small matter of my fetching water from the reservoir ultimately led to a major movement. Seeing this increased my confidence and courage. I began to realize I could do more to help my community lessen its misery and troubles.

In Umrer our community was on the outskirts of the town next to the meadow that served as an open-air latrine for most villagers. There was no sanitary sewer system, and therefore even the more well-off people with toilets could not flush their waste away. The mehtar sweeper caste would collect human excreta from the toilets in black drums and load it in bullock carts to deposit nearby. Hence there was always a foul smell in the air. Adding further olfactory insult was the presence just a furlong or two away of a leather processing unit. The smell of rotting flesh combined with the shrill cries of carrion birds, vultures and crows, was often unbearable. In the rainy season it smelled unimaginably worse.

Flush from the success of the water satyagraha, I resolved to meet with the municipality officer, Mr Naidu, and tell him about our plight with the waste dumping and stench. He listened sympathetically, and then asked why I had left the fresh clean air of my village of Sathgaon to live here. I told him that education – and not the air – was what had drawn me to Umrer.

I invited him to visit our neighborhood and experience our plight firsthand. Although very busy he agreed to come sometime when he was free. When he did arrive, as soon as he reached the outskirts of the town he realized what a world of difference existed between the rest of Umrer and our neighborhood. I covered my broken cot with a torn blanket and invited him to sit in our yard. Just then, a gust of wind brought a sharp burst of odor. He sprang to his feet, pulling his handkerchief over his nose, and exclaimed that he now understood our plight. When he returned to his office, he immediately changed the permissible location for dropping off human waste to several miles away. In this way, I gave our neighborhood a break from foul hell. Out of this victory sprang a deeper interest in social reform.

From wrestler to bodyguard

I was about to hand in my ninth grade annual exam when I noticed that the other students were writing invocations to the Hindu gods on their papers such as, *Sri Ganeshaya Namaha* or *Om Namaha Sivaya.* I decided in turn to write upon my exam paper in big letters *Jai Bhim,* the dalit slogan proclaiming victory to Dr Babasaheb Ambedkar. This happened to be 14 April after all, the celebration of Babasaheb Ambedkar's birthday. But upon seeing this, our well-meaning teacher Jheerkunthwar Guruji warned me, 'You should erase what you wrote and only write your roll number. Otherwise the grader will know instantly to which caste you belong.'

I answered quietly, 'Sir, if you first tell the other students to erase what they wrote, then I will erase my words.' Although none of other students erased their invocations, I could hear them muttering angrily at my impudence.

One of them hissed at me, 'Just wait till we finish the exam, then I'll show you!' Sure enough, after the exam was over, a student named Dande and his friends caught up with me. They encircled me, shouted at me and then started pushing me around. I was young and strong from hard work in the field and had often wrestled playfully with my uncles; but I was but one against seven or eight. Although they were city boys, I was no Hindi film hero to employ martial arts moves, so I fought back as best I could while yelling for help.

At length, in a sea of blows I fell to the ground on my face, and blood spurted from my nose. The gang of upper-caste boys kept beating me. Unless I did something drastic they would pulverize me into chutney. My ancestor Ganba had succumbed to a tiger in the forest, now here I was being attacked by my own kind in the city who did not even recognize me as such. It was this realization that hurt more than the rain of blows that kept coming. Then something clicked in my mind. As a wrestler, I knew adversity requires a radical change in tactics. I grabbed the student closest to me, and pressed him under me in a bear hug, concentrating all my strength on him, not worrying about the continuing kicks and punches from the others. A minute later, the poor soul could barely struggle. He gasped out to his friends to let up on me or he would surely die. Then they dropped me and fled.

In the meantime, someone heard the commotion and called for help. I was taken to the hospital for bandaging.

That evening, a festive program had been planned in the mahar pura to celebrate Babasaheb's birthday. Many dignitaries had arrived including the District Collector from Nagpur and Dashrath Patil, the social reform worker from Bela. People spoke out about the injustices and indignities inflicted upon untouchables, and the need for solutions. My younger sister Rukmini, who had accompanied my father, got caught up in the atmosphere and bravely ran up to the stage to speak.

'Babasaheb's inspiration has stimulated our society to awaken, so we will move forward and progress,' she said. 'There is no doubt about this. Today some students shed my own brother's blood. They beat him without mercy for expressing pride in our community and our leader. Oh higher-caste people, listen carefully. Today you subjugate us. But we are now awakened. Our society will progress and we will surpass yours with much fanfare. In this way we will avenge ourselves.' This boldness won Rukmini much applause. Dashrath Patil patted her back and praised her generously. My heart overflowed with happiness and pride in her.

A few days later, at the Hindu festival of Ram Naumi, a few of my friends and I tracked down some of my recent assailants in the festival crowd near the lake and gave them a good whipping. Tensions mounted in our neighborhood and school. Our high school headmaster served as intermediary between the opposing factions, and eventually things calmed down.

Regarding my sister, I wish I had happier things to relate. Rukmini was brave, beautiful and intelligent. Unfortunately, as soon as she passed fourth grade, relatives started planning her marriage. Since they could not immediately find a good match, they agreed to let her continue into fifth grade, but soon after, they found a boy from Nagpur for her to marry. I, like many others, felt he was not a good match for her as he was less educated than she. Even my own parents did not find the match suitable but we were unable to oppose the decision of my grandparents.

It is so painful for me, even now, to think of how tragic and disastrous this marriage proved to be for my dear sister Rukmini. Her husband was a policeman, and by nature was cruel and easily angered. Rukmini could never achieve happiness, peace, or understanding in her husband's house. She had a daughter – a ray of hope for her forlorn life – but the infant died within a year, and it broke Rukmini's heart. After that, she felt suffocated in her husband's house. There was no love, only their harsh expectations. She started to get sicker. I took some time off from my studies once to take her to the hospital. But after she returned home, she became seriously ill again and never recovered. Finally, six years after her marriage, she died. Only death brought her release from her hardships. Had she been able to continue as a pioneer in girls' education I think her life and the community would have turned out for the better.

OUR SCHOOL WAS dominated by the Rashtriya Swayamsevak Sangh (RSS) group, which always hectored us to join them. I attended some of their meetings but did not find its nationalistic and militant Hindu ideology to my liking, but my friend Chaitaram Rahate, of the cobbler caste, pressured me to stay on with them for a while. He said that we could learn from their organizational skills and strict discipline and eventually form our own association. He went on, '*Arrey* Namdeo, you have a chronic shortage of money and good clothing. If you join the Sangh, they will give you a good shirt and half-pants. After we get the goods, then we can quit.' So, out of economic desperation, that is precisely what we did.

Without money, a person can become helpless and humble—as we experienced repeatedly. I recall another revealing incident when I was in sixth grade, in Umrer, in the rainy season. I once happened to meet Sri Hari Savji of the goldsmith shop where my father had worked, and he said to me, 'Namdeo, I heard that your father is not well back home in Sathgaon, and there is no good doctor there.' I ran home and told my brother Ankush. We felt it was urgent to get to Sathgaon quickly—we could travel by train to Bhivapur, and then run on foot to Sathgaon. But since we had no money for the train ticket, we boarded the train hoping no one would notice us. At Bhivapur, as we left the train, the ticket checker caught us. We explained my father's illness and our urgent need to be with him, but this had no effect, and he took us to the stationmaster's office.

We repented for our foolishness in traveling ticketless when we could have walked. Finally, after two hours, the ticket checker took compassion on us and let us leave. By then it was night, and we still had three rivers to cross and a long walk through mud to get to Sathgaon. So we stayed overnight with family friends in Bhivapur and left early in the morning. We saw our father and were overjoyed to discover that he only had an ordinary fever. The next day we humbly walked all the way back to Umrer.

One afternoon at home, I was grinding grain on a millstone. The head clerk at Vithoba Savji's goldsmith shop came to call on my father. Seeing me, he said, 'Namdeo, you study in high school, you have come far in your studies, and yet you grind grain into flour! This takes a lot of your energy and time. Here, take this one anna and go to the nearest grinding mill.' He insisted on giving me the money, despite my objections. After he left, though, I still ground the grains at home. It would have taken me time to go to the bazaar and back, carrying the grains on my head; and because of the crowds, I would have had to wait a long time at the mill. So self-sufficiency with grinding the grains at home saved me both time and money.

In the goldsmith shop there was also a Muslim sheikh, a respected elder, who did *vasuli* work (collecting overdue accounts from customers). He became a good friend of my father's, and being widowed, he would come over quite often to pass time with us. If he had aches and pains or other small ailments, I would massage his limbs and his back. He would be very satisfied and would say contentedly, 'Namdeo, when you grow up you will be so well educated that you will earn more than 200 rupees a month!' This seemed impossible to me—after toiling a whole day we would earn far less than a single rupee. Yet in 1952, when I got my first monthly salary in New Delhi, it was 240 rupees, and I thought fondly of the old sheikh's prediction.

During high school summer holidays I would find various jobs to augment the family earnings. Once I worked as a bookkeeper at a sugar ration store for Kareem Seth, where a whole day's work would earn me eight annas. After a while I asked for a raise. Seth replied, 'You should not complain. Your eight annas are earned with honest work and have prestige value beyond monetary worth. You know a prostitute can earn five rupees in one hour—but those rupees have no dignity or value.' What could I say in the face of such worldly wisdom? As the Hindi proverb states, '*Pativrata to bhukan mare, pedhe khyaya chhinal*' (The virtuous wife may starve to death while the prostitute feasts on sweetmeats). I just lowered my head and continued working quietly.

IF I FAIL to mention the crucial and loving help that my paternal aunt Bhaga extended during our school days in Umrer, it would be an unforgivable omission. She was the younger sister of my father and resembled him in physical beauty. She had a happy married life, living with her well-to-do in-laws in a good house. I used to help and serve her father-in-law, by massaging his limbs to relieve his arthritis. He was very happy with me and immensely proud of my studies. Our primary school was near their house, so she and her husband Motiram saw us schoolchildren often.

When I used to gather bundles of grass to sell for animal feed, Bhaga would actually put some of her gathered grass into my bundle so that I could earn more money. Sometimes they would insist that I eat with them, especially on feast days when they had cooked mutton. She would place a lot of mutton pieces on my plate and conceal it with rice, to increase my share of the feast.

When our family's economic status had deteriorated, and even our odd jobs barely helped feed us, Aunt Bhaga would always ask if we had eaten yet. Being the oldest, I would always politely decline, but she could tell otherwise from the wan looks of my siblings, and would insist on feeding us. When I would serve her father-in-law, she would send me home with some grains or vegetables. Sometimes, on her way to fetch water, she would first fill her empty vessel with grains and give them to us on her way to the well.

IN 1942, WHEN I was in ninth grade, I heard that Dr Ambedkar would be appearing at a conference in Nagpur to establish the Scheduled Caste Federation. So far, I had only heard of Dr Ambedkar but never seen him in real life. Was there really a real man behind the myth? Could just one man be the most learned person in the entire country and still have time to serve as our emancipator? I was full of anticipation to see and hear this legendary Babasaheb. I was so determined to attend the event that I raised the conference entrance fee of one rupee and twenty five paisa by doing extra work in the fields. I earned enough to cover the entrance fee with just ten paisa to spare. It was not enough money to buy a train ticket. Therefore, I walked the twenty-nine miles from Umrer to Nagpur. I stayed with my relative Shri Baburao Meshram, who was a social reform worker and a poet. He had been our host years ago during the episode of our nearly ill-fated tribute to the fierce Maharaja.

This was my first trip alone to the metropolis. I walked around in amazement at the city of Nagpur, looking at the stream of humanity in the streets. This city had once served as a capital for a major part of the British Empire in India. Being centrally located, all train routes between north and south and between east and west criss-crossed the city. The British had built several beautiful administrative and university buildings here.

On 18 July, the first day of the three-day conference, a crowd of some 75,000 had gathered. There, too, was Dr Babasaheb Ambedkar on the dais. He stood out immediately because of his height and robust figure—his dark hair swept immaculately back over his head, framing his prominent forehead. His spectacles flashed with intelligence. His voice boomed whenever he spoke over the loudspeaker.

I felt great pride when my own relative Shri Baburao Meshram welcomed Babasaheb to this large gathering with a song he had composed and now recited over the loudspeaker:

> 'Baba Ambedkar kya kahoon shaan aur shaukat teri,
> *Aur bus gai hain Bhimrao dilmein murat teri.'*
>
> (How can I express your aura and magnificence, Baba Ambedkar? We keep your image in our hearts.)

Those three days were full of enthusiasm and hope, and for me, a venue to learn about the context of my own sufferings. Every day, the Federation rose with new inspirations, ideas, and plans. Dr Ambedkar proclaimed the aim to unite all the subcastes of the untouchables in one association. But his ambitions went even further, touching upon the plight of women in India. It was telling that the crowds of people were not just bedecked in dhotis and pants and shirts, but also in saris. About 30,000 of the 75,000 delegates were women, led by Sulochanabai Dongre. Dr Ambedkar was very pleased, and spoke about the need for women to contribute boldly, beyond just the domestic sphere, to the affairs of the community. Indian women of all castes and creeds in this and previous generations often lived lives of subjugation, being subject to customs ranging from purdah to sati, living in near-universal illiteracy. Babasaheb said:

> I want our women to strive for education and progress—an educated woman will move ahead and bring forward both

> her family and her community. Women should be organized and support the education of the children. They should not discriminate between boys and girls. Girls should not be rushed into marriage. One very important thing is to limit the number of children to better the outlook for all members of the family and community.

In this way, Dr Ambedkar stressed the importance of women's rights and family planning long before it became national policy. In 1936, when Dr Ambedkar had brought up the topic of family planning in the Bombay Assembly, he was ridiculed by Congress and other parties. Truly, Babasaheb had tremendous foresight and understanding, and it is telling that the lot of women in the dalit community was advancing far more than in most other sectors of India.

Because of a recommendation from my relative and host Baburao Meshram, I was able to serve as one of Babasaheb's special bodyguards in Nagpur, and even escort him on his walks. I felt with pride that all my days of manual labor and wrestling in the village had paid off. After the conference, Dr Ambedkar set off from his hotel on foot with some colleagues to attend a grand party in his honor, hosted by the Mayor of Nagpur. At the hotel gate, we bodyguards tried to forge a path through the crowd for him. Three women in tattered saris accosted our party and asked, 'Which one is Babasaheb Ambedkar?'

Dr Ambedkar identified himself, and one of these women stepped forward to garland him with marigolds. Babasaheb, being quite tall, had to stoop very low. The women said, 'We are very poor and have no money to afford the entrance fee. So we have been waiting outside here for many hours, in the hopes of seeing you. We are now blessed by this darshan.'

Deeply moved, Babasaheb asked how they could have afforded the flowers. They related how they had sold extra bundles of grass and firewood to afford their modest gifts. Babasaheb's eyes moistened. Choked with emotion, he said:

> Mothers, when I was very young, I lost my mother. I do not know what she was like from personal memory. But looking

> at your devotion and love, I can feel the maternal love and compassion she must have had for me. I promise you, just as I earned my education, I will do my utmost to help your children progress so you can have a peaceful, fulfilled and respectable life. If I cannot do this, I will take my own life with a gun!

Hearing these words, we were dumbfounded by his passion. On that day, Dr Ambedkar had received thousands of garlands made of roses, jasmine, and many other fragrant flowers, but it was the modest little marigold garlands that touched his heart the most.

IN UMRER, SOME of us dalit high school students formed an association called the Tarun Udayakal Mandal (Progressive Youth Group). We worked to create a strong and active organization engaged in healthful activities ranging from sports to literacy promotion. We sponsored clinics for physical activities ranging from soccer to self-defense using lathees. We pooled our books to create a library and even received book donations from the philanthropic Maharaja Gaekwad of Baroda, who had started a mobile library. We also established a small Ambedkar Library.

Our members would speak in the surrounding villages about the importance of education and we would also spread the word about Dr Ambedkar's social progress movement. On one occasion, about eight of us students went to the village of Dhurkheda to present a skit about the evils of alcohol. Villagers always found it more entertaining to have the plays done in hard-hitting pure village dialect.

In one scene, my friend Eknath was playing a drunkard buying country liquor from a vendor in bottles that we had earlier filled with water. Eknath and other "drunkards" bought this fake alcohol and drank it with gusto on the stage. As it turns out, Eknath was actually extremely intoxicated, as he had decided to heighten his performance by drinking several bottles of real alcohol to start out with. When all the fake liquor ran out, Eknath cried for more. 'Don't fool me saying the liquor is gone!' Much to the delight of the audience he then vigorously cursed the "shopkeeper."

We signaled Eknath in vain from behind the curtains that the fake alcohol was really all gone, but he could not understand us. Fully caught up in his role, he was on the verge of coming to blows with the shopkeeper. We were in a quandary since the villagers were too absorbed by Eknath's performance to fetch us more water. And to drag the popular Eknath off stage would have upset the audience, with potential danger to us.

Finally, in desperation, some of my colleagues urinated in a bottle back stage and passed it to the alcohol vendor. Eknath seized upon the "freshly made liquor" with relish and raised it to his lips. After a few great gulps he gasped and sputtered a mouthful all over the stage, tears in his eyes. The audience cheered wholeheartedly at his accurate portrayal as he tottered around the stage, spilling the rest of the brew.

The next morning, we set off for Umrer elated by the success of our program. We laughed and chatted until Eknath suddenly asked, 'By the way, the last bottle you gave tasted peculiar. Where did you get that bad water?' The pact of silence we had created beforehand could not long withstand his persistent questioning. Finally, helpless with laughter, we revealed the secret of the last bottle. Eknath boiled over with fury, and it took many miles of travel before he eventually calmed down.

I HAD MADE many friends in Umrer because I had studied there from third grade through high school. My friends ranged from being well-read to completely illiterate. I befriended several boys from subcastes even below ours such as the Rahate brothers from the cobbler caste, and Baliram Wankhede from the barber caste. Of course, my friendships could flourish most when Grandmother Saguna was away at our village.

One friend was Pandurang Navnage. He had not studied much, and by nature he was naughty and carefree. His parents tried very hard to encourage his friendship with me, thinking I would be a good influence on him. Unfortunately, sometimes the reverse proved true, and his antics and schemes would occasionally place me in a precarious position. Fortunately, at the other end of the spectrum was Tularam Dongre. More than a good friend, he was also a faithful guide and adviser. We were distantly related, and he was also the cousin of the social reform worker Sadanand Dongre, who had started the satyagraha for asserting our rights to water in Umrer. Tularam was the only son of a well- to-do, good family and had started his education at a more appropriate age. He was already studying at the prestigious Morris College in Nagpur when I was in ninth grade.

I was fast approaching the stage in the Indian educational system when I had to choose my "major subject." When I confessed my perplexity to Tularam he told me that most students from our community had all chosen subjects in the Arts faculty; for sake of balance, the community needed students to go into the Sciences. I took his advice, and ended up choosing chemistry, physics, and mathematics.

Another influential friend was Lakshman Nagdevte, a pleasant sportsman who always took a major role in social reform programs. In 1942, during World War II, Lakshman heard Babasaheb in a speech hector young people of our community to sign up for the army's mahar battalion to enhance the reputation of our community, as well as make a good living. Impressed by this speech, Lakshman left his studies in ninth grade and enrolled in the army.

Lakshman would return from the military during holidays and tell us about his adventures. His thrilling stories gave us goose bumps and made us want to join him. Adding to the allure of adventure, were ever-present newspaper ads and billboards that declared, 'Whether you pass or fail (your matric) you can join the army!' But we also had to keep in mind the wishes and dreams of our families, and thus we remained in the village. Lakshman would thoughtfully pass on his old military clothes to me every year when he got new uniforms; he knew about my desperate circumstances.

Visions of the "Queen's Palace", the College of Agriculture in Nagpur: a foolish boy's dream?

Of course, I was also greatly influenced by friendship with relatives as well. One strong influence was my uncle, Dayal Mama, who had bought me the cap with gold thread once upon a time. He lived on his fields outside the Umrer town limits. One day, after passing ninth grade exams, I visited Dayal Mama. He was filling his bullock cart with firewood to sell in Nagpur and asked me to accompany him. I immediately agreed.

After making our delivery, near the middle of the city, we saw a very majestic, beautiful building with whitewashed columns, palm trees, sandy driveways, and a grassy court and garden. Impressed, I asked Dayal Mama about it. He told me that it was called the *Rani ka mahal,* or Queen's Palace. I was astonished because I did not recall any queen living in Nagpur. He thought that perhaps in the olden days there may have been a queen here, but now it was the College of Agriculture. I decided that I should like to study in this majestic building someday. But that was just a foolish boy's dream.

IN 1945, AS MY matric exam came closer I began to panic. My brother Ankush had been helping me by working to cover expenses and doing his share of the housework, and Grandmother Saguna had gone back to Sathgaon. So I had grown accustomed to spending time with my friends—swimming, debating, wrestling, and doing social reform work. Now I had to give all that up and focus on studying to make up for lost time.

I should mention that other, unforeseeable distractions had also arisen over time, as Umrer grew in size. Other huts had started springing up around ours, because the land in the outskirts of Umrer was relatively affordable. Instead of being isolated, we were now in the midst of a booming community and a growing neighborhood. The people multiplied even faster than the huts. The old peace and quiet was vanishing. One could hear household quarrels and bickering, children fighting and yelling, and occasional drunkard husbands beating their wives. These became the sounds of everyday life. Whenever I would open my books to study, invariably, another commotion would spark up somewhere. Not only were we chronically short of money, but we were now short of precious peace and quiet.

But still, the quarrels and arguments often proved entertaining. Just behind us lived a most quarrelsome, ill-spoken woman. I still remember a fight in which she had addressed her neighbor in the vilest of terms, and her neighbor replied with equal enthusiasm and crudity. Then they spat streams of invective not only at each other, but at their previous and succeeding generations of family members as well. Finally the quarrelsome woman tucked in her *palloo*, the loose part of her sari, girding herself for action, and she took this solemn oath as we listened spellbound:

> Hey mistress, here I come! I will crawl up your womb from below, and will take up residence and kick my feet inside you. I'll grab your liver and swing on it. In fact, I'll enter during the spring Holi festival and I won't leave until the autumn Diwali festival! Don't think I am any ordinary woman—I will wreck your life and leave your body in such ruin that in all your years you will never forget me!

A tragic love affair also unraveled nearby. A woman had an affair with a man whom her brother disliked. One day the brother hid outside the hut until he spied his sister's lover. Then he proceeded to thrash him mercilessly. The lover somehow escaped, but then later sneaked into his assailant's hut with a knife and murdered him. When the case went to court, the woman surprisingly took the side of her lover and claimed he had struck in self-defense. Later on she became known as *Bhaumaree* (brother-killer).

I still cannot understand how we managed to study in this disturbing, riotous neighborhood. The only solution was to study very early in the morning when it was quiet. The habit of rising early that Grandmother Saguna had inculcated in us proved quite a boon in this situation.

In any case, I studied very hard towards the end as exams approached. Then a distracting incident occurred while the exams were in full swing. One evening, my friends Buddha, Pandurang, and Mahadev Meshram came to see me. They told me about a deeply distraught cook who had just lost his fourteen-year-old daughter to an illness. He had recently moved to Umrer, so he did not know many people. Because he was from the *somvanshee* subcaste of the mahar community, the mahars of Umrer were unwilling to help him arrange a funeral procession to the cremation grounds. How could our people, scorned and oppressed by others, likewise scorn one of our own? This old narrow-minded orthodoxy upset us all.

My friends said that some young and broadminded people needed to step forward to help him. Usually I would be the first to volunteer, but I had an annual exam the next morning, and I felt that my whole future hinged on that crucial exam. But they implored me to help, and eventually, they prevailed. It was late at night when I returned home exhausted. I had no energy for eating, let alone for studying.

The next day I headed off to take the exam after studying a little in the morning. It did not go well. But still, with the exam was over, my mood lifted and I went with my friends to Bhivapur to observe Ambedkar Jayanti, a program in celebration of Babasaheb's birthday. Our community leader Janbandhu Guru made me the president of the program saying that it was time for young people to come forward to leadership positions. My friends were elated to see me elevated to that status and enthusiastically chanted, '*Nimgade kare pukar, Babasaheb ki*

Jayjayakar,' meaning 'Nimgade is giving the call for all to shout the praise of Babasaheb Ambedkar.

When the exam results were announced, I had passed some exams by a narrow margin, but had fared exceptionally well in other subjects. What counted, was that overall, I had passed this battery of qualifying exams.

IN 1945, I WENT with friends to Nagpur to attend a conference of the Scheduled Caste Students' Federation. Of all the speeches, I still remember one by a man named Kamble, who always spoke in English. His English was so inspirational, flowing, and natural, that people started calling him "Michael" Kamble. Kamble said,

> This beautiful, magnificent building, and the other halls and colleges we see here today did not rise up out of nothing. It was the labor of our people that built all this. Our forefathers, our uncles, and our brothers toiled here, in the mud and the dirt; they built these buildings with their blood and their sweat. But can we come here freely to enjoy all this and study in these same buildings? No, we are barred by caste discrimination and poverty from coming here. Our community must right this great injustice by educating ourselves, our children, and our grandchildren!

The next meeting of the Conference was to be held in the town of Chandrapur. In order to make that possible, several students, including myself, volunteered to collect funds. It was a welcome opportunity for me to travel from one village to another collecting donations. I had no money to spare, so I went on foot. In this manner, I walked about four hundred miles that summer, to visit about two hundred villages across the Nagpur, Chanda, and Bhandara districts. On some days it would be extremely hot, with the sun directly overhead, and with my feet almost directly in the shadow of my head.

In every village in the evening I would hook up with local social workers and we would assemble everyone and tell them about Babasaheb Ambedkar—about how he had educated and advanced himself, and about the social movement and the progress that he championed. The village people were poor, hardworking and could not afford much, yet they still gave according to their ability—some just one or two annas, some one or two rupees.

In Brahmapuri, the district official, Nagdavne, who was from the mahar community, fed me, housed me, and also gave a good donation. In addition, he gave me five extra rupees, saying, 'You are a student, and yet you still walk from village to village in this hot and harsh season. It may give you sunstroke and sap your strength. I want you to use these rupees to travel with.'

However, I still went on foot, not wanting to spend a single paisa on myself while doing social work. I came to understand village culture and their unique customs, traditions, and faith firsthand. I learned the songs women sang as they ground their grains on stonemills at home; I learned abhangs and bhajans, proverbs, and village idioms; from a holy man Sant Gadge Maharaj and his disciple Kaykade Maharaj I learned the art of giving *kirtan* and *pravachan*—sermons and religious discourse. Afterwards, all these helped me in my writings and speeches. I learned which villages were more progressive and which were backward, and I met and learned from many social reform workers. Along the way, I also made many friends. If you have a sweet tongue, the Marathi proverb goes, you will have friends anywhere in the world.

Finally I returned to Nagpur to hand over the collected funds to the well-known community leader, Advocate Sakharam Meshram, whom I had heard speak at several assemblies. Before accepting the donations he asked where I was from. When I said 'Umrer,' his curiosity was piqued. 'Have you heard of this boy from Umrer who has been canvassing villages on foot, not spending a single paisa on himself? Many other volunteers will collect ten rupees and spend five on themselves. The boy's name is Nimgade. Do you know him?'

'I am Nimgade,' I shyly said, and handed him 115 rupees. He looked at me with surprise. Then he barraged me with questions about my background and struggle. This was our first meeting, and we were to become good friends.

Advocate Meshram told me that the conference planned for Chanda had been postponed. The Scheduled Caste Federation and the Student Federation meetings would be held in Bombay. A delegation of students and social reform workers was going, and he said that I should join them. I humbly declined because I had no money. Then he took fifty rupees out of the 115 and said, 'Since you labored so hard in the harsh heat to collect these funds, I myself will take out fifty rupees for your expenses and tickets to go to the Bombay conference.' I was very thankful and impressed by his consideration and his appreciation of my hard work.

When I returned to Umrer and briefed our Udaykal Mandal members about the developments, they were also surprised and impressed by Advocate Meshram's thoughtfulness. Seven of them agreed to go to Bombay with me.

The Bombay conference, held in May 1945, drew delegates from all over India. We were all housed at a local school. Dr Babasaheb Ambedkar was very pleased by the number of participants. He said in his speech:

> My dear fellow *samaj bandhus* (brothers of our community), this is a very important milestone in the progress of our Scheduled Caste Federation. We had set up the Federation in 1942, only three years ago, in Nagpur. We have made much progress since then and most of our untouchable brethren are coming up under one flag. This has made me very happy. However, we have no resources, not even a newsletter. The injustices committed on our fellow untouchables cannot be documented or reported. Without money, it is difficult to provide education for the poor. Therefore it is crucial to come together to fight to overcome our difficulties.

In this speech Babasaheb introduced his famous call to action – *Shika, Sanghatit Vha, Sangharsh Kara* – 'Educate, Organize, Agitate!'

The next day, at the same venue where the Scheduled Castes Students' Federation met, Babasaheb Ambedkar delivered a stirring speech in which he said, 'As I have gotten my education, so can anyone else with hard work and determination. One person can progress individually and then pull the whole community forward.' This made a very deep impression on my mind and soul. I made a very clear commitment to myself that whatever the difficulties ahead, I would persevere with strong determination and hard work to gain higher education.

AFTER THE CONFERENCE was over, my seven fellow Umrer delegates and I explored the metropolis of Bombay. Thus far, Nagpur had been the largest city I had ever visited. But Bombay was a city on a world scale. It housed the film studios that had made India the largest film industry in the world, and its tall buildings swept all the way down to the crescent-shaped Marine Drive along the Arabian Sea. Nagpur seemed a village in comparison.

For us, however, a highlight of the trip was a visit to Babasaheb's bungalow. Dr Ambedkar had already returned to India's capital city of New Delhi, where he was a minister in the government. His nephew Mukundrao showed us Babasaheb's bedroom, library, and study. We noticed a pet cat, and we felt that she was more blessed than us because she could stay and roam freely throughout Babasaheb's house and grounds. Upon seeing this beautiful and majestic residence, we were filled with respect for and pride in Babasaheb. Babasaheb's bungalow, which he had named *Rajagriha,* compared favorably to higher-caste residences in the posh neighborhood.

All of us came from poor families, and we had to watch our money carefully. In those days, for eight annas one could get an all-you-can-eat special. We landed at a restaurant one afternoon, paid our money in advance and sat down to eat. We were famished, having not eaten since the previous afternoon meal, and devoured the first serving of food. While awaiting the next serving, we ate up all the roti even before the dal arrived. After it did, we ate it up before the rice made it to the table. By the time the vegetables finally arrived, we had finished the rice. We stayed there, eating more and more, until we finally finished all the food in the restaurant, leaving all the cooks and serving staff completely exhausted.

We heard later that the next day some other people from Nagpur had gone to the same restaurant. When the proprietor found out where they were from, he immediately said, 'I am sorry, Sirs, but no Nagpurians allowed!'

Wandering around so busily with my friends, I completely forgot about the forthcoming results of my exams. By June, however, when the results were announced, I came to my senses. I passed in the third (lowest) division and this distressed me. I blamed and cursed myself for having roamed around with my friends, swimming, wrestling, traveling to fairs and weddings. I started to repent for all the valuable time I had wasted on frivolities when I should have been studying. The mind truly resists focusing because it wants something different at every moment, as the Hindi proverb points out: '*Manke matta chalieyen nahin, palak palak man aour.*'

Then I consoled myself that at least I did not fail. All the effort of the last year did not go to waste. I should be able to get admission to a college somewhere or other. This hopeful thought led me to start seriously thinking about where and how to study next.

My friends were also happy that I passed, and knowing my financial circumstances, they collected funds for a graduation party for me. Some friends said that on such occasions, it was permissible to drink alcohol. Although I had limited experience with alcohol, we started off in high spirits to purchase *sindi*, made from fermented palm juice.

That day clouds filled the sky. Suddenly a bolt of lightning struck a nearby house. We were blinded and deafened for seconds, and then we heard loud cries and wailing. We ran to help. This house had been the scene of a happy occasion with people preparing for a wedding. The women had gathered

The stately buildings of Nagpur University.

upstairs with the bride, talking happily and singing traditional songs. Then lightning struck that room, killing the girl who was preparing the bride. Many women were injured and many had fainted from fear. We took the injured on cots to the hospital. The hospital, being small, had only one doctor and one physician's assistant. With so many patients, they asked us to stay and assist them. And so our party to celebrate my passing of the matric exam was forgotten.

My parents were overjoyed that I had passed the matric exam, and had thus vindicated their hard work and sacrifice and their faith in me. My father said, 'Namdeo, my son, you have studied as much as you can. Now is the time to make the most of your life. You should be able to get a good job now.' My father's Muslim friend Pinjari agreed, saying that now you can easily land a good job as a police officer and eat well. But Babasaheb's had sowed the idea of higher education in my mind at the Bombay SCF meeting and I did not want to settle into a job; by now I had a burning desire to get higher education and perhaps even study at the Rani ka Mahal, the Queen's Palace—the Agriculture College in Nagpur.

I asked my father for his permission to study further. I promised that I would somehow find a way to pay for my education, without asking him for anything more than my admission fees. Father was understanding and sympathetic. Always a progressive thinker, he had already helped a boy from a neighboring village who had failed his matriculation exam. My father persuaded the boy's father to give him another chance and even housed the boy at our home so he could study. The only thing the boy's father provided for his son's support was some rice once and some dal another time. My father even took a collection from friends to cover the boy's "supplementary exam" fee.

With my father's blessing, I excitedly filled out the Nagpur University admission application form. But one of the items to fill out was about how much acreage the applicant's family had under cultivation. I immediately became dejected and worried that I would be rejected outright because our family of landless laborers had no fields. Finally, some friends suggested that I bring along a social reform worker to meet with the principal of the agricultural college to explain why it was essential for landless students to learn about agriculture.

Hemchandra Khandekar, a social reform worker from the mahar community, agreed to accompany me for this task. At Nagpur College, we met with D.V. Baal, who was substituting for the principal, Mr Churchill, who was in England for summer holidays. Mr Baal was convinced by our explanation that landless laborers could make an impact on farming practices, and he recommended my admission. He must have subsequently communicated at this very point to the vacationing principal, because that year, of the six Scheduled Caste students admitted, four were landless.

PART II

THE CITY

The moneylender and the Queen's Palace

Once I gained admission to the Agricultural College the question of funding arose, because in those days all students had to pay fees—there were no scholarships. For this matter I wrote a letter addressed to the kind-hearted citizens of Umrer, requesting financial assistance for an ambitious student hungry for education. Bearing this letter, I approached several affluent and philanthropic townspeople. Many people rewarded me with sympathy and advice, and a few gave me a rupee or two. How could I afford college on that meager amount? I then asked my father to help me find a loan. The two of us approached the moneylender Helwatkar Sahukar. He laughed at us with contempt and said, '*Arrey*, you people don't have enough to eat, yet why do you hunger for education? Would it kill you to get a job?'

My father pleaded with him, but the hardhearted man remained untouched, even when my father prostrated himself, touching the moneylender's feet.

'Go away,' the moneylender said, shrugging off my father. 'You don't get money by shaking a tree. How can I lend you anything? What security do I have that you will pay me back?'

I was shattered to see my father humiliated. It is no wonder that Dr Ambedkar referred to the Indian moneylender as

> the worst parasitic class known to history... He does not use his money for production. He uses it to create poverty and more poverty by lending money for unproductive purposes... he is told by his religion that moneylending is the occupation prescribed to him by Manu, he looks upon it as both right and righteous. With the help and assistance of the brahmin judge who is ready to decree his suits, he is able to carry on his trade. Interest, interest on interest, he adds on and on and thereby draws families perpetually in to his net. His

> grip over the nation is complete... The whole of the poor, starving, illiterate India is mortgaged to [him].[1]

Yet a new burning desire grew within me to not only educate myself well, but also to teach such people to lose their intoxication for money and wealth.

I believe that those who have firmly made a decision, and work hard, with self-confidence, sincere effort, and concentration, can achieve the most difficult ambitions in life. My father and I kept trying for funds. The concept of *prayananthi parmeshwar* – of repeatedly striving for success – is what sustained our efforts. Vithoba Savji gave me twenty-five rupees. I collected another twenty rupees from Karim Sethji, Mansukh Sethji, and Govindrao Munimji. We even sold my mother's silver bracelets and other items to earn another thirty. In total I now had seventy-five rupees, while the Agricultural College fee was forty rupees a month.

Since the Agricultural College hostels were expensive, I could not stay there. Instead, I stayed at the Chokhamela Hostel, which cost only eight rupees a month. The hostel was established by forward-thinking social reformers, to house poor students from neighboring villages. The Chokhamela hostel was named after of the devotional, untouchable fifteenth-century poet, who had to stand outside the temple to worship the deity Vitthal. The hostel was about four miles from our college. I did not have a bicycle, so I had to walk. I would have to leave at seven a.m. for laboratory practicals, and then return to eat and wash up, then again report to classes at 11 a.m. and finally return to the hostel at 5 p.m.

To cover my other expenses and avoid burdening my father, I started tutoring two boys from a Bengali family for ten rupees a month. I picked up an extra two rupees a month tutoring a girl from a Christian family. Her house was on the way to my college. Her mother would give me a cup of coffee, which removed the

---

[1] *Dr Babasaheb Ambedkar Writings and Speeches*, (Bombay: Education Department, Government of Maharashtra, Ed. V. Moon 1991) vol. 9: 201–17.

fatigue of the day. The girl was weak in studies and just her expression led one to believe that she was not very bright.

One day I was very tired. I had been trying very hard to teach her, but the task was like trying to pour tea into an upside-down cup. That session proved a test of my endurance and patience. Frustrated, I finally snapped and slapped her cheek, muttering, 'I have been trying to explain things to this *dari* for so long, but she is not learning anything.'

Tears gathered in her eyes. 'You are not here to slap me,' she said. 'My father gives you money to teach me.'

'I am sorry, I didn't mean to hit you. Today I was very tired. It won't happen again.' Remorsefully, I touched her cheek lightly.

Just then, Doctor Pereira, a family friend who always called on them, entered the room. Embarrassed, I quickly removed my hand. He chuckled, 'Please carry on your tuition.' He must have thought that he was witnessing a romantic moment!

After he left, she asked, tearfully, 'Why did you scold me, calling me *dari*?' The word dari is a village term meaning 'good for nothing' or 'idiot.' I became frightened, thinking this could have ended my tuition job.

Thinking quickly I said, 'In my village language, they say dari because they cannot pronounce the English word *darling*.' Slowly, she started to smile, and sighed with relief.

In this way my daily routine of learning and teaching proceeded. My father used to send one or two postcards a month to keep me updated on family matters and to encourage my studies. After my move to Nagpur, my brother Ankush was left all alone in Umrer. My mother and my younger siblings therefore moved to Umrer to be with him. My brothers Rambhau and Prabhakar and my sister Anjani all enrolled in Umrer schools. Thus the family base shifted to Umrer from Sathgaon and we could no longer be considered a rural family. Umrer seemed far more accessible because of the railroad, and I started returning to Umrer for all holidays.

One day at the Chokhamela Hostel I received a letter from my father informing me of my grandmother Saguna's demise. My eyes were filled with tears and my heart was heavy with sadness. I remembered my childhood years with her, when I would quail before her stream of insults, proverbs, and abusive poetry. I recalled how we would laugh heartily when her stream of invective was directed at grown men. Now I yearned to hear them from her lips again. More than just a grandmother, she was also a second mother to me who inculcated in us the qualities of discipline and self-respect.

My father had not informed me that Saguna died because they did not want to interfere with my studies. She had hurt herself while laboring in the mango orchard, recovered from the injury, but limped a little. A few days later she relapsed and knew her condition was worsening. Ever practical to the end, she extracted a promise from the family not to call anybody and to not disturb my studies; we were not to hire a band for the funeral procession, we were not to spend money on new clothes for her body, and we were to bury rather than cremate her, as this was cheaper.

On Saguna's last day on earth, Grandfather Budha bathed her and combed her hair. He got her fresh jalebi from the bazaar, and cradling her in his lap he fed them to her. Hearing this story about their deep affection for each other, I could visualize the scene perfectly and it brought tears to my eyes. Saguna's entreaty to be buried and not cremated made me remember this Hindi couplet:

> *Prana mere nikal rahe hain, gam no karna prannath,*
> *Mitti bharte bharte hogi, akhri mulakat.*
>
> (My life is leaving my body; do not mourn, dear husband, lord of my life/ As you pour the soil over me, that will be our last meeting.)

I WAS SOMEHOW funding my education and keeping my expenses to a minimum. Since I had no good clothes, I wore what my military friend Nagdevte had given to me. For two annas or so, I could buy pants and a shirt from the rag market. I could also buy used notebooks which still had some blank pages. Buying new books was inconceivable. I only bought used books that were absolutely essential for agricultural subjects. I bought books for no other subjects—not even English. Grandmother Saguna would have been proud of me.

The specter of prison

In those days colleges enjoyed a month of holidays in the fall for the Dussehra and Diwali festivals. Instead of returning home, I used those holidays to work for our political candidates in the upcoming 1946 elections. On 27 September 1945, I went to the village of Pavni to attend an election rally. Following a stirring speech by Advocate Sakharam Meshram, the chief guest from Nagpur, and other social reform workers including myself, had a chance to share our ideas and talk about Babasaheb Ambedkar's mission.

I spoke about how in the Puranas, it is said that God, even to help one devotee, appears on earth as an avatar. But seventy million untouchables are suppressed and oppressed, mired in poverty and ignorance, and yet no god has appeared on earth to show compassion for them. Really, instead of worshipping these stone idols, let us follow the advice and example of Dr Ambedkar, who has lifted us from the bottom of the social order to lead us to salvation and progress. We must live with self-respect, not as slaves. In order to better our lives, we must work for knowledge and higher education. We must not feel defeated and inferior; instead, we must uphold the ideal of the hero Karna from the Hindu epic, the Mahabharatha, who suffered many indignities because of his low birth. We would do well to keep in mind the Sanskrit sloka,

> *Sutto wah, sutton puttron wah, Yo wah, kow wah, bhavanmeyin hum*
> *Deivaya yetta kulay janman, madha yetthai cha paurusham.*
>
> (It is not in our hands to choose our birth, caste, or family;
> But it is in our hands to choose action to earn merit.)

I continued along these lines, saying that dragging dead

animals to dispose of them, eating decaying meat, and entering into the slavery of bonded forced labor were some of the traditional practices that we should relinquish. Going to the temple was not necessary. I spoke against the caste system, and criticized the people who observed the system blindly and propagated injustice by humiliating and harassing other human beings. Except for some of the higher-caste people who came to listen out of curiosity, everyone appreciated the speech very much. Some of my Nagpur classmates, A.D. Meshram and Baliram Waghmare, then set up a program for me to speak in their native village of Kaurambhi.

There, near the town of Pavni, we swam in the Wainganga river and then hiked up a nearby hill. We walked by a temple dedicated to the Hindu god Shiva, or Shankar. Untouchables were not allowed to enter Hindu temples, as their very presence would be defiling. Some of us suddenly had a yearning to enter the temple; after all, if even birds and beasts could freely wander in and out, why not us? The impetuous blood of youth beckoned us. More than a matter of exercising our religious faith, we wanted to exercise our rights as human beings. We were on the verge of entering the temple when we caught sight of Dagoji Bankar, the brother-in-law of A.D. Meshram. He stood some distance outside the temple and with great reverence began to prostrate himself on the ground to worship. We surrounded him and began to ask him questions. One of us said, 'What's in the temple anyway?'

Dagoji replied, 'God.'

'Which God and what kind of God—one who lets injustices be committed against us?'

Dagoji had no answer. Others chimed in, 'How can he really be a God if he sits in the temple and merely witnesses all that happens in the world?' Or, 'Why should we worship such a God?'

As these questions became more and more heated, the son of the village landlord came walking by. He was also a college student, but unlike us, he was a follower of orthodox traditions. Now our discussion turned towards him and intensified. We severely criticized the Hindu gods and religion, and we could see a deep anger kindling within him. We ended up leaving without entering the temple.

Later on I heard that the son of the village chief had spoken to all the higher castes in his village and had poisoned their minds against us. Some of them were so enflamed that they themselves went to the temple under the cover of night to break and throw idols of the sacred bull Nandi and the lingam pind representation of Shiva. They then went to the Pavni police station with their own false eyewitnesses and accused six of us – Mahadev Meshram, Arjun Meshram, Baliram Waghmare, Ramteke, even the pious Dagoji Bankar, and myself – of committing this crime of desecration.

I knew nothing of these developments since I was elsewhere presenting another *kirtan* and *pravachan* in the village of Bhuyar. Suddenly, on 2 October 1945, the Pavni police arrived in Sathgaon and began inquiring about me. In our small village the news spread like wildfire. In the higher-caste area, people magnified my powers, saying, 'It's good that they are looking for Nimgade, otherwise he might also have attacked our famous Dattatreya temple!' Others felt that the mahars nowadays were getting too insolent and should be taught a lesson or two. A poisonous atmosphere of caste discrimination, mistrust, and hateful blind faith now replaced any remaining feelings of friendliness or neighborliness. Even villagers who had taken pride in my educational accomplishments now despised me.

Grandfather Budha, who was probably about ninety years old but fit and strong in every way, suddenly sat down as if his back had been broken. Thereafter, in fact, he appeared to need the support of a cane for the first time in his life. Weakly he muttered, 'Oh Namdeo, I always used to advise you to be very careful and diligent. Even the mighty tiger is watchful and wary, and suspicious about even his own shadow. I have lived so long and I have never had to confront the police on anything. Remember that you should always go behind the police station, and never in the front. What have you done, Nama?' Hearing his lamentations brought tears to the eyes of everyone in the family.

By now, most of the people of the village had assembled near our hut. Even small children abandoned their games and came to watch. It was a blessing in a way that my mother was away in Umrer and that Grandmother Saguna was not living, so they did not have to see this. My mind was full of worries about my reputation and my pursuit of education. I felt that my parents' sacrifice was now wasted; their hopes and ambitions were now ground into the dust.

My father said, 'Namdeo, do not lose heart. You have not stolen, or gambled, or murdered anyone. You went to Kaurambhi to spread the message of social reform. I have faith in my Namdeo; he would never do such a destructive deed. Go now, son: I will accept for now that I have three instead of four sons.' Hearing his loving words of encouragement, my heart was overwhelmed and my eyes moistened.

'Nama, tears in your eyes?' My father asked gently. 'If you work for social reform, you will have to endure many things. The truth will prevail. Do not weep.'

I replied, 'Father, these are tears of happiness after realizing how fortunate I am to be the son of such a lofty-hearted man. Seeing your faith in me, I vow that I will always preach the message of Dr Ambedkar. I will serve my community and will never let anything blot our family honor.'

The police took me to Pavni. A lot of people had gathered there because only four days ago, I had given my speech wherein I had criticized the Hindu religion and the caste system. The atmosphere was very tense with supportive and sympathetic members of my community on one side and angry, vengeful upper-caste people on the other. Fortunately, the police subinspector was a promoter of education and was very considerate. He said, 'I feel you are innocent, but had I not arrested you, I feared communal riots might have erupted here. So please cooperate with us and help us avoid rioting.' Bail was set at 200 rupees for each person. Raghunath Waghmare of Pavni, brother of Baliram Waghmare, put up my bail.

In Pavni this was the only topic of discussion. The entire town churned with various permutations of the story. The untruth, after all, spreads like wind, far faster than truth. The news even reached Nagpur where the *Navbharat* newspaper headline read, 'Followers of Dr Ambedkar desecrate Hindu temple.' One rumor held that a pig had been killed and thrown in the village well. When rumors stretch the truth, the Hindi proverb warns, a foot-long cucumber ends up with a nine-foot seed. Word was spreading that the mahars had become very insolent, seeking education and trying to touch the sky.

A Hindi proverb summarized my condition well: '*Ek to karela, upar se neem chaddha*' (The bitter-gourd vine now climbs the bitter neem tree: meaning bitterness upon bitterness). First our financial misery, then the struggle of college studies, and now to top it all, this court case and the constant need to appear in Bhandara district, which was about an hour's journey by bus. I felt that all the troubles and anxieties of the world had fallen on my shoulders. I was so spent with worry that I could not concentrate on my studies.

> *Peeche bhee jaun kahan, age badhna bhee hai katheen,*
> *Andhkar hai ghanghore, lagta hai eksa raat din.*
>
> (There is no place to retreat, and it is difficult to go ahead, I am engulfed by the intense darkness, day and night look alike.)

Until now no one from my clan had ever gone to court for anything. On the days we were called to court we would have to leave our college obligations and travel to Bhandara. It was natural that our studies would suffer. My state of mind was so low that my friends and family were quite alarmed. I had no desire to groom myself and I let my hair and beard grow out. Even in this disturbed and distressed condition, I somehow managed to maintain my grades and successfully completed my first year of college.

According to my nature, even with the court case, I did not stop the work of visiting local untouchable neighborhoods to enroll students there in the Scheduled Castes Students' Federation. It brought me some relief from my own worries. The membership fee was a modest four annas in those days, but even this posed a hardship for people. There was such an intense desire for education, thanks to Babasaheb's inspiration, that from almost each untouchable hut people were sending their sons and daughters to school. Now, even farm laborers, roadside workers, and coolies joined the ranks of the educated. Our people were awakened to the need for education.

The Chokhamela Hostel was near the house of Advocate Sakharam Meshram, himself an alumnus of our hostel. Therefore, he got to know all the students there very well. Advocate Meshram would gather us together in a nearby park on Sundays and discuss Babasaheb's books such as *Who were the Shudras* and *What Congress and Gandhi have done to the Untouchables*. His belief was that all Scheduled Caste students should be able to discuss and state their viewpoints fearlessly and skillfully. He therefore made students take opposing viewpoints on certain subjects to practice debating. With practice, all of us gained verbal confidence to match our desire to fight injustice and affect social reform. Many who left this hostel went on to become staunch social reform workers and revolutionaries and earned good names for themselves. You will see this in the paragraphs to come.

On 24 January 1941 Chokhamela Hostel celebrated its Silver Jubilee. The organizers felt that inviting Gandhi as the chief guest might help secure a lot of grants. But many of our students were strongly opposed to this idea. This may surprise many readers, who have likely grown up reading generally positive things about Gandhi. And who could argue against stated sentiments such as 'I would rather that untouchability die than Hinduism live?' Gandhi was no doubt a brave man, not only for his opposition to the colonial rule of India but also for maintaining a simple garb that led Churchill to refer to him as a 'half-naked fakir.' In his simple lifestyle, he maintained a standing with the common man that no politician could match. It is no wonder that Gandhi would become a convenient symbol for the Congress party. But he was not always a convenient symbol for the party, coming to differences over the direction India should follow, with Gandhi favoring rural values and Nehru favoring industrialization. Perhaps the best summary of the complex character of Gandhi is provided by the writer George Orwell, who labeled Gandhi as 'a saint among politicians, and a politician among saints.' If the symbol of Gandhi has inspired some of his followers to discard casteism, then some good has come from Gandhi's ideas.

Initially there was much hope on the part of our community that Gandhi would work in our interests, since he said many of the right things about the evils of untouchability. With the Poona Pact of 1932, however, Gandhi snatched away all the separate electoral rights for the untouchables that Babasaheb had fought for and folded them into the joint electorate. This ensured that even with political seats reserved for untouchables, successful candidates would have to appeal to the interests of other communities, and not truly represent the downtrodden. But perhaps our community's greatest opposition to Gandhi came from his challenging Babasaheb's status as leader of the untouchables. At the famous Round Table Conference in London, aimed at transitioning toward independence, Gandhi had opposed Dr Ambedkar's representing the untouchables. To gain his way, Gandhi would often resort to fasts unto death, a political tool tantamount to soft blackmail that exasperated Babasaheb and our community. Even the illiterate villagers of our community often made colorful and cutting remarks about these tactics and would joke about how our community saved Gandhi time and again from death by giving up our rights.

While Gandhi wanted to appear to lead the untouchables to emancipation, his actions often suppressed our progress. Gandhi, you see, while opposed to the violent excesses of casteism believed in the hereditary system of caste. He thought reform should come about through compassion of individuals rather than, as Babasaheb thought, through attainment of political rights and political equality. At Gandhi's ashram in

Wardha, Maharashtra, he had a brahmin lad sweep the compound to show the sweepers that their hereditary work of sweeping was socially important and meaningful; he was less interested in letting sweepers advancing up the rungs of society.

In 1938, Gandhi was unhappy when our state Prime Minister Dr N.B. Khare of the Congress party appointed R.U. Agnibhoj from the untouchable cobbler community as a minister in his cabinet. On 26 July, Gandhi called a Congress Working Committee meeting at Wardha and accused Dr Khare of not keeping the discipline of the Congress party. He claimed that untouchables were not even worthy of becoming county officers, let alone ministers. Dr Khare was so disgusted with this statement that he resigned his post as Prime Minister of Central Provinces and Berar and thus the whole assembly was dissolved. Thus ended the first ministership of a member of the Scheduled Caste community.

Gandhi's actions reminded many of the proverb: '*Muh mein Ram, baggal main churee*' (the holy name of Ram on the tongue, but a concealed knife in the hand). Gandhi himself may have heard about the opposition to him, so this may be why he traveled past Nagpur, got off the train at a small station, and then came back by car to Chokhamela Hostel for the festivities. The untouchables waved black flags and carried out a peaceful demonstration, but some goons disrupted the event by striking the protesters with lathis and throwing stones at the event tent.

Sensing a growing danger, Advocate Meshram, N.H. Kumbhare and other social reform workers surrounded Gandhi and the Principal D. Churchill with their open umbrellas, and safely escorted them outside. The protesters then vented their frustration on Advocate Meshram and broke one of his ribs. They were about to throw him in a well when some social reform workers rescued him. The untouchables were held responsible in newspapers for all this trouble, while in fact we ambedkarites saved Gandhi from harm.

The atmosphere in Nagpur had grown tense.

Riot!

When Lord Linlithgow was the Viceroy of India, he appointed Dr Ambedkar to his executive council. As a British gentleman, he respected the wisdom of Babasaheb Ambedkar, and once remarked, 'Dr Ambedkar, you are the equivalent of two hundred graduates.' 'How?' asked Babasaheb.

When Lord Linlithgow was unable to readily answer, Dr Ambedkar furnished an explanation: 'It is because I have acquired my knowledge with tremendous determination, devotion, and hard work. In this manner I acquired a deep knowledge of many subjects.' He then went on, 'I want to provide the same quality of higher education for my fellow untouchable people. Please, you must make this possible by sanctioning grants to aid their education.'

Dr Linlithgow accepted his proposal and in 1945, sixteen dalit students from India were given scholarships to go to England for higher education. Three of those sixteen were former residents of Chokhamela Hostel. The hostel gave them a grand reception. I kept wondering that if I had started school at the proper age, at six instead of fourteen years, I perhaps might have been honored to join them in England.

ON 12 DECEMBER 1945, Babasaheb Ambedkar came to Nagpur in connection with the provincial elections. The All India Scheduled Caste Federation, the Samata Sainik Dal and the untouchables of Nagpur gave him a grand welcome. I served as one of his bodyguards. Babasaheb's growing popularity made us increasingly fear for his safety in this potentially explosive atmosphere. Sometimes we guarded him so closely that we would step on his feet, but often we could offer only mental apologies.

The assembly was held in a central location, at Kasturchand

Park. Babasaheb warned that in this election, we should elect candidates worthy of representing our interests, and that the Congress party, aligned with Gandhi, should not meddle with our representation. Without political power, there would be no future for us. We must be awakened and alert to protect our rights. Through his speeches and writings, Babasaheb truly touched many lives; even those of villagers who could not read his writings or even hear him. The Hindi proverb reminds us why: '*Surat se kierat badhi, bin pankhon se udhjaya.*' (Good deeds and fame spread far and wide without wings.)

The untouchable people were so anxious to hear Babasaheb Ambedkar that they would endure any pain to do so. An example of this devotion is provided by a distant relative of ours named Dattu Mama, who made his living chopping firewood and always walked with his ax hanging from one shoulder. On this day he was excited to hear Babasaheb Ambedkar after a day of hard work. When a drunken man stopped him and asked him to chop some firewood, Dattu Mama politely refused, stating that he was going to hear Babasaheb talk. This answer infuriated the fellow, and he again insisted that Dattu Mama chop wood for him. Again Dattu Mama refused. Suddenly the man grabbed the ax from Dattu Mama and brought it down on his shoulders, cursing, 'How dare you refuse to work for me? What will you get from this speech of Ambedkar?' Poor Dattu Mama was badly wounded and never got a chance to hear Dr Ambedkar's speech.

When I heard what had happened to Dattu Mama, I went to the hospital to see him. His physical suffering and mental agony touched me deeply. I immediately gave him the two rupees that my father had recently forced upon me to replace my torn shirt.

'Dear Namdeo,' my father had said, 'now you are studying in college these torn clothes do not suit you anymore.' The next month my father came again from Umrer to see me, and I happened to be wearing the same torn shirt which I had repaired with needle and thread in many places. Upon seeing this, he said, 'Last month I gave you two rupees to buy a shirt but you disobeyed me!'

I told him what had befallen Dattu Mama, and Father was also stricken with sorrow for our relative. We both went to see Dattu Mama at his house. He welcomed us, and with tears of gratitude said to my father, 'Your son Namdeo is very compassionate. He has a boundless sympathy for the poor, and he is willing to help with deeds, not just words.' On hearing this, my father's face lit up with pride.

Two days after Babasaheb Ambedkar's appearance in Nagpur the Samata Sainik Dal held a conference where people spoke out about injustice against the Scheduled Castes and the necessity to fight for rights. The Secretary of the All India Scheduled Caste Federation, P.N. Rajbhoj, said, 'The Congress Party is systematically trying to divide and rule the various Scheduled Caste groups and they are resorting to false means to get their own candidates elected on reserved seats (seats reserved for Scheduled Castes). In recognition of their deceit, I declare that I will burn the sign of Congress, the Gandhi cap.'

A virtual Holi festival bonfire was lit, as many of those assembled threw their Gandhi caps into the flames. I took my father's white cap (commonly worn by villagers to protect against the harsh sun) and threw it in the flames. It brought to mind the incident from my childhood, so long ago, when Congress party miscreants in at a bonfire Sathgaon had snatched my gold thread cap to burn, and I felt avenged. This was somewhere around the same period that H.N. Hardas proposed using the slogan, *Jai Bhim*, meaning, "Victory to Bhim (Dr Bhimrao Ambedkar)" be used by untouchables in place of the usual greetings, "Ram Ram," "Johar Mai Bap," or "Namaskar." Although the phrase had not fully caught on yet, Mr Rajbhoj now reminded us again about the term "Jai Bhim." It subsequently caught on and has been used ever since.

Reading about the conference proceedings in the newspaper the next day, the higher caste people of Nagpur were infuriated. Caste tensions mounted. Random incidents of lathi beatings, insults, stone-throwing, molesting of women, and stabbings started to become more frequent.

In Nagpur, many of the mahars worked in the textile mills and were supporting Advocate Sakharam Meshram, who was contesting an election. The Congress party called for a strike in the mills, so as to cause difficulties for Meshram's supporters. They hoped that under financial pressure, many of the mahars would leave their mill jobs in Nagpur to find work elsewhere. But the mahars had deep endurance and pooled their resources to support each other, and even half-starved themselves to make victory possible.

In the Sitaburdi locality of Nagpur, Radhabai Kamble, a mill worker herself, inspired women laborers to fight for their rights with her powerful oratory. She organized the workers to go to work as a group because solitary workers were easy prey for caste-conscious goondas. The women would hide red chili powder in the folds of their sarees to throw in the eyes of would-be assailants, in order to save their modesty and honor.

Nagpur became a very frightful and dangerous place. In the end, the higher castes resorted to another trick to stop the untouchables from voting. They put the untouchable polling stations in high-caste neighborhoods. Their hope was to harass the untouchables as they came to exercise their franchise and to discourage them. But there is a limit to how much violence and injustice people can tolerate. Groups of wrestlers and fearless volunteer workers from our community escorted our women to the voting booths. They found, however, that the higher castes had their own pahalwans and goondas ready for combat. The sparks of this fighting grew into raging flames. Fighters from both sides were ready for a blood bath, carrying knives and swords and other weapons.

On election day, there were fights and beatings everywhere. We heard a rumor that Advocate Sakharam Meshram had been surrounded and arrested by the police. Upon hearing this, many mahars got together and converged on the police station. The police started a lathi charge on the crowd. Several people were wounded, and the crowd became uncontrollable with rage. The police started firing shots, first into the air, and then into the crowd, causing a stampede. We scattered in every which way to save our lives, but many died and many more were wounded. Right in front of me, near a bridge, I saw my friend Ramdas Dongre, who had just recently been married, get shot and die.

In this riot, two brave workers, Sampat and Husein, fought with courage, and ultimately fell while battling several ruffians. In their honor, Baburao Meshram, the poet with whom I was staying, composed this Hindi couplet:

> *Sampat, Husein dono, vaha veer the hamare,*
> *Kar vaar dushmone pein, rana mein gayen hai mare.*
>
> (Sampat and Husein were our bravest soldiers / They killed many enemies and were ultimately themselves killed.)

Several unfortunate individuals of all castes were trapped in the wrong place at the wrong time during the riots. In our neighborhood I ran into Bhivapurkar Koshti, member of a high caste of Umrer, who was stranded there. He had come to Indora to cast his vote. On seeing me he said, trembling with fear, 'Namdeo, you have appeared like God before me. Please save me, my brother!'

I felt sorry for him. I said, 'Brother, if you wear your Gandhi topi here, you will not survive. Please give it to me.' I took his Gandhi cap and escorted him to Baburao Meshram's house and hid him there until the riot calmed down. When all was quiet I escorted him out of the area.

For days afterward, casteism poisoned the air, with scattered beatings, fights, stabbings, and murders. Some young men went underground to escape police persecution and arrest. A boy named Raut was so intimidated and frightened that he stopped coming to Agriculture College. We students would try our best to go out in a group, and avoid going anywhere alone. However, I often had to go out alone for my tutoring jobs. The Chokhamela Hostel superintendent, Mr Tumpalleewaar, hailed from a higher caste and was warned to leave the hostel for his own safety. But he would say, 'I have great faith in the students here. They will protect me.' And he remained safe.

It took some time for the atmosphere to calm down in Nagpur. One day, as usual, I was walking home from college when I met a man I knew. I greeted him with the usual, 'Jai Bhim.'

His eyes suddenly darted all around him and he whispered, 'Don't use that greeting outside our neighborhood. Who knows who might be listening in the shadows and attack us!' Another day, a friend and his son were watching a parade in a park. Upon seeing me, the young boy, who was sitting on his father's shoulders, greeted me with 'Jai Bhim.' His father immediately covered his son's mouth and warned, 'Don't you dare say that again on the open road! If an enemy heard us, we could easily be beat into chutney!'

Sometimes good comes out of bad circumstances. During the communal emergency, all the mahars were united as if they were children of one mother, and they were ready to take on any enemy. They forgot their subcaste differences and other misunderstandings. Even the women and children stood ready to protect the community. Our men took to patrolling the neighborhood at night in groups of four or five. The mahars earned the reputation of taking tremendous revenge—one death from hooligans would be avenged by two hooligan deaths. The fame of mahars as fearless and brave warriors spread to outlying towns and villages, making people hesitate to instigate trouble with the community.

Just as Kurukshetra was the battlefield of the great Mahabharatha epic, the mahar-dominated area of Indora – site of most of the gunfire, beatings, lathi charges, and killings – became known as the battlefield of the Nagpur riots. After the riots, when anyone asked me where I lived, instead of saying Chokhamela Hostel, I would announce with great pride, 'I live in Indora.' It would please me to no end to hear the surprised reactions and admiration, '*Wah*, the people from Indora are fearsome and brave.'

The 'Temple-Destroying Nimgade!'

Because our temple desecration case was still underway, I gained undeserved notoriety as "*Mandir Todne Walla Nimgade*" or "the Temple Destroying Nimgade." As a result of this publicity, social reform meetings and conventions even outside Nagpur would always invite me to participate. I would attend these events during holidays from college. In 1945, I was invited to the Vidharbha Kotwal Parishad, an organization covering four districts, concerned with the welfare of village kotwal, lowly officials from the mahar community who served as watchmen to village chiefs. Prominent revolutionary and social reform workers were present, as was the chief guest, Dadasaheb Gaikwad from Nasik, a close associate of Babasaheb Ambedkar. Dadasaheb Gaikwad was a powerful orator who could switch effectively between refined Marathi and colorful village dialects. A generous characteristic of his was that he offered promising students and young social reformers chances to speak. On this occasion, he asked me to present my thoughts.

I said enthusiastically that because I came from a village, I knew the problems facing the village kotwal. Despite being given a heavy work burden they had been socially neglected. Kotwals had to perform sundry tasks ranging from removing bodies of dead animals to reporting robberies to the police to serving as luggage porters for any visiting police inspector to doing the bidding of the village chief. The kotwals had to live on whatever payment was given, which was usually inadequate. Furthermore, sometimes their excess workload had to be undertaken by their wives and children as if they were bonded laborers or slaves. In my short speech, I said that to gain relief from this servitude and injustice, the kotwals must be given an exact list of their duties and stick to only those specified duties. Furthermore, they must not be treated as slaves and should be paid according to their workload.

Dadasaheb Gaikwad appreciated my speech and he congratulated me heartily. We formed a friendship that continued when he went on to New Delhi later and served in the Rajya Sabha, the upper chamber of India's parliament. I was privileged to enjoy his friendship and affection until his death.

In August 1946, the Nagpur Scheduled Caste Students' Federation held elections. As I had done a lot of work canvassing for this group in many areas in Nagpur, I was elected to a leadership position by an overwhelming majority of votes. In December, we organized the All India Scheduled Caste Students' Federation Conference at Kasturba Park in Nagpur.

We requested Babasaheb Ambedkar to be the chief guest, but he was very busy writing the Constitution of India, which had to be completed in time for India's scheduled independence from England in 1947. Jogendranath Mandal, a prominent leader of SCF from Bengal, agreed to be our chief guest. I was appointed mess secretary, and that kept me very busy with meal arrangements for all the delegations. Although I did not get to attend all the proceedings, I was happy to see that the conference was a great success.

During the efforts to enroll students for our students federation, I had to visit many wards in Nagpur. In the Dharampeth area, I met a family of four sisters, living with their mother and grandmother. They told me that they missed their brother, who was away in Delhi, and so they asked me to stay for the evening meal with them. I agreed. The youngest girl was a high school student, at Saint Ursula School. She asked me to help her with her Botany class. She was an intelligent girl and her voice was melodious. I found myself going back to their house again and again to help her.

I began to feel a growing attraction to this girl. Using some precious funds from my tutoring work I bought some cloth, and took it to a tailor in their neighborhood to have a shirt made. In those days, tailoring involved interminable delays. I took advantage of this to come often to check on my shirt, and then I would go and see her. Her face would light up when I would come by. My friends would to tease me, calling me "Romeo." Unfortunately, with this blossoming romance and my court case, my attention to my studies was suffering.

One day when I went to visit her, the girl was not there. Instead, her grandmother sat me down and lectured me. She told me that exams were coming near; and neither of us students could afford to take our attention away from our schooling. She said that I was from a poor family, and I had come to Nagpur to study, and that was what I should focus upon. She forbade me from coming to see them anymore.

I was devastated. As I walked away, I saw the young girl. I told her of what her grandmother had said. She said nothing, but quietly, with tears in her eyes, she turned away and she went home. I knew it was over. I heard a Hindi film song from a radio in a nearby restaurant, *'Tera khilauna tuta balak, tera khilauna tuta hai, kismet ne loota.'* (Your toy is broken, child, broken, stolen by fate.) I felt that the song was about my dreams, and I hurried away from there. And then I heard from another radio the sad voice of K.L. Saigal singing a song from the classic romantic tragedy *Devdas*, *'Jab dil hi tut gaya, hum ji ke kya karenge.'* (When my heart is broken, what in the point of living.) Thus, I felt like the leading man Devdas himself, who had to let go of his love, and then had to spend the rest of his life empty and in pain.

One of my friends must have told Advocate Sakharam Meshram about my problems. He summoned me to his house and then exhorted me to put my mind to my studies. He said, 'This is an important year for you. First of all, you are in dire financial circumstances. Then there is a temple desecration case going on against you in the courts. Stop wandering here and there being distracted by romance; just concentrate on your studies. If you fail, think about the devastation and disappointment for your mother and father. Can you really afford to lose a year? Son, listen to me carefully. To be a serious and worthy student you must keep these five principles in mind: perseverance, concentration, light sleeping habits, light eating habits and no distracting thoughts of home. These are the *vidyarthi panchlakshanam* (five rules for students).'

As I listened to Advocate Meshram, the memory came rushing to my mind of how the moneylender Helwatkar Sahukar had rebuffed my request for an educational loan and had scoffed at my aspirations and humiliated my father. At that time I had vowed that I would pursue higher education; I would place education as the highest good, and thus show those rich people that there are better values to enthrone than wealth alone. In order to vindicate my father's faith in me and to clear the grave insult he had suffered, I had to work very hard. But now there had been so much damage done to my studies from both external and internal factors that I did not know where and how to start making amends. In the words of the Sanskrit proverb, '*Chinta chitta samanasti.*' (Worry and wood kindling for cremation are the same; they both burn and consume the human body and mind.)

On top of my other problems, I did not even have some necessary course books. One day the bungalow of a Parsi family close to our hostel caught on fire. As I ran to help, the thought occurred to me that if I were injured or burned while fighting the fire, I might not have to appear for exams. Heedless of my own safety, I rushed into the building. With the help of the neighbors and students, the fire was vanquished in no time and my plan was dashed. Now the only flames I fanned were those of worry.

In my perplexity, an idea dawned on me about how to study. I said to my fellow students, 'Friends, I have a proposition. I have no money for textbooks. But I will clean your clothes, make tea for you, and the like; and in return, please share with me whatever you read from the books.'

Five friends at the college agreed to help me by giving me their class notes to read and by explaining anything difficult. Two of the engineering school students helped me with mathematics; some students helped me with the English exam. One day I found that a book called *Real Achievements* was needed for the English exam the next day. My good friend Tularam Dongre, the same friend who had advised me to go into the sciences, immediately used his own money to buy the book, and he tore it into three parts. He and two other friends read each of these three parts and then summarized the contents for me. In this way, many of my friends in the hostel came to my rescue, and I will never forget how they helped me concentrate my body, mind, and will on studying.

In Chokhamela Hostel, the lights were shut off at ten p.m., and everybody had to to study until that time and then go to sleep. Because of my village roots, I could not adjust to this schedule since my eyes would start closing around eight p.m. Then I realized that I could wake up at four a.m. and study in the kitchen, when the staff turned on the kitchen lights and started their work for the day. The kitchen staff, being friendly and considerate, would minimize noise by whispering and using soft utensils so that I could concentrate.

I somehow managed to sit for exams in a fairly well-prepared state—but certainly not as well-prepared as I should have been. After the exam was over, I felt a huge burden had been lifted. My fickle mind immediately thought of returning to my social wanderings. I had missed my town of Umrer. My thoughts also turned to the family at Dharampeth, and the youngest daughter there. But the words of her grandmother came back to me, and I struggled to control my feelings. That road was closed to me, and it was best for me to forget it. I looked for some work to do, and I found a menial position in an office, sprinking water on the *khaskhas ki tattee*, a curtain of plant fibers that kept rooms cool in summer through the process of evaporation. Then, using some of my new earnings, I proceeded home to Umrer. After weeks in Umrer, wandering and laughing with friends, swimming in the village pond, reading in the library, and relaxing with the relatives the summer vacation disappeared in a flash.

That year the Ambedkar Jayanti was celebrated with great

pomp and splendor. Babasaheb Ambedkar gave such a powerful speech that one of his main critics, the prominent brahmin writer Acharya Atre, had a change of heart. He published a special issue of his *Navyug Patrika* (New Era Journal) with articles praising Babasaheb Ambedkar and his speech. Acharya Atre wrote, 'After this, I will never again criticize Dr Ambedkar; I have broken that pen which used to criticize him.'

We untouchables were full of pride. This special issue was priced at eight annas, but there was such a demand for it in our community that it would sell for five rupees. When my good friend Lakshman Nagdavte came home for holidays from his military service and got married, I gave him this special issue as a wedding present. He was delighted, saying this was the most precious of all the wedding gifts he had received.

As the exam results were to be announced soon, I returned to Nagpur. I was now getting worried about how to face my family and friends if I had failed. As soon as the exam results came out, I opened the newspaper with trembling hands, searching for my name. I knew that very few students pass this intermediate exam, so it really made no sense for me to think that I had passed. My mind crazily persisted looking down the list of names that had passed. Suddenly I saw my name on the list. I could not believe it. I blinked and looked again. Yes, it was still there. I felt astonished and elated, remembering all the confusion and chaos of the exam day.

Some 125 students from our Agricultural College had sat for the exams. From these only 33 students had passed, and I was proud to be among them. Out of about 25 students from Chokhamela Hostel, Kathane and I were the only ones to pass. Later that year, in the wake of India's independence from the British, there was a supplementary examination to retest many of the failed students, and many ultimately passed.

Although all my friends were surprised to hear of my success, the Chokhamela Hostel Superintendent said, 'Actually, I am not surprised that Nimgade passed. He used to wake up at 4 a.m. when all of you other students were fast asleep, and he would study by the light in the kitchen.' Of course, hearing of my success, my parents, family, and friends in Umrer were also overjoyed.

AT THE END OF 1946 I won two scholarships. One, from the Harijan Sevak Sangh, amounted to fifteen rupees per month, the other, from the Central Provinces and Berar government, amounted to twenty five rupees per month. Since I was not allowed to keep both scholarships at the same time, I told the superintendent that I wanted to surrender the Harijan Sevak Sangh scholarship. It was the smaller of the two, and moreover, I preferred not to be called Harijan. This term, meaning "children of God," was coined by Gandhi to refer to the untouchables and Scheduled Castes, and we saw it as condescending.

The superintendent was very kind. He said, 'Keep both scholarships for now. We are not going to inform on you. Don't turn your back on any money. Next year you can cancel your Harijan Sevak Sangh scholarship.'

Forbidden romance

When I passed the intermediate exam, my close friends in Umrer took me to a movie to celebrate. In those days we did not have a proper cinema hall, and the movie was screened in the open air. During the intermission, I noticed a beautiful girl in the midst of a group of girls. Especially in my pleasant state of mind, she appeared like an angel to me. I asked my friends, 'Who is that beauty over there?'

They told me that her name was Tara, and she was from the Lodi (a higher caste) community. I was astonished when I realized that she was the same girl who had cursed me many years ago for touching her Ramayana book.

I thought that this little village girl, with her fair complexion and fine features, could have been a film star. Why had I never seen her in our small town before? My friends told me that this was because she had gone away to the city for school, and had returned just recently.

One day when I went to visit my aunt Bhaga, I was thrilled to see Tara standing in the front yard of a house nearby. I went forward and introduced myself. I reminded her of the incident from our childhood, when I had touched her Tulsi Ramayana book, and how she had abused and cursed me profusely and told me to leave. After a while, she also remembered this with embarrassment. She asked me to forgive her, as back in those days she was a child and did not have guidance about what to say and how to behave. And then we both laughed wholeheartedly. After this, whenever I would visit Umrer, I would go and meet her.

As time went by, our friendship grew. I would be so anxious to see her upon reaching Umrer, that as soon as I reached my family's house, I would drop my bags there and rush off to her house. My friends used to tease me about her. Tara's mother was no longer very orthodox. She always welcomed me very warmly and would inquire about my studies. My aunt Bhaga would tell me that Tara would often ask her about when Namdeo would be coming to Umrer to visit; and this would make me very happy. There is a couplet in Sanskrit:

Yuvateesya leela yena, Yesya na dravate chitam
Sa sadhu muddho wa pashuhu.

(To see the frolic of a lovely woman, without a stirring in the heart / A man must be a sage, or a eunuch, or a beast.)

Caste was a barrier for us; there was no possibility for us to marry. But I still had feelings for her. One day, I came home to Umrer from Nagpur, and as usual, I went immediately to meet her. It was hot and dusty, and I was very thirsty. She looked so lovely in her new saree, as she graciously offered me a glass of cold water, that I could not resist taking her hand in mine along with the glass. I myself was astonished about how it happened. I had never behaved like that before in my life. I held my breath. After a moment, she withdrew her hand. I waited, head downcast, for the inevitable screams and recriminations that must ensue for this breach of propriety.

But they did not come. Instead of cursing and abusing me, as she had in childhood, she softly said, 'Namdeo, we are from two different castes and our marrying is out of the question. Why do you behave like this, so rashly? Our love is pure, let it remain so. That is the best for us. Now we can talk to each other anywhere and in front of anyone; we have nothing to hide. If we make some misstep, the openness of our relationship will disappear; it will bring dishonor to our families. We will be left with only misery.' On hearing the words of wisdom and sincerity, I was astonished. God had given her not only beauty, but also intellect and understanding.

A Muslim to the rescue

When I was in my third year of college, I applied for a central government scholarship which had been established by Dr Babasaheb Ambedkar but my application was denied. The Ministry of Education informed me that the scholarship was meant only for students in technical subjects such as medicine, science, and engineering. Agriculture was not considered a technical discipline, and so I had no chance for the scholarship. I was stung by this rebuff, and I decided to take up this issue with the education minister.

My friend Keshav Gajbhiye helped me draft a letter in which I tried to prove that agriculture is indeed a science and a technical subject. Further, I showed that most of the agriculture students came from poor families from rural areas and hence had great need for such scholarships. I ended with, 'Sir, when fatherly affection will encroach upon your mind, then you will forgive me for these harsh words and feel the pain for a tremendous injustice your ministry has caused to us, by the wrong interpretation that agriculture is not a science.'

I sent copies of the letter to the Education Minister, to Dr Ambedkar, and to Babu Jagjivan Ram, an influential politician from our community. As sending a letter, with copies, was a costly affair in those days, I sought financial help from my colleagues. Instead of helping, they teased and mocked me for tilting at windmills. They were from moderately well-to-do families, and so didn't have to worry about fees and costs for books and clothing.

Then weeks later came a stroke of good news that made me proud: my efforts yielded fruit! The scholarhip was opened to agriculture students. My friends who had teased me were excited and happy. I was delighted, until I found that unfortunately I was not eligible for the scholarship as my marks were not high enough. So here I was in a perplexed mood; I could not decide whether I should celebrate or mourn.

In dire need of this scholarship, I decided to take up the issue again with the Education Ministry and wrote a letter indicating my appalling economic situation and the valid reasons for my low percentages on examinations. I further added that my juniors received the benefit of the scholarship whereas I felt that I had been virtually punished. Somehow, my words had an impact, and I succeeded in my mission, receiving the scholarship award that gave me much relief from my financial worries. However, I still had others. We were still facing the criminal trial in court. Advocate Sakharam Meshram, Nashikrao Tirpude and Hajarnavis were arguing this case on our behalf. As this case was in the Bhandara court, some 50–60 miles away, we had to leave Nagpur to attend the case every time we would receive a court summons. One day, as I was waiting for my turn in the court, a strong and imposing stranger came up to me and asked me to step aside with him. I felt scared when he walked me to a spot where nobody could overhear us.

He whispered, 'I am Fago Ustad, I have killed several Hindus in the recent riots in Nagpur between the Hindu and mahar communities. I heard that some students of my community have been falsely implicated in the case of the temple-breaking incident. I was tremendously annoyed to hear of this injustice against our boys. I came here to help. As we stand here, just point out to me your accusers. I will take care of them. The police are already looking for me, so I don't care if they punish me for one murder or for a hundred murders. I will finish them all.' From the folds of his clothing he pulled out a glinting, sharp knife. I felt a strange mix of emotions: fright because of the danger he represented yet genuine admiration for his daring attitude and courage and for his support for students of the community.

Fago Ustad was known to be a very good wrestler, and had a good status in the community as a champion during periods of unrest. During the communal riots in 1946, he had saved several of our people from caste-based beatings and killings. While the police were searching for him day and night like a hunted dog, the financial condition of his family turned from bad to worse. In December 1946, when I was the secretary of a Scheduled Caste Students' Federation seminar in Nagpur, we had given the leftover food to the family of Fago Ustad. And so, when Fago came to know about my false implication in the case he came to my rescue.

Somehow, a calmer mind prevailed, and I spoke to him hesitatingly, trying to think of how an elder person with considerable judgment and experience might speak. I suggested that if our opponents were killed, everyone would assume that we were guilty, and the charges of murder would be added to our current ones. It would become even more difficult for us to pursue our studies. I told him to await the result of the case. Our cause was just and we would certainly win. I told him to not worry about us, but to go away and maintain his flight from the police. I had to repeat my plea for him to save himself before he finally left.

On 22 January 1947 the verdict of the case was delivered, and it went against us. We were fined 200 rupees and, if unable to pay, we were subject to six months imprisonment. The other five paid the fines and were set free, but I had no money to pay. My father heard this news and he was beset with worries for me. My father's employer, Vithoba Saon the goldsmith, noting his perplexity, asked about what was worrying him so much. Upon hearing the reason, Vithoba immediately gave him the 200 rupees. And to this day I treat Vithoba like a messenger of god who paid my penalty and allowed me to continue my studies.

Advocate Sakharam Meshram advised us to move our case to the high court to appeal the verdict, as any person convicted by the court is not entitled for any government service. Three of my convicted colleagues – namely Bankar, Mahadev Meshram, and Ramteke – being illiterate and with no scope anyway for government service had no desire to pursue an appeal. However, for the other three – namely A.D. Meshram, Baliram Waghmare,

Namdeo Singh? Shortly after winning my "temple desecration" case and just before cutting my hair.

and myself – it was necessary to pursue this appeal. Meshram and Waghmare, however, rushed off to their home villages for summer vacation; they did not worry much about the case as they came from more well-off families.

On the advice of Advocate Sakharam Meshram I summoned up my courage and met with Advocate Nisar Ali, a very successful advocate in those days. After listening carefully, he asked me for one thousand rupees towards the fee. The blood rushed from my face and I nearly fainted when I heard the amount. After collecting myself, I narrated the entire story of my financial condition and the difficulties I was facing in pursuing my education. Finally he accepted my request on a contingency basis.

On 30 January 1948 Gandhi was assassinated by Nathuram Godse, a Maharashtrian brahmin. People of all communities, including ours, were shocked. Despite the political differences between Gandhi and Babasaheb, I did not hear anyone say anything against Gandhi at this time. A few days later, riots erupted in various parts of the country including Maharashtra. This time, brahmins were targeted indiscriminately for beatings by commoners. In Umrer, I came across the figure of my high school headmaster, a brahmin gentleman named Lambe, bleeding in a small ditch. I had always the fondest memories of Headmaster Lambe, since he had taught Sanskrit with love and inspiration. Once upon seeing me coming to school in the monsoon downpour with a thatched makeshift shelter, rather than an umbrella, he said, 'That Nimgade is not afraid of anything; he will go far in life!' Other people, in contrast, would laugh at my improvisation.

Two friends, and now I, tended to Headmaster Lambe. He moaned to us, 'Please don't stay with me otherwise they will come to beat you also.' I said, 'No harm will come to us, Guruji.' We carried him carefully to the nearest hospital. I was very pleased that he recovered fully.

Later in the year, Advocate Nisar Ali fought our case with full zeal and sincerity, getting the court verdict overturned in our favor. In October 1948, we were acquitted. The advocate and I were overjoyed. We were able to pay his fees through the fines that were returned to us. This court decision now kept the door open for any government jobs for me.

I HAD LEFT my hair and beard unshaved while fighting my court case, but now I decided to cut my hair and beard. My friends, being in a celebratory mood, prevailed on me to pose for a portrait sporting a Punjabi turban. While at the photography studio, my friends noted a photo of a gentleman with long hair and beard that bore a striking resemblance to me. The studio owner told us that this was the likeness of the famous Guru Golwalkar, founder of the Rashtriya Swayamsevak Sangh. Since then, to this day, my agricultural colleagues of various castes enjoyed addressing me as "Guru."

The new judgment of the court brought joy to all my kith and kin. In my celebratory mood, I enjoyed the comments from my friends and professors about my new look. Some confused professors thought I was a new student. On recognizing me, they said that I looked "smart" now. My professors Mishra and Gupta even said, 'What a surprise! The godly man, the sage, has become a gentleman!'

Food and friends

With the court case behind me, with my long Sadhu-like hair now shorn, and with some scholarship money under my belt, I could now experience a slightly more normal college life. In those days, due to food shortage in the country, we were served a limited amount of food in the hostel. We asked our hostel warden to increase the ration. He claimed that the ration was sufficient. We then invited him to visit our dining room. That day, we used my ability to be a big eater when the occasion allowed – a survival skill so essential in the feast-or-famine rural environment – to good effect. I demonstrated how I alone could devour the rations meant for feeding five to six students. On seeing this, the warden was sufficiently impressed by the meagerness of our rations, and, through subsequent intervention with the Governor, both our food ration and our student grants were increased.

While our Agriculture College library had plenty of books written by great personalities like Jawaharlal Nehru, Mahatma Gandhi and other scholars, there were no books by or about Dr Ambedkar. When I brought this matter up with the librarian, he advised me to see the principal, P.D. Nayar. I gathered my courage and met with the principal. He was a man with a towering personality but was also kindhearted and polite. I told him, 'Sir, in our college library, we have numerous books on different subjects and also of distinguished authors, but not a single book on Babasaheb Ambedkar. He listened patiently and said, 'Dr Ambedkar is not an easy author to understand. His material requires advance reading and lot of general knowledge of various subjects. For instance, in his recent book *Thoughts on Pakistan,* it will be difficult for our students to understand discussion on the territorial demarcation of partition.'

After my repeated requests about this matter, the principal consented to include books involving Dr Ambedkar in the library. He then enquired about my studies and my student life. I told him how I would walk four times roundtrip between the hostel to the college for a total of 16 miles per day. He felt bad that I did not have a bicycle and offered me a job tutoring his young daughter. I thanked him, and told him that I was already doing some tutoring near the hostel.

In the third year of college, we had to prepare intensively for exams. During that period, every day we had two exams. After a morning exam, I was studying in the garden. A cool soothing breeze was blowing and I was lulled to sleep. When I awoke, I found myself alone. All the students had gone to the classroom for the exam. Terribly frightened, I rushed there to find everybody already busy in solving the paper. I narrated the entire episode to Mr Mishra who was supervising the examination. He was kind enough to allow me to sit for the exam. But I was flustered and not able to concentrate, and I decided to return the paper blank. Mr Mishra encouraged me write something on the paper, and, if needed, to meet and ask the principal for a re-examination.

My meeting with the principal was futile, and no re-examination was conducted. I still had a slender chance of passing, because students who failed in one subject, but passed with good marks in all other subjects were eligible for academic promotion. On the day the results were declared, I was quite nervous and I paced desperately. Finally my friend Shende came to me and announced that I had passed the examination. After all the dread and worry, I could not really believe this until my friends pulled me to the notice board to see the printed results. That was perhaps the happiest moment of my life.

During my fourth year of studies, I decided to move to the college hostel instead of travelling 16 miles every day from Chokhamela Hostel to the college. But in the college hostel, life was not so easy. The students there were mostly from rural areas where the caste system was strictly observed. They were hesitant about eating with me, and even the mess attendant was reluctant to pick up my plate and wash it along with the other plates. I took this matter to the hostel warden, but he remained silent about the matter.

When I was in Chokhamela Hostel, the food was certainly not as good, but it was served with dignity and respect. I told my story to the hostel sweeper and offerd to pay him to serve food to me at his residence. He readily agreed. When the hostel warden found out, he finally broke his silence about casteism. He thought that the dignity of the college had been lowered by having a student take meals with the hostel sweeper.

The hostel warden summoned the sweeper to his office and warned him that he might be fired if he continued serving food to students. He also called me to his office and asked why I would eat at the sweeper's house. There was, after all, another student of Scheduled Caste, but he ate in the student mess with the others. I told him that I lived with my caste identity and that I could not hide it. The student he referred to was a gosai of the mahar caste, who had changed his surname to the brahmin-sounding "Goswami." He was passing as a brahmin and was taking part in Hindu activities such as the Rashtriya Swayamsevak Sangh training camps. My friend A.D Meshram, who was also studying in the College of Agriculture, took his meals at the Institute of Science where the more urban students did not rigidly observe the caste system.

To prevent Munnalal, the sweeper, from losing his job because of narrow-minded and heartless casteism of the so-called well-educated people, I resorted to cooking my meals outside my room on a makeshift fire-pit based on three bricks. This proved very time-consuming and tedious. Fortunately, I had two understanding roommates, Divekar and Warangaokar. They were both from the brahmin caste, but never objected to the portrait of Dr Ambedkar I kept beside my bed. Warangaokar felt sympathy for me when he saw me cooking outside the room on a fire of twigs and sticks. He was a married man who went home to his village every week. One day he brought a kerosene stove from his home for me and also taught me its rather complex operation. This proved far more convenient, and I expressed my deep gratitude to him for his thoughtfulness.

One evening, I was alone in the hostel studying for an examination. Three middle-aged women came to my door. I inquired if I could help them, as they were probably tired and hungry from their trip. One of them was the mother of a fellow student, Deotale, who was away somewhere else on campus. I offered to take them to the student mess to eat, but they were traditional villagers and felt it improper to eat with men. So I offered to let them use my stove, but they were afraid to use the contraption. I was in a bind; I had to study, but I felt obliged to extend hospitality to these women. So I started cooking food for them on my stove and I tried going back to my studies.

In the meantime, Deotale's mother started talking with me about my village and my family. When the meal was ready, she suddenly recalled that she kept fast on that day, and therefore she would take no food. The other two women ate and thanked me for my hospitality. One of them said to me in private, 'Do you know why she does not want to share your food? When she found out you are mahar, untouchable, she lost her hunger.'

I was happy that I could help, but pained that one woman refused my food because of my caste. I narrated the entire episode to my friend Deotale. He apologized for her behavior, and explained that she was still living in the village and had not yet shaken off old prejudices and ignorance. It reminded me at once of how my own grandmother Saguna did not want to feed my friend from the scavenger community at my home.

The humane behaviour of my roommates, who treated me just like a brother, provided much consolation. Divekar was a fun-loving fellow with an interest in drama. He was very fair, thin, and had a slender nose. For one college drama, since we did not have female students, Divekar put on a sari and make-up and played the role of a woman. One day after the drama program was over, Divekar rushed home to the hostel, but as he was still in female costume, our hostel watchmen forbade him from entering!

One day when I was about to start cooking my food, Divekar stopped me, and said, 'Namdeo, today you are joining me for the feast of your life!' Apparently, Divekar had an arrangement to eat his meals at the home of a brahmin lady, and he knew that she was preparing some special treats today. I was hesitant, as I was afraid of offending that woman if she came to know about my caste during dinner. From my speech pattern alone, she would be able to tell that I was from the mahar community. 'Look,' he said, 'your friend Balkrishna Wasnik came with me the other day. He speaks very cultured Marathi, why don't you?'

I told him that Wasnik came from Nagpur, where he learned a refined manner of speaking; whereas I came from the village. But Divekar insisted that I join him. 'Namdeo, it is true, your rough village language may cause trouble. But this food is not to be missed. Just do this one thing: do not open your mouth for any purpose other than to eat. No speaking!'

I agreed, and I went with him. When I entered the house, I was amazed by the sweet fragrance of incense sticks mingling with the delicious aromas of the food. A wide variety of dishes was beautifully arranged, all prepared with ghee—quite an extravagance. Back in Chokhamela Hostel, the food was very simple, even on festival days: rice, lentils, one vegetable and sorghum roti. Luckily, everyone's attention was on the delicious meal, and at no time was I called upon to speak. I ate heartily and left safely contented.

In the grassy area surrounding my hostel there was a small makeshift temple that was created by assembling some roadside stones on a pedestal and anointing them with religious colors. Passers-by would bow to the stones and sometimes even make sacrifices to them. It was that easy to manufacture new deities all over India in those days! One day, when I was about to start cooking my meal, two worshippers walked by with brass water vessels that they wanted to fill up. I directed them to Maharajbag

Garden for water. A minute later, I realized that it would prove far more convenient for them to use the hostel tap. I called them back.

They were very pleased, and we started talking. It turns out they were cooking a goat meat feast in honor of their stone gods and invited me to share their meal when it was ready. I readily agreed because this way I could study instead of having to cook. After they went off to prepare their feast my colleagues Deotale, Warangadkar and Lakhe came by and were surprised to see that I was not cooking as usual. They asked whether I was observing a fast.

When I told them about my upcoming feast, the three of them wondered if they could join me, as goat meat was not allowed at the hostel. My new friends cooking the feast were happy to oblige. The four of us college friends feasted happily on the food cooked in the open air. After our lunch, I asked them to tell me whether they observed any change in their personalities. 'No,' they replied, but they were happy and energetic.

Then, I explained that the food which we had eaten had been prepared by people from the mahar untouchable community. Because this food had done them no harm – in fact they seemed happy and energetic – what sense did it make for me to cook and eat separately?

They said that they had absolutely no objection to my joining everybody at meals in the mess; they did not observe untouchability. I took much consolation from their statement. All four of us then discussed the issue of how to convince the other college students as well as the dining hall staff about the need to end casteism.

Eventually, we decided to start a new dining hall for those who did not observe caste barriers and untouchability. Initially we received a cold response as few students joined our mess. Slowly, we started educating them about the new government laws against untouchability, and more students signed up for our mess. These efforts proved a boon for me as I could start dining with all my colleagues regardless of caste. Many of the newly enlightened students then became my best friends. We went together to movies and festivities and forged many long-lasting friendships.

MY FELLOW STUDENT N.K. Shende, who was fond of dramas, asked me to join him for a Marathi drama at the annual function of the locally prestigious Morris College. I agreed with great pleasure because Morris College was coeducational at a time when no girls were allowed to study in our Agriculture College. Before entering, we admired from afar the Morris College girls in their chic silk sarees, gold earrings and jewelry and perfumes. I felt as if I were entering a new world full of romantic possibilities.

At the entrance to the hall, several Morris College students were welcoming the guests. One of the girls looked up and down at my worn clothing and long beard, and remarked sarcastically that now goondas were trying to attend the festivities. My pride was stung. Hot-headedly, I yelled, 'I am poor, is it a crime to be poor? If I had come here clean-shaven and nicely dressed, any girl from your college would be ready to marry me!'

Other students, hearing the commotion, approached us. My friend Shende tried to calm me down, but still angry, I shouted, 'Today, I have determined that when it is time for me to marry, I will select one of *you* from Morris College to be my wife!'

We proceeded into the hall, and had just occupied our seats, when we saw some Morris College boys approaching us with a look of menace in their eyes, brandishing folding chairs as makeshift weapons in their arms. Shende and I, sensing danger, looked frantically about for an escape route. We were two against the entire college; we were surrounded like the hero Abhimanyu in the epic Mahabharata, cut off from his troops deep within enemy ranks. At this moment the power failed.

While other audience members cursed the darkness, we prayed to providence as we crouched down the aisle and then through the door. We made good our escape from Morris College.

A few days later, I ran into a classmate named Kamble. He asked me about my recent visit to Morris College. Then, with a smile on his face, he admitted that he was working backstage at the Morris College hall handling the lighting work for the drama. When he saw the real-life drama unfold before his eyes and sensed our danger, he cut the lights.

On hearing this, I offered my profuse thanks. Shende was similarly surprised and grateful. He exclaimed, 'In mythological stories, when a devotee prays, God comes to his rescue in one form or another—in our case he took the form of Kamble!'

'I am not a coolie!'

Occasionally, we agriculture college students were taken for educational field trips to visit progressive farms around India and learn about doing soil surveys. I always enjoyed these trips as they allowed a village boy to explore the larger world. On one such trip in 1949, in my final year of college, after a farm visit in Bengal, I took a side trip to Calcutta to take in sights such as the Victoria Memorial and the Botanical Gardens. I visited some Calcutta students who had come to Nagpur for the conference of the All India Scheduled Caste Federation. They welcomed me with open arms and made my stay comfortable. I also visited Hemchandra Naskar, a Scheduled Caste member of the Drafting Committee of the Indian Constitution. Just as impressive was my meeting Radha Mohan Gadnayak, the famous poet who had failed his high school examination 14 times but now could find some satisfaction in having his poems included in university syllabi.

On the return trip, after an excursion to Bhubaneshwar which features distractions such as the Konarak Sun Temple and Lord Jagannath Temple I reached the train station in time to find that my train was pulling away without me. This did not bother me, since I felt I did not have any pressing obligations for several days anyway. I decided to go and enjoy the seashore for a while, as I had never seen so much water in my life. While strolling along the beach, a big black dog furiously rushed toward me. In my fear, I cried out in my mother tongue, Marathi.

The owner quickly ran over and controlled his dog. Then he turned to me with a pleased expression. He was delighted to hear his mother tongue so far from home. He was Kamble, also a mahar from Nagpur, working as cook to a European officer who managed a railway hotel.

Mr Kamble insisted that I come home with him, as his wife

was very eager to converse in Marathi. He also wanted to introduce me to his boss' wife (his boss had returned to England for a while). He passed me off as his cousin to impress his employers by showing his family was indeed educated. His boss's wife was lovely and kind-hearted, and meeting her was my first opportunity to talk with a European lady. I ended up spending four tranquil days as a guest of Kamble in a nice hotel room overlooking the ocean. During my stay, his boss's wife taught me how to swim in the ocean and look for starfish and seashells. This was my first encounter with anyone from outside India. I wondered how the people beyond our seas lived and mingled among themselves.

WHEN I RETURNED to Nagpur my friends were worried about me, as they had no idea where I was. It was the month of March, with final exams approaching. It was also time for the festival of colors, Holi. On this day, people celebrate with great gusto by smearing each other with colored powders and spraying each other with colored water. As I had very few clothes, I stayed inside my room all morning to avoid ruining my clothes. At last, however, I came out for a stroll through the garden towards the dining hall.

As I was about to enter, a Hindi-speaking student approached me with a dozen of his friends to anoint me with colors. I politely said, 'Please, look at me, I am a poor boy, I have few garments; please don't throw any colors on me.' But they did not heed my plea and soon I was covered with colors.

Terribly angry, I pushed forward and slapped the ringleader on the cheek. The climate became silent and tense. I was alone and surrounded, but I did not want to back down or run away. I shouted with all my courage and strength, 'I warn all of you. Don't come forward, or the consequences will be dire for you. If I had a weapon at hand, surely I would kill the first ones to come at me.'

'Oh! You are our friend,' one of them tried to mollify me. 'Don't get annoyed.'

'I agree with you, yes we are friends,' I replied. 'However, I still remember the days when all of you were not letting me eat food with you. Even the servant in the dining hall refused to clear my plate. At that time, was I your friend? Was I one of your colleagues? And now I become your friend, when you people want to dump colors on me?'

Feeling my anger and indignation, they fell away in silence. A lot of students eating in the dining hall witnessed this event. I had been known up to now as a quiet and peaceful student. People were amazed at both the depth of my anger and my courage. I emerged a local hero from this incident.

I WAS STUDYING in the hostel with full concentration, enjoying the calm of its tranquil grounds before entering the storm of the examination hall. But, as before, during my prior key examinations, history repeated itself and a mishap occured. I was about to leave for my chemistry exam when I heard a scream from the main road. An old beggar woman was crawling on the street, apparently after a vehicle had struck her. The vehicle had disappeared, and in its place a crowd had gathered. But nobody was willing to step forward to help the woman.

I could not tolerate her misery, so I helped her sit up and examined her for injuries. Her ankles appeared to be sprained. I did not want to leave her alone in such situation although I was worried about my exam. I pleaded for some kind-hearted people in the crowd to help, and finally some of them took her to the nearby hospital.

Then I hurried off for my examination. When I entered the examination hall, Dr Tamhane the external examiner who had come all the way from Delhi, asked me why I was late. When I explained what had happened he kindly permitted me to take the examination. When the results of this examination were declared, surprisingly I topped the class by a wide margin.

In this manner, after a successful series of exams, I succeeded in receiving my B.Sc. I was slightly upset for not doing my best and not passing first class, but nevertheless I was very proud of my achievement. I wanted to convey this good news to my parents and kith and kin. I decided to take the train to Umrer to see them. Along with a maternal uncle, Nagdevte, I took a train that reached Umrer station at 9 p.m.

At the railway station, we were greeted with torrential rain and lightning. I saw a young, well-dressed couple with a small baby who had arrived by the same train. They had some heavy baggage and were desperately looking for a coolie. But there were no coolies to be found, and no type of conveyance. Umrer, being a small town, had essentially closed for business on this stormy night. I saw the worry on their faces and decided to help them.

'Uncle,' I said. 'This family is in trouble and they need help. What is the use of my youth and my strength, if I do not help them in their difficulty?' I took off my shirt and trousers to keep them dry and handed them over to my uncle. In my undergarments, dressed like a laborer, I went to that couple and asked, 'Sir, Where do you want to go? Give me your luggage.' Their faces shone with relief as they told me the address and loaded their luggage on my head. The rain had let up a bit, but it was dark and wet. We hurried off to their house. I was touched to see the tender care with which the mother was protecting her baby from the rain and cold.

When we reached their destination, the gentleman pulled some money to pay for my labor. I declined it. He misunderstood me and thought that I wanted more money, so he offered more. Again I refused politely and said. 'Sir, in fact I am not a coolie, I am a college student and I have just graduated from Nagpur College. I came forward to help you when I saw your plight, with your luggage and baby in the rain. I just did my duty as one human being for another. I am Namdeo Nimgade from this town.'

'Oh! I saw your name in the newspapers today; you are the same boy who has qualified the B.Sc. Agriculture degree examination! You are a grandson of Budha Mahar of Sathgaon village. I am from the goldsmith caste, from your neighboring village of Shankarpur. I am grateful to you for your help when we needed it so much; and I promise you that we will make every effort to eradicate the evils of untouchability.' He added, 'Your community cannot fail to progress, when it has a youth of good heart like you.'

I felt elevated on hearing these good words about my community. I immediately went back to the railway station, to Uncle Nagdevte. I put on my garments and rushed home. I bowed to my father and touched his feet, and told the wonderful news about my degree. I saw great happiness and pride on his face.

PART III

CASTE ASIDE

The holy stepping stone

'What should I do now?' I asked my good friend and fellow student Damodar Patil. Damodar was a short, clean-shaven young man with a round face and good physique, who also came from the mahar community. It was 1949 and I was at a crossroads in life, a hard-earned B.Sc. in hand, and desperate to continue my education. Nagpur did not offer advanced studies in agriculture, so I would surely have to move far away to obtain a higher degree. But my father and mother had a different plan in mind for me and insisted that I should get married and settle down with a job. How was I going to justify continuing my studies with our precarious finances?

Damodar's benign appearance belied a steely determination and mastery at planning. To further his own chances at earning first division marks he decided to appear for the final examinations the following year. In my case he knew that my sights were set on studying at the Indian Agricultural Research Institute (IARI) in New Delhi, the crown jewel of the national agricultural education system set up by the British after a series of severe famines had devastated India. But my marks were not up to par for the heavy competition to secure admission at IARI. Damodar suggested then that I apply to Banaras Hindu University, also a prestigious institution in the northern state of Uttar Pradesh, for my M.Sc. degree. Knowing that I had barely managed to scrape up enough money to finish college, and had no financial resources to study at Banaras, he suggested I consult his father for financial help.

Damodar's family was very affluent in those days when most of the community was under the grip of severe poverty. His father was a gracious, compassionate, and considerate person, very interested in education. So I met his father and, explaining my dire circumstances, requested 300 rupees as an educational loan to tide me through until I secured a scholarship. His father fell silent; he wanted to help me, but he appeared to not have had ready funds at that time. Damodar's stepmother was listening; she immediately came forward and offered her gold bangles to her husband. 'Please mortgage these bangles and arrange for some money for Namdeo to continue his studies.' I was surprised and touched and felt very elevated by their kindness and confidence in me.

I returned to my village with 300 rupees and related this story of its generous origin to my parents. I said that my decision was firm to try for the postgraduate course at Banaras. My parents were compelled to accept my choice. My relief was mixed with a tinge of sadness, as this plan would lead me far away from my family and my native place.

GREAT LOCAL excitement greeted my admission to the Banaras Hindu University for the M.Sc. course in Botany. Banaras was one of the holiest cities for Hindus, and many were astonished that one from our lowly community would have a chance to go there. Before proceeding to Banaras I went to my village Sathgaon to meet with my relatives, friends and villagers. With great pride and joy, all our friends and relatives came to the border of the village to bless me and give me a warm send-off.

Banaras was a new and unknown place for me. I was allotted Room 182 in the Dhanrajgiri student hostel, sharing the room with another student, Majoomdar. He was a chubby fellow with a great fondness for sweets. One of my few possessions was a portrait of my hero, Dr Ambedkar, which I proudly displayed in the room. I was both happy and relieved that Majoomdar did not object to it.

Banaras Hindu University is a very famous university, known for its excellence in education. Pandit Madan Mohan Malviya, a veteran leader in Indian politics, established this university in 1916. Many kings and philanthropists donated generously for its development. I remember an incident regarding the famous

Baroda Library, named after his highness, the King of Baroda, Sayaji Rao Gaekwad. Once Pandit Malviya came to Bombay and went to meet Dr Ambedkar. He was amazed to see the huge book collection in the personal library at Dr Ambedkar's Rajgriha residence.

'Dr Ambedkar, I bow before you, you are really a son of Saraswati, the goddess of wisdom and learning,' Pandit Malviya exclaimed. 'I had heard about your library and I wanted to see it. Today I am truly fortunate and surprised to see how magnificent it is. I need your library for the benefit of my students at the university that I have established and will offer you the sum of 200,000 rupees.'

On hearing this generous offer, Dr Ambedkar quickly replied, 'Thank you for the honor of your request, Mr Malviya, but I am sorry. Your purpose is very good. I would like to donate this library to a champion of education of your stature; however, I cannot live without it. This is not just a collection of books but this is the sum of my lifetime achievements and my precious wealth.'

I was hoping for a scholarship at Banaras but was only able to get a "free-ship" (remission of tuition fees). My total expenditure was limited to about 25–30 rupees per month, so I had no resources for extra clothes and other luxuries. On the advice of my friend Captain Sharma I joined the National Cadet Corps (NCC) so that I could wear a good uniform that they provided. I enjoyed several other benefits of the NCC—the parades and drills, camaraderie, and wholesome food.

I was content in Banaras, but in my heart, I yearned for even more. If I were to have my way, Banaras would be but a stepping stone...

The lion's den

On 3 October 1949, just months after starting my higher studies at Banaras I took the overnight train from Banaras to New Delhi, the nation's capital. My destination was the Indian Agricultural Research Institute (IARI) for an admissions interview. This was the nation's premier agricultural institute, an oasis of research farms, greenhouses, and laboratories at the far end of Delhi. Beautiful red brick buildings in the British Raj style and bougainvillea bushes lined the well-laid out roads of the institute. Throughout my months at Banaras, I had reminded myself that my ultimate educational goal was to study in New Delhi, the seat of power in newly independent India. Having done well in my first few courses, I took the plunge and applied to the institute.

Unfortunately, the admissions interview summons had come suddenly. I had taken the first available train out, and arrived without enough time to shave or bathe; I had to go straight from the train station to the exam hall for my interview. Seeing my bedraggled state, the secretary of the director's office could not believe I was there for an interview until I showed him my interview letter.

Seven interviewers faced me, and I felt like a goat in a lion's den. To make matters worse, I had not eaten since the previous night. The Director, Dr J.N. Mukherjee, resplendent in a suit and tie, asked me, 'Why are you coming to Delhi? You are already at the prestigious Banaras Hindu University, one of the top institutions in India.'

'Sir,' I replied, 'If I come to Delhi to study at your institute I will be able to get a better post with which to serve my country and my family better.'

Dr Mukherjee then commented, 'You are underqualified; you

only have a B.Sc., and you passed with ordinary grades. You do not even know the ABC of chemistry.'

'Sir, I fully accept the fact that I am fresh, but if you provide me the opportunity to study here, I will do my best to learn my ABCs all the way to XYZ. I have already proven myself with my work at Banaras.'

The interviewers were startled by my confidence despite my unkempt appearance. I was able to field a series of technical questions posed by other interviewers. Finally, Dr Mukherjee could not resist asking, 'So, why are you appearing here so shabbily dressed?'

I explained that I had to rush from the overnight train.

'Very well,' he said. 'Please wait for us outside.'

I sat outside in the waiting room for several hours, feeling faint from hunger, as they deliberated their admissions decisions. Finally, I was summoned in to see Dr Mukherjee. He said, 'Your director at Nagpur Agricultural College, Dr P.D. Nair, has recommended you very strongly. Therefore, we have decided to admit you... but on probation.'

I felt a great sense of relief. But then he went on, 'You will have to pass the six monthly examinations. If you fail, you will have to leave this institution. Now, you can pay your fees.'

My relief was as quickly replaced by a huge sense of worry. I had already spent all the money that I had borrowed while at Banaras. How could I even live in the nation's capital, let alone pay the fees? Fortunately, some kindly Maharashtrian students at IARI came to see if any of the newly admitted candidates hailed from Maharashtra. I recognized some of their faces and we lapsed into our mother tongue. Some of the older students, who knew of my economic circumstances, lent me money for my initial fee deposit. Thus I gained admission to the prestigious Indian Agricultural Research Institute.

Beggar's clothes in the nation's capital

Even with my supplemental income, I could not meet my tuition and expense obligations of 150 rupees. In addition, I still had earlier education debts. I had left Banaras suddenly, before securing a firm scholarship. To my parents I would always write, 'I am satisfied here, with no worries but my studies.' I would write carefully so that my tears would never fall on the letter. Fortunately, I was able to concentrate on my studies. There was no other choice. Always worried about money, I was never able to purchase good clothes. Seeing my threadbare clothes, a library guard once denied me admission until I mentioned the names of several other students.

I was fortunate in having as my academic guide a Bengali scientist named Dr S.P. Raychaudhari. A thorough gentleman with intelligent, piercing eyes, he helped me in countless ways with his consideration and thoughtfulness. To help me financially, he hired me to tutor his own two sons. His sons were bright, wonderful, and motivated. (This was in pleasant contrast to another student I tutored who channeled his disinterest in education by querying me about irrelevant hypotheticals such as "If I bump into a pretty woman in a crowded marketplace, is that a sin?")

With regard to food, I was fortunate to have formed a good friendship with my fellow Maharashtrian K.C. Sahare. Sahare served as the all-important mess secretary at IARI and he allowed me to eat there for free. Unfortunately, his tenure did not last forever and the new mess secretary decided to charge me for dining privileges pro-rated all the way to my first day. Fortunately, Dr Raychaudari quickly intervened and had the mess forgive my fees.

On one occasion, I was participating in a student play, cast in the role of a beggar. On the day of the performance, I arrived late, leaving the cast worried that I would not be able to make my costume change in time for the curtain opening. I said, 'Do not worry, give me a few seconds.' Backstage, I simply stripped off my borrowed trousers and shirt and then stepped onstage in my old and torn undergarments. The other students in the beggar roles had had to tear their clothes to fit the part. Our ensemble won first prize! Despite this one advantage of poverty, it became apparent that makeshift tactics to meet ends meet would not serve me in the longer term.

In desperation, I went to the Education Ministry, where I was elated to discover that I had qualified for a scholarship. Unfortunately, it was good only for Banaras Hindu University and I would have to reapply for one of few remaining scholarships for IARI. I panicked, thinking about what would happen if I did not get a scholarship, especially as winter was starting to set in. I would need warm clothing and blankets.

One day, in the library, I came across a newspaper article announcing an All India Scheduled Caste Federation meeting at Dr Ambedkar's house in New Delhi on 14 November 1949. Thinking to present my case for a scholarship, I raced to the meeting, with hope rising in my chest. The chief luminaries of our community had gathered there. After the meeting, I tried to meet Dr Ambedkar, but his secretaries dissuaded me. I pleaded with them, and they finally advised me to intercept Dr Ambedkar on the verandah on his way to his office. I introduced myself and told him of my difficulties. This was my first opportunity to speak to him directly. Some years ago, when I had served as one of his temporary bodyguards at Nagpur, I never had the opportunity to even speak to him through the thick crowds.

Dr Ambedkar now listened with grave concern. Then he said, 'You should meet with Dr Panjabrao Deshmukh, who heads the scholarship board for Scheduled Castes. I am so involved with writing the Constitution that I cannot pay attention to anything else. Tell him I sent you.' Despite his inability to help me at this time, I was so happy just to have these words that in the evening,

With Dr Panjabrao Deshmukh, who was there to help me when it mattered.

I excitedly wrote a letter to my parents which included a poem I composed in Babasaheb's honor.

Two weeks later, with Babasaheb's advice ringing in my ears, I walked six miles to see Dr Deshmukh at his residence at Delhi's Constitution Club. It was briskly cold, and I was wearing my dhoti and a shirt; I had nothing warmer. I had not shaved, since I did not have money for razors. Dr Deshmukh was not home. His door was locked. I sat shivering at his doorstep in my ragged clothes. Finally, at about 10 p.m., a short, balding, middle-aged gentleman in homespun woolen clothing appeared, deep in thought. His eyes sparkled with intelligence, and I realized that this might be Dr Deshmukh.

'Who are you?' he asked, 'and what brings you here? You appear to be a fellow of determination to be sitting here. Are you looking for a job?'

With good reason, considering my bedraggled appearance, he did not believe that I was a student at IARI. I mentioned the magic name of Dr Ambedkar, and he understood immediately. I explained my plight. He listened carefully, probing me with questions. Finally he pulled out twenty five rupees from his pocket to give me.

I refused the money, saying, 'There are a thousand other poor students like me, who may need to leave their studies not because of intellectual deficiency but because of financial hardship. Can you please do something to help the greater cause of all of us students so we can persevere in our studies?'

My plea touched him. He asked me to document my plight. It was 11:15 p.m when I took my leave, wearing a sweater and muffler given by the kind Dr Deshmukh. At 1 a.m, I reached my hostel. A few weeks later, he published my life story in the January 1950 issue of *Sandesh*, a weekly dedicated to helping the downtrodden. This was the lead story and was published in three parts. This story helped motivate the Scholarship Board to increase the scholarship funding from 750,000 to 1,000,000 rupees.

With a scholarship in hand, my situation improved. But I still spent money sparingly so that I could send some back home to help reduce my family's debt. Because of a delay in receiving the scholarship money, several friends from all castes lent me bedding and clothing. Chandrapal Gupta gave me a blanket. Dr Raychaudari, in the meantime, served as a beacon for my studies, ensuring that I passed my six monthly exams with good marks.

Into the melting pot

Delhi was a melting pot of different cultures. While Hindi was the primary language heard in the streets, one also heard a mix of tongues ranging from Punjabi to English to South Indian languages to Bengali and occasionally even Marathi.

One day, when I was wandering in the beautiful agricultural institute grounds, a tall, well-dressed fellow in a horse-drawn carriage pulled up and in a booming voice asked me for directions to the hostel. I tried to explain the way to the carriage driver and I ended up sitting next to him to provide directions. He was a new student, A. K. Pradhan, from the eastern city of Bhubaneswar, and this ride became the basis for a life-long friendship. He was a rich Christian from Orissa and I was a Hindu from Maharashtra. So deep was Pradhan's concern for me that he would even leave his wardrobe open for me to use his clothes as I wished. This was but one of many friendships forged across the boundaries of state or creed or caste.

In the nation's capital, all the Maharashtrian community gathered, regardless of caste, for certain cultural events. A subgroup of Maharashtrian Scheduled Castes also met separately under the banner of "The Siddhartha Welfare Center" to discuss matters of social concern and hold cultural events such as a large yearly picnic.

On one occasion, all the Maharashtrian hostel students invited Dr Panjabrao Deshmukh to dine at the mess. To everyone's surprise, he accepted. We had a wonderful dinner program with him, with a frank dialogue between the Minister and us lowly students. The very next day, word reached the institute bureaucrats, who were horrified that such a distinguished visitor had been feted in such a lowly manner. We received a stern warning about the need to inform the institute about any such plans in the future!

DESPITE THE PRESSURE of studies, I had a steady flow of visitors, primarily consisting of needy students visiting the capital city. On one occasion, a distant relative who fled home on account of a domestic dispute took refuge with me. My colleagues were surprised that despite my pressures, financial and otherwise, I could remain hospitable. I also helped visiting students through the scholarship application process. Most were grateful, especially when they saw how meager my resources were, and they would leave me useful items such as bars of soap.

Only once did I have a bad experience: a distant friend of a friend stayed with me, and dined heartily every day in the mess. I assumed he was paying his own bills, but only after his departure I discovered that the mess bill was under my name!

On seeing this, a friend exclaimed: 'Nimgade, how do you tolerate all this?'

I said, 'I am practicing what our Indian culture teaches: the guest is god!'

I also kept in touch with the Scheduled Caste community by talking with the sweepers and servants in the hostel. Occasionally, I would even visit their houses. With a fellow social reform worker named T.D. Kamble we worked to encourage education within these illiterate communities by setting up an evening school, the Bhimrao Night School for working adults. This helped me take my mind off my personal challenges.

Some sweepers and servants did not believe that such a highly educated person such as Dr Ambedkar could come from our community. In order to help persuade them, I took one community representative on a borrowed bicycle to see Dr Ambedkar himself, on 14 April 1950, at his birthday festivities. After hearing Dr Ambedkar's speech, this community representative became a believer, and helped spread the message to his own village. In this manner I helped spread the word of Dr Ambedkar in the greater Delhi area.

Babasaheb Ambedkar among his admirers on his birthday in 1950. I was the only one who heeded Mrs Savita Ambedkar's admonishments for people in the front to be seated.

On 15 April 1951, we celebrated the opening of our community center that became known as the Ambedkar Bhavan, built on over an acre of land in the heart of the central government area in New Delhi. This land was donated by Dr Ambedkar himself for the upliftment of the Scheduled Caste people of Delhi. (The inauguration was not held on his actual birthday, the prior day, because Dr Ambedkar did not like the idea of celebrating his birthday.) Rafi Ahmed Kidwai, the Agriculture Minister, a highly regarded Muslim, inaugurated the center.

The foundation stone created by the society read:

> The foundation stone of this building was laid by Hon Dr Babasaheb B.R. Ambedkar, M.A, Ph.D, DSc, Bar-at-law, London Minister of Law, Government of India, The Saviour of Untouchables of India
>
> (Delhi Scheduled Castes Welfare Association)

When Dr Ambedkar saw the stone he was horrified. He said, 'I do not like the idea that my name should be given to this building! The person who seeks accomplishments does not want fame; and the person who seeks fame does not accomplish anything.'

That day he exhorted the several thousands in the audience to seek education for themselves and their children. He advised equal education for both sexes. 'Only education will take our community to the pinnacle. Be truthful and bold!' Later he would say, 'Educate. Organize Agitate: secure your futures by yourselves!'

An adventure at the Asian Games

Another inauguration I attended was for the newly constructed National Physical Laboratory, which abutted our agricultural institute. Here, Prime Minister Nehru himself appeared and exhorted the audience, 'These scientific laboratories are the modern temples of India! Scientific progress will take our nation ahead.'

As he wandered with the crowds through the newly opened laboratories and grounds, I approached him for his autograph and said humbly, 'Sir, I have a question.'

'This is not an appropriate time,' said the Prime Minister. He was dressed immaculately in his long tailored jacket and white cap.

'Sir, this is the most appropriate time for me,' I countered. 'I am an agriculture student of humble origins and I want to know if these modern temples will be open to all castes, because entry to temples of god is still prohibited to the Scheduled Castes.'

After hearing this, Nehru smiled and patted my back. 'Yes, of course! Anyone can come and work here. I wish you much success!'

I was proud that despite my hardships and woes, I still enjoyed my student life to the fullest and could savor those memories of boldness and adventure.

I WAS TO see Prime Minister Nehru once again, for I found myself drawn to several of the inaugurations and spectacular events going on in Delhi. In 1951, Delhi hosted the Asiad, the Asian games. There is a Hindi saying, '*Padhogay likhogay, banogay nawab, Khelogay, kudogay, to banogay kharab.*' (If you read and write, you will become a prince magnificent, but if you play and jump around, your life will be misspent.) But I preferred the western attitude to life: "Work while you work, play while you play."

Nimkar, another impoverished student, shared my philosophy. He and I hit upon a plan to view this Asiad spectacle cheaply. An adventurous fellow with an inventive mind, Nimkar bought one ticket and then, once inside the grounds, tied it to a stone and hurled it over the wall, where I retrieved it. Thus, we each entered at half-price. While we were enjoying the games, a loudspeaker announced that Prime Minister Nehru would inaugurate the swimming competition at the Olympic pool, for which separate tickets would be required.

I remembered that an old friend of mine was stationed at the army compound adjacent to the Olympic pool. We quickly went, only to find that he was no longer stationed there. Our inquiries had taken us well within the army compound. Looking up, we realized that, providentially, only a low wall now separated us from the swimming area. Wasting no time, Nimkar thrust himself over the wall. Several young soldiers saw him and followed suit to see the games for themselves. I also put my hands to the wall and pulled myself up. But a policeman arrived and he grabbed my feet.

'Officer, I am guilty!' I exclaimed. 'So, why should you be at my feet when by rights it should be the other way around!'

The policeman started to laugh and he let me proceed over the wall. Safely inside the swimming compound, we found ourselves in a thick crowd. We could not see a thing. Press photographers arrived with their large cameras and tripods, but the crowd would not allow them to proceed. Inspiration struck us again. We said to the photographers, 'Let us help you!' Then we grabbed their tripods and swung them like police lathees, shouting, 'Stand back for the Press! Stand back!'

Soon we reached the front, near the Prime Minister and foreign dignitaries. We helped the photographers set up the tripods and then enjoyed a better view of the swimming races than did most of the VIPs. What excitement and spectacle!

Later, the diving competition started. This time, to ensure

the best view, we grabbed some towels lying by the swimming pool and proceeded in an authoritative manner toward the diving area. Once there, we started toweling down the wet athletes. No one challenged us or asked us for credentials. Thus emboldened, we even climbed with towels up the diving tower, assisting athletes once we reached the top. From high above, I could now view the thousands of spectators. Closer below me I could see the Prime Minister and dignitaries; but I had an even better view than they did!

Unfortunately, other spectators started coming up the platform, and it gradually became crowded. A loudspeaker blared out, 'Please get off the diving platform; there is danger of bodily harm if anyone falls the wrong way into the water.' I realized our moment of glory was ending, but I wanted to savor it until the last. 'Let me see what it is like to be like a diver,' I thought to myself. I stripped down to my underwear and handed my clothes to Nimkar. I felt a moment of anxiety, but then, in front of the thousands of spectators and dignitaries, dove off the platform.

Lost in the jungle

During my first summer holiday in 1950, I went home to my village in Maharashtra. I was pleased to hear about the upcoming wedding on 1 May of my dear friend Damodar Patil, whose family had lent me money for my Banaras education. There was no time to walk to his village, so I rented a bicycle. The villagers tried to stop me because the path went deep through the famous Tadoba jungle, where tigers, bears, and wild boars roamed. I ignored their warnings—so great was my desire to attend Damodar's wedding.

As I proceeded, the forest grew thick. I reached a fork in the path and realized I had lost my way. Evening was approaching, and soon I heard the footfalls and howling of wild animals. The story of my ancestor Ganba, who had died while fighting a tiger, came to mind. In the growing darkness, I was startled to see pairs of eyes in the forest. The trees rustled. I got goosebumps. I stood very still, and was then able to make out what sorts of creatures were looking at me. To my great relief, I saw the figures of deer standing or walking calmly, not fleeing in alarm as they would if they had sensed a predator nearby.

Wondering and worrying about which way to go, I suddenly heard the sweet tinkling of small bells in the distance. I concentrated on following this sound, walking as quietly as I could in the darkness so as not to lose it. Surely, it would lead me to civilization. I felt great joy when I came across a herd of cows, and then a small village. I approached the villagers and told them of my plight. I was quite hungry by now, and they fed me. Then I said that I had to proceed to the wedding.

The villagers warned me against traveling further this late in the evening. But I insisted that after coming so far, I must make it all the way to the wedding. Finally, I convinced five or six village men to accompany me, and I offered to pay them. Together we proceeded, with lathis, spears, and flaming torches, conversing and laughing as we walked through the jungle. Finally, we heard the sound of the wedding procession. Damodar, the groom, was surprised and overjoyed to see me, and he embraced me as a brother.

'OH LADIES, SOME water, please, just a little water please.' The next day, when I returned to my home village of Sathgaon, at the village outskirts I saw some women of the mang community pleading for water at a high-caste well. One or two were grudgingly given some water, but the remaining mang women got none. I felt great sympathy for them, remembering my travails in high school in Umrer when I had to get water for our household.

I invited these mang women to draw water at the well some distance away in my mahar community. But my reception at home was lukewarm, since many mahar people opposed this. They argued that the mangs should dig their own well just as the mahars had. But I knew that the very small mang community did not have the resources to dig their own well.

I argued that we Scheduled Castes should unite. After all, it was our agitation for water rights in Umrer that had allowed us to draw water from higher-caste wells. My arguments for unity and social justice instead of the blind following of tradition prevailed. Ever since then, the mangs and mahars have drawn water from the same well.

LATER THAT SUMMER, I helped our family arrange and celebrate the wedding of my younger sister Anjani. It was a joyous occasion, reuniting our family. But at the same time, despite keeping expenses to a bare minimum, it further indebted us. A steady stream of visitors from nearby villages placed a further drain on our meager food supplies. My father would often refuse to eat, claiming he was fasting, and in this manner stretch the food to allow guests to eat. I felt guilty, because my stubbornness regarding my quest for education had added to our family debt.

A few weeks later, while visiting R.R. Patil, a close friend in Nagpur, I beheld a beautiful girl drying handmade noodles in the sun outside her house with her mother. She was a slender teenager with lovely eyes and a gracious manner. I thought that if I could marry a girl like her, I would be most happy. What better way to find out who she was than by asking her herself? With her mother nearby, it was not a breach of modesty or propriety for the girl. She did not even look up, but continued with her work while answering my questions. I found out that her name was Kamal, and that her father was Madhavrao Sontakke, a government officer. She was in tenth grade, which meant she was about fifteen or sixteen. Obviously, she was too young for me. Furthermore, I had my education to finish and no employment. It was not in my destiny. I suppressed the thought and went on my way.

Soon after I returned to Delhi, I found that my name was growing in recognition, due to my community service and the publication of my biography in Dr Deshmukh's journal. Solicitations for marriage had begun to pour in from several families with daughters. But I wanted to defer marriage a few more years because of my educational mission.

IN DELHI I always kept my village roots in my heart. My parents and I exchanged letters, which took about a week to reach each other. In times of calamity I could not rush to their help because over a twenty-four-hour train journey separated us. Instead, I would have to remain calm and pray for the best. It was with this spirit in 1951 that I had to receive news through a letter from home stating that my grandfather Budha had passed away on 15 August.

Now, hundreds of miles away in Delhi, I could not believe the news. I had rarely even seen my grandfather Budha sleep. Rising before us in the morning, Budha was a hard worker who ceaselessy took care of his family. My dream was to reciprocate one day and buy him nice clothes and help take care of him when I finished my studies. Therefore, it was a deep shock when I received the news. My eyes welled with tears.

Later, I learned that he had developed diabetes. He had insufficient food to eat, and yet he would somehow still walk two miles every day to the clinic for treatment. On his deathbed, he thanked his gathered family and even mentioned me. He predicted happy and prosperous times ahead and expressed his faith in my educational goals. He was an estimated 101 years old at his death, living six years past the death of his wife Saguna. The era of my older generation had truly passed. A pillar in my life had been removed. The next few weeks, I could barely concentrate on my studies. I rued that I could not even attend his funeral.

Learning from wasps

'What are you doing outside so drenched? Go home and change – I'll wait until you come back with dry clothes!' This was my concerned advisor, Dr Raychaudhari, admonishing me to get dry as soon as possible. It was 1951, and I was consumed entirely with writing my thesis. Dr Raychaudari was very busy with official duties, but had saved the three-day Independence Day holiday weekend for reviewing my thesis. I brought my precious draft to his bungalow, but on the way I was caught in heavy monsoon rains. I clutched my thesis to my chest and bent over to protect it. The rains had stopped but I was entirely soaked when I reached his door.

I said, 'Please do not worry, I am used to this since my village childhood. I will dry out soon under the fan.'

'Your childhood state is one thing, but now as an adult you may catch a cold. You can borrow a bicycle to get to your hostel.'

I was forced to admit that I had no other good clothes to change into. He looked shocked for an instant but then gave me his own pajamas and shirt to wear. 'Since it is the holidays, why don't you just eat and sleep here while we revise your thesis.'

'But I am an untouchable and living under your roof may offend your wife,' I said.

Mrs Mira Raychaudhari was a gentle woman who wore the traditional vermilion powder in her hair and modestly covered her head with the edge of her sari in the presence of men. Dr Raychaudhari then took his wife aside and asked her opinion. She replied, 'I do not care what caste he is. He tutors our children so well! That is all I care about. He is a big brother to my children, and a son to me.' In writing my thesis, thus, I gained not only knowledge, but also a generous, open-minded family from Bengal.

Hiring a typist for the thesis proved expensive, since it required

With my mentor Dr S.P. Raychaudhari in 1973.

four bound copies. I was now beset with worrying about how to meet this expense. I lay on my hostel floor one morning still brooding when I noticed a wasp building a nest on my wall. I worried now about what would happen if I were to get stung, on top of all my other problems. With this in mind, I broke the nest and went out for a walk.

When I returned, the wasp was back, building a nest in the same site. I again broke the nest. By evening the wasp had successfully rebuilt the nest. The perseverance of the small creature amazed me. If the wasp could work so hard without giving up, then surely I, with the intelligence of a man, could not admit defeat.

One day, inspiration struck. Why not write to some charitable foundation for support? I composed a letter for several foundations. About a week later, I heard from the Bombay Tata Foundation. They granted me 300 rupees. With this grant, and the confidence that came with it, I successfully produced and defended my thesis.

So important was agriculture to our newly independent

nation, that Prime Minister Nehru personally presented us our diplomas. Because of his busy schedule, the diplomas were presented right at the seat of government, in Parliament. I puffed out my chest with pride in my graduation robe as I received my diploma.

An even bigger thrill awaited me as I left the hall. Crossing the verandah was none other than Dr Ambedkar. For a moment I felt embarrassed, since my achievements seemed so meager next to those of Dr Ambedkar's. But still I ran to intercept him and bowed at his feet. He said, 'Oh no, my boy—this is Parliament!'

Arising, I said, 'Thanks to your inspiration and blessings I have become an agricultural scientist.'

He beamed at me and I felt immense satisfaction.

Nimgade the 'Guru'

Now I was a graduate, but without employment and without a place to stay in the hostel. I did not know what to do next. Dr Raychaudhari advised me to obtain an honorary research fellowship at the agricultural institute through the institute director. He further suggested that I consider the fellowship topic of fractionation of organic phosphorus. I felt like a blind man receiving sight.

My hostel neighbor, Balgovind Prasad, a brahmin, invited me to stay in his room, thereby saving me from paying rent elsewhere. A slightly built, mild-mannered and thoughtful man, Prasad was a devout follower of the renowned Hindi writer Premchand. Writing in the early 1900s, Premchand departed from conventional stories involving the rich or the royal by writing in the language of common people about the plight, dignity, and determination of poor folk. Prasad embodied the noble teachings of that great soul through his hospitality to me. He would even bring me milk to drink. I reciprocated by giving him some academic advice and helping him with occasional errands.

One day, Dr Raychaudhari dropped by at the hostel and informed me that there would be an employment interview the next day. I was struck by his deep thoughtfulness and concern for my welfare. It was unheard of for a division head to ever visit the hostel. Any other high-ranking official would merely send such a message through a servant.

The next day, on the basis of Dr Raychaudhari's advice and the strength of his recommendation, I presented myself at the interview, and proved successful. Thus, on 10 May 1952, I became the proud recipient of the title "Research Assistant" at the Indian Agricultural Research Institute. I could heave a sigh of relief. I thought that this might mark the end of my financial troubles.

THE PROPHECY OF the Muslim colleague of my father had come true, that some day I would earn over 200 rupees a month—my first month's salary was 240. I sent 200 rupees of this to my family, pleased with how this would help everyone.

By coincidence, after my friend Prasad graduated, his room was allotted to an incoming Maharashtrian student. This was Nilkant Bhure who would soon become a close friend. Bhure urged me to stay on in his room for free. Thus, even after starting employment I continued to stay at my student hostel. Now, I could enjoy hostel life, without the financial and educational pressures.

One day, a Gujurati friend named Mangukia asked me to accompany him to meetings of the Bharat Sewak Samaj (India Service Society), held at the Prime Minister's residence.

'What qualifications do we need to join?' I asked.

'Youth,' he replied.

'What is the advantage to joining?'

'One can see many pretty women,' he replied with candor.

With youth being my primary qualification, I agreed to join my bachelor friend Mangukia to provide him moral support. Later, I learned the Bharat Sewak Samaj was started for youth volunteers across all castes and creeds in service to our young nation. In those days there was relatively little security at the Prime Minister's residence, although we did have to pass by a few guards with rifles as we walked up the sandy red driveway into the magnificent whitewashed Raj-styled mansion. The society met in one large room that could hold a hundred people. Although several earnest young women were there, all eyes rested on the Prime Minister's daughter, Indira. Indira was a lovely young woman, who always appeared in a graciously draped saree. Because of her shyness, however, no one could ever dream she would herself become prime minister one day. In fact, in those days, her father wanted to shield her from politics. Indira was keenly intelligent and knew something about each of us.

Closer to home, I mentored many incoming Maharashtrian students regarding academics and social life at IARI. Students from Nagpur, remembering my old moniker from my "temple-destroying" days, referred to me as "Guru," and the use of the term spread. I also enjoyed writing amusing poetry and narrating it in the hostel mess. Soon, the students started inviting me to become part of the entertainment at social functions. Sometimes, if I did not show up, students of all castes and creed, would ask, "Where is Guru?"

Sometimes my compositions would satirize religious orthodoxy, but in a gentle and fun manner, and no one took umbrage. In fact, even to this day, at meetings and reunions these former students, who are now high-ranking officers, still ask me to repeat several poems and slokas from the days past.

Often, they would ask, 'Guru, you have a job; why have you not yet married?' For this question I composed the following reply:

'Oh dear God, bless this true devotee,
Take the form of a girl and please marry me!'

Mother takes precipitous action

I kept sending a large portion of my salary home, thinking that all was well in our village. Then I received a letter from my brother Ankush who wrote, 'Our mother is so anguished that she does not have a daughter-in-law and does not have any grandchildren, while her sisters and friends have become grandmothers. Once, her pain was so deep that she jumped in a well thinking to end her life. But then she had a change of heart and tried to climb out, holding onto a vine, but she was too weak. She cried for help and was finally saved by some villagers. I think, dear brother, now you should think about marriage.'

The letter alarmed me. Mother had always been a calm, quiet, hardworking woman, never drawing attention to herself and her needs. I had thought to work another two or three years to accumulate some savings before settling down, but now had to consider her desperate state of mind. I wrote back to my family, 'Please go ahead and start the process of searching for a bride for me. I will abide by my parents' choice.' But while I wrote these words, I kept remembering the lovely girl Kamal Sontakke whom I had seen in Nagpur.

My guide, Dr Raychaudhari, meanwhile, encouraged me to publish scientific papers in order to progress further in my career. He said to me, 'I have seen many young scientists gain fame, but no one's achievements please me more than yours, because you have crossed many hurdles. Let other people think themselves big, bigger, or best, but you should remain humble and walk on the ground. Do not unnecessarily fly in the air!'

Following this, I submitted a paper for publication and was happy to see it accepted. I was invited to present it in a scientific congress in Lucknow. I was nervous when I stepped up to the podium in front of our nation's leading scientists, but I was successful.

I took advantage of my leave from duties to visit my home village. I went straight to my mother who was still weak, but recovering from her misadventure in the well. She admonished me to bring home a daughter-in-law, now that I was employed. I assented, but asked for some more time while I settled into my new work. I also dropped by our friends, the Patils, in Nagpur, hoping to catch any glimpse of the exquisite girl Kamal who lived nearby. But I was disappointed.

When I told my Uncle Patil about my thoughts regarding marriage, he said, 'Oh, just in this neighborhood, there is a suitable girl who is very pretty and well mannered. She is in her first year of college.'

I replied, 'I come from a poor village; she is an educated city girl. Her family will never allow it.'

My aunt intervened, saying, 'You appear a good match in my mind, so I will ask her father.'

I also asked another friend, Wagdhare, about whether the Sontakke family would ever deign to give me their daughter's hand in marriage. He said, 'Why not? Anyone would be pleased to have a literate and employed man like you in their family. Mr Sontakke is in my office and perhaps I can approach him.'

I asked my brother Ankush to help represent me in case any suitable brides should turn up. I told him that my top choice was Kamal Sontakke. The family and our well-wishers by now had created a plan to settle the issue. We sent an emissary, Uncle Patil's daughter, to the Sontakke household, on the pretext of soliciting a magazine subscription. Kamal appeared at the door without the benefit of make-up or preparation. Kamal in her natural state so pleased our "spy" that the family decided to stop the bride search right there.

Our syndicate now approached Mr Sontakke through Uncle Patil. My friend Wagdhare provided a character reference as well. In the meantime, I was nervously awaiting the news, even as I pursued my research. One day, Ankush wrote me, 'The

Sontakke family states that they have never met you, and therefore cannot make any informed decision on this matter.'

It would be difficult to take leave so early in a new job. But, on the other hand, for a girl like this, there would be many candidates, and time would be of the essence. Therefore, with trepidation I applied for a leave.

My guide Dr Raychaudhari advised me, 'Before marrying, make sure that the parents of the girl can maintain her for a year or two at home, because you will surely have a chance to study abroad. Anyway, do not delay marriage now, since a late marriage can create several new problems. So, hurry on!' I was astounded by his kind advice and particularly because this was this first time anyone had mentioned that I could study abroad.

Thus, on 3 May 1953, surrounded by my father, Ankush, and two uncles, we proceeded to Mr Sontakke's house. Kamal herself greeted us. Her attention was focused on serving tea, but everyone's gaze was on her. Then, the interrogation started. Mr Sontakke questioned my relatives closely and then engaged in a long conversation with my father, whose manner and charisma appeared to have pleased him greatly. In fact, to my surprise, he assented to the match and even fixed an engagement date of May 10. Perhaps he recognized in me a fellow devotee of education. He himself was among the first five Scheduled Caste college graduates in central India.

The engagement was a brief ceremony in the Sontakke courtyard in which Kamal and I barely saw each other. Her face was partly covered with her sari border and that must have obscured her view. Furthermore, we were not facing each other during the ceremony. The engagement was really more of a binding together of two families than an introduction between future man and wife.

Because the horoscope cast by my father showed that the name "Kamal" was not auspicious, both parties decided it was best to resort to using her birth name of "Hira." Thus, I always teased her about transforming her from a lotus (*kamal*) into a diamond (*hira*).

'Who are you?'

I returned to the village to share the news with family and well-wishers. Then I came back to Nagpur on a bus to see Kamal. On a luggage rack above me, somebody had stowed a can of cooking oil which leaked onto my head and my clothes as I napped. The rural bus spewed dust and smoke onto its crowded, sweating passengers. By the time I reached the city, the dust, oil, and sweat had combined to make me look a mess. I had a growth of stubble on my face, and to make things worse, I had a pimple on my cheek, which I had covered with a small bandage. But I was excited to see my new fiancée Kamal, and proceeded straight to her house.

I was in a sorry state, perhaps looking like a pirate or a brigand by the time I knocked on the Sontakke household door. Kamal answered, and looked bewildered. I asked for her father, and was told that he was at the office. As it turned out, her mother was also away. Kamal said diplomatically, 'If you return at five p.m, you will surely catch them.' She retreated into the doorway.

A neighbor who was related to the Sontakkes stepped out of her door and scrutinized me. Finally, she called out, 'Oh, you are the new son-in-law! You must have just arrived.' Then she turned to Kamal and said, 'Do you not recognize your own future husband?'

Kamal looked in disbelief and then blushed. Finally, with a shocked expression she scurried back inside. The relative, however, had invited me in by this time. I immediately dropped my bags inside and rushed to the outdoor bathing area to remedy my appearance. I scrubbed myself hard with soap. Then I shaved and donned clean clothes. I sat respectfully in the front room wondering about whether she liked me or not. After some time, however, Kamal appeared, still unsettled. But in her hand was a tray of food: rice and besan, a chickpea flour preparation, a simple, quick meal.

My mouth watered at the smell of the food, for I had not eaten in hours. I looked forward to the first food from the hands of my future wife. Before I could say anything, Kamal left. At the very first bite, I realized there was absolutely no salt in the food. I ate slowly, hoping she would return so that I could ask for some salt, but she had already taken my dirty clothes to wash. Later on, when her younger brother Babu sat down to eat, I was told that he yelled, 'What is this bland nonsense! There is absolutely no salt in this food!'

After eating I went to the household water tank to strike up a conversation with Kamal. But she answered each of my questions monosyllabically and shyly. Fortunately, her mother returned soon and greeted me very warmly, and a few hours later, Mr Sontakke came back from work and was equally gracious. But my mind was in a tumult because I had not even had a conversation with Kamal. With this in mind, I braced myself and asked Mr Sontakke, 'Tomorrow, I have to leave for Delhi. I would like to take Kamal to a movie tonight.'

The Sontakke parents did not assent immediately. Instead, they conferred in the kitchen for a few minutes. In those days, it was unheard of for an unmarried man and woman to socialize. But quite likely they took pity on me. Mr Sontakke said, 'You go several blocks away and wait for me. By that time, it will be dark and I will bring Kamal. And when the movie is over, immediately return home with her. This way, no one will know.'

I could barely concentrate on the cinema. Finally, on the walk back home, I could talk. I could not contain myself from asking Kamal, 'Why did you not recognize me?'

She said, 'How could I? My cousin had pointed you out to me in the crowd at the engagement ceremony, and she had pointed to a man with a goatee who appeared the life of the party with his jokes.'

I laughed, 'That was my brother Ankush! And then why did you run away when I first came to your doorstep?'

As it turns out, Kamal had almost fled from me earlier this afternoon, because she had thought that either I was an imposter or, given my rustic appearance, that I had lied about my education. Because of her agitated state of mind she had left out the salt, the most important spice in the food. But, to her credit, she said later, 'Because you ate my unsalted besan without even the slightest complaint, I think you are a most tolerant man.'

OVER THE NEXT few months, I was pleased to receive congratulations from friends and colleagues. Yet, on the other hand, I began to realize that the poor economic condition of my family would put a strain on our marriage. I was, after all, marrying a city girl who was accustomed to higher economic standards than my humble rural family. I had hoped to improve and stabilize our family's financial condition within the next two years.

PART IV

MY TIME WITH BABASAHEB AMBEDKAR

Visiting Babasaheb's bungalow

At this point I must digress from my own story to focus on my time spent with Babasaheb Ambedkar. He was like a father to us students, praising us when appropriate and also getting angry when he felt we strayed from our primary purpose in life: education. What I learned from him has influenced the course of my life, as well as important personal and professional decisions I was to make. I was fortunate to have spent spent much of my free days and holidays – hundreds of hours – at Babasaheb's ministerial homes in Delhi. After Babasaheb resigned from his ministry in 1951, I would visit more frequently without any appointment in the evenings.

I would arrive by bicycle and greet the armed sentry and then sign the bungalow registry. In the 'purpose of visit' column I would usually write 'darshan.' I was seeking blessings. I would park my bicycle outside the wall. On an ordinary evening there might be five to ten bicycles of visitors already parked here, but the number of people coming by foot – usually poor villagers – was probably five times the number of bicyclists.

I would then walk the 200 or so feet on the red sandy driveway to the porch enjoying the well-kept lawns and bougainvilleas. Conspicuously visible were the experimental plots carved out of the lawn that Babasaheb dedicated to all sorts of horticultural experiments of his own—so keen was his desire to see India free of famine. As an agriculturist, I was impressed to hear him recite Latin botanical names of his crops and plants. I once asked Babasaheb, 'Why don't you let us give you a tour of our Indian Agricultural Research Institute sometime?' He laughed, 'You are unaware, but I have already been there several times. Sometimes I go early in the mornings with my driver and walk the fields there. Several of my specimens and plantings here are from your institute.'

On entering the bungalow itself, I would greet the private secretary or personal assistants, all of whom I had befriended. I would also greet and talk with other individuals waiting to see Babasaheb. Sometimes we would wait in hushed tones on one of the dozen folding chairs in the front hall or the spacious verandah that could accommodate 25 or 30 people. In the summer evenings everyone including Babasaheb would sit directly on the cool green lawn. On hot nights an assistant might run a table fan outdoors plugged into an extension cord. Around 9:30 or so, an assistant might announce that Babasaheb's dinner was ready. The rest of us would then leave. The rest of the night, from what I understood, Babasaheb would be reading or writing, catching just a few hours of sleep.

While outwardly Dr Ambedkar's bungalow was much like that of most high-ranking ministers, inwardly it was rather different due to the continual presence of many visitors from humble stations in life. Another difference was the vast number of books. He had numbered bookcases with glass doors in most of the rooms in his house. Even from his verandah overlooking the lawn, where we often talked until late in the night, one could see bookcases. And this was only a portion of his library; the bulk of it was housed in Bombay. Once, I mentioned to him, still remembering the story of how Banaras Hindu University had sought Dr Ambedkar's library, 'I hear your personal library is one of the best in the world.'

Babasaheb laughed. 'I cannot vouch for it being one of the best in the world; but certainly it is one of the finest in our country. I have 33,000 books, some of which are quite rare and unique.' His books covered topics ranging from politics to poultry and from the Theory of Relativity to Buddhism. He had researched topics ranging from architecture to agronomy for his above-mentioned horticultural experiments. Dr Ambedkar was comfortable talking about concepts ranging from large-scale irrigation to atomic energy to coal mining. When I once asked

Babasaheb, 'How do you relax from your long hours of study?' he replied, 'To me it is relaxing merely switching from the study of one topic to an entirely different topic.'

On one telling occasion, a British commission had scoured the entire country in search of a certain report, but with no luck. Finally, they came to know about Dr Ambedkar's library and they found it there. He let them borrow the report on the condition that they return it immediately when they were finished. More impressive than the library itself was Babasaheb's memory. On one rare occasion, Babasaheb needed a reference for one of his writings but could not find it in his library or anywhere in India. Finally, he called a student he knew at his alma mater, Columbia University, in New York City. When the book did not turn up, Dr Ambedkar told him to forget about the card catalogue and just go to a certain shelf in the large library and look for a book of a certain size and a certain color. And there it was.

Babasaheb's high standards for preparation extended to all facets of his life. I recall hearing about how he once turned his car back because his hat was not right. He was particular about his pens, too. On one occasion, when I handed him my pen for obtaining his autograph, it did not work properly. He handed it back, saying, 'I do not want to spoil my handwriting for you.' He then found his own pen.

Parliamentary political opponents learned quickly not to underestimate Dr Ambedkar's preparedness. Once in parliament, Syama Prasad Mookerjee, a minister, challenged Babasaheb, saying, 'Yesterday, I was not in parliament, and it appears that Dr Ambedkar passed a portion of the Hindu Code Bill hurriedly and ran away.' Dr Ambedkar replied, 'I do not want to sink to such a low level in criticizing my opponent. But as far as law is concerned, you are simply a rabbit in front of an elephant. Therefore you cannot make me run away!'

During a debate on a national language for India, in which Babasaheb, to many people's surprise championed Sanskrit, the root of many Indian languages, Professor Mitra, a Sanskrit scholar and Member of Parliament challenged Babasaheb's knowledge by posing a question in Sanskrit. Babasaheb replied in Sanskrit, and thereupon ensued an hour-long debate in Sanskrit following which Mitra declared, 'Dr Ambedkar, you are a master of Sanskrit.' This was all the more remarkable because Babasaheb had been prevented early on from learning the language, because of caste injunctions. Ambedkar eventually studied Sanskrit to the point of being able to remark, 'Sanskrit is the mine of literature. Brahmins did not learn this language properly and did not allow others to study it either!' From Babasaheb I gained a deeper appreciation for Sanskrit aphorisms. But Babasaheb also spoke several other Indian languages, as well as foreign tongues such as Persian and even German.

Another time in Parliament, Babasaheb angrily dismissed the Scheduled Caste Commission Report with the words, 'This is not a Commissioner's report; it looks like a servant's report!' At this point, the Home Minister, K.N. Kutju, himself a Ph.D. and barrister-at-law and a relative of Nehru, stood up and suggested, 'Perhaps Dr Ambedkar has not read the report thoroughly.'

To this, Dr Ambedkar replied, even in the presence of Nehru, 'It is not in my blood to make blind criticism. You can ask me about any point in the report from cover to cover. You may not know my reading habits. For your information, I must tell you, the number of books which I have read surpasses not only what you have read, but also the combined amount read by your forefathers, your present generation, and your coming generations for many years hence.' The next day, the national journal, *Shankar's Weekly*, showed a cartoon depicting Kutju sweeping a street in front of Dr Ambedkar, who was seated like a learned brahmin wearing a sacred thread.

ON OCCASIONS OUR visits to the bungalow would involve waiting for hours for Babasaheb to appear on the lawn or verandah. His assistant Sudama would relay to us information about his whereabouts, or say 'Babasaheb is writing' or 'Babasaheb is on the phone' or 'Babasaheb is taking a bath.'

I befriended Sudama and learned about his fascinating life

story. As a child, Sudama was abandoned by his father at Dr Ambedkar's bungalow in Bombay with these words: 'Sir, you are our leader. I am desperately poor and will leave my child in your care.' Before Babasaheb could even reply, the father fled. As Sudama grew older under Babasaheb's fatherly care, he said, 'Babasaheb, you have taken care of me, now I only want to serve you.' And thus, Sudama tended to Babasaheb for perhaps a quarter century.

Such was their mutual respect, that once, Sudama, upon returning from a late night movie realizing that his entering the bungalow might disturb Babasaheb who was engrossed in work, fell asleep outside the door. When Babasaheb stepped outside for a breath of midnight air, he spotted the sleeping figure and tiptoed away. The next morning, Sudama awoke to find himself draped in Babasaheb's own overcoat.

Conversation with Sudama and others would thus consume our time while we waited on the verandah. When Babasaheb did eventually arrive, usually in a comfortable white kurta pyjama or a white Bengali lungi with loose Bengali shirt, his voice would boom as though he were addressing a large rally, *'Kasa ahet, ba?'* or 'How are you all doing?' He would address my group of fellow agricultural students in Marathi, Hindi or English; sometimes with quotations from Sanskrit or Pali, often lapsing from one language to the other, and often highlighting key points with a repetition in different languages. With strangers he might break the ice with a joke. 'What is your name?'

'My name is Singh.'

'Singh? That means lion! I am afraid of lions! What brings a lion here?'

'I am here for your darshan.'

'I am very ordinary, and my parents were quite ordinary. I am just like you. If you want to take darshan, go to other political leaders. They are always ready and anxious to give their blessings and are stretching their legs forward so that people can touch their feet. Don't come to me for darshan; instead, give me work to do. Tell me what I can do for you.'

Usually a personal assistant would jot down notes about work to be done on behalf of different visitors. In this manner, Babasaheb blended social work with socializing in a relaxed atmosphere. In this informal setting, we students ('my boys,' as he often called us) were privy to facets of his life and work that were not seen by other people. Even here, however, Babasaheb could become impatient if someone asked him to repeat a point, or curt if anyone pontificated without a good base of knowledge.

Although as Law Minister Dr Ambedkar had a monthly entertainment budget of about 500 rupees, refreshments most often just consisted of water—every last bit of his resources were being diverted into expanding his library! But what kept us coming was the inspirational conversation. There was an air of idealism and hope, and so it was with an uplifted heart that we approached Babasaheb's abode. The fatigue of the journey of eight to ten miles would disappear when we arrived.

Once, I was bicycling with a fellow student, M. Wanjari, on my back seat. Not far from the bungalow, we were overtaken by a pretty young woman bicycling quickly. Wanjari, from the comfort of the back seat remarked to me, 'How is that girl overtaking us? Are we not strong men?' His words spurred me to action. I picked up the pace and raced the woman for a good mile or so before overtaking her. Only upon seeing Babasaheb's bungalow did we slow down. Savoring our victory, we entered the bungalow and sat down to wait.

In a few minutes we spotted Babasaheb on the verandah with his sleeve rolled up for his insulin injection. To our horror we recognized the nurse administering the injection as the very same young woman we had overtaken on bicycle. We felt like delinquents engaging in a childish race while this nurse must have been racing to administer a possibly life-saving injection. We crept away towards the door when Babasaheb recognized us. 'Come, come!' he boomed, with his sleeve still rolled up. 'Why are you running away!?' The woman saw us over her syringe. To our immense relief she said nothing, but merely smiled.

'Do not get tempted by power'

Babasaheb took time from his busy schedule to continue hectoring me about my educational progress. He was proud that I had come from an entirely illiterate background and yet had caught the fever for education. In some ways, our backgrounds could not have been more dissimilar: Babasaheb's father had a good post in the British army, and thus he had a cosmopolitan outlook from the beginning. He was always well dressed, and in parliament was considered along with the Muslim leader Jinnah as one of the best-dressed Indian statesmen. For myself, regarding clothing, my rural roots were often apparent. As a child, Babasaheb did not face the beatings that I did at the hands of upper-caste individuals. But he did face ostracism and numerous humiliations, especially early in his career. Interestingly, because his mother had died early on, his family took pity on him and he was also spared disciplinary measures at home. 'I was quite mischievous as a child!' admitted Babasaheb. 'Sometimes I would climb onto the roof and cause mischief. Even if I broke roof tiles I was spared any beatings.' It was thus a sense of empathy and outrage that powered Babasaheb's mission that led him to bombard the very basis of Hindu society.

Starting from the very beginning, Babasaheb obtained several educational scholarships. Of course, in large degree, that was because of his formidable mental powers combined with an intense focus on studies that contrasted with my distractible nature and family obligations that time and again almost derailed my educational pursuits. Perhaps sensing this, Babasaheb would enquire from time to time about my academic progress. He warned me several times, 'Be careful and work hard. Carve out enough time for your own research, even if you must do so on holidays and weekends. You must pursue higher education beyond a B.Sc. or an M.Sc. and even beyond a Ph.D.! Degrees are just stepping stones.'

I once countered, saying, 'But there is no end to knowledge.'

Dr Ambedkar bristled. 'You educated people just want to get a job with a salary and then forget about education and everything else including your society! I think I have been able to help some students; but it pains me that I could hardly do anything for the common, illiterate man. I ought to have devoted more time to illiterate untouchables.'

Even while engaged in research and work, I continued going to Babasaheb Ambedkar's bungalow for community meetings. On one occasion, I ran into a new person there dressed in a Maharashtrian dhoti. Recognizing a compatriot, I engaged in a long conversation with him during which I talked about my educational struggles. It turned out he was Kannamwar, a prominent Congress party secretary. He was looking for an educated Scheduled Caste candidate to fill a vacancy in a state legislative assembly seat in Maharashtra. Then, to my astonishment, he offered me the ticket. I was dumbfounded. After all, I had no political background or intention, and I told him so.

'So many people would die for such a chance!' he laughed.

I said that I would have to ask my father's advice before taking such a step, but he told me that there was not enough time for a consultation.

'Then in that case, I will ask my father here, who is Babasaheb Ambedkar. He has been my inspiration in life.'

Later that evening, I sought Dr Ambedkar's counsel. He shook his head. 'Becoming a Member of the Legislative Assembly is quite an ordinary thing when you compare it to what you can accomplish as a scientific role model for our community. We are very weak economically and socially, and we need strength in all fields. We must be a well-rounded community. Do not get tempted by power and politics.'

I once heard Babasaheb field a telephone call from a Punjabi politician that perhaps reveals some of Babasaheb's cynicism about politicians. This politician stated that he was interested in joining Babasaheb's Republican Party. 'It is good that you want to join us,' Babasaheb's voice rang out, 'but pray tell me about when you plan to abandon us!'

On one occasion, in 1952, I volunteered to canvass for Babasaheb in the Bombay elections for the seat of Member of Parliament. But instead of being happy with this, he said, 'The best students should not waste their time! I do not seek victory at the cost of my best students!' His use of the term "best students" inspired me, and I resolved I would pursue my education with full vigor.

And so, I remained a scientist for the rest of my career, but have always worked actively as a social reform worker at the same time. From time to time I would show Babasaheb posters from programs being held by our Scheduled Caste community in Delhi. He would be very pleased, saying 'These kinds of activities are just what we need. If a man wants to live alone in the jungle then that is fine; but by working in concert, one's efforts are magnified: one and one becomes three.'

BEING INVOLVED WITH social reform work, I was open to help with all sorts of causes that could distract me from studies. One day, an elderly man, a rustic fellow from the villages, came to visit me. Though a laborer of good build, he had tears in his eyes. He had heard about the work that I had been doing in our community. Apparently, his niece had recently been married to a man who appeared to have a very pleasing personality. But inwardly he was of bad character. His financial situation had gone sour, and in the pursuit of easy money, he had apparently sold her for a thousand rupees to a house of ill repute at G.B. Road, the red light district near Sadar Bazaar.

I told him that I knew nothing about this element of society and could not help. But then he explained further, that his brother, on his deathbed, made him promise to take care of his daughter. I was still hesitant to help, but his sobs melted my heart. Reluctantly, I agreed. In the evening, we set out to G.B.

Road, with myself posing as a customer. I felt very ill at ease but had to remind myself of our noble mission. We passed several stores of every description including bookstores. Finally, from the street, the uncle pointed out the stall where she worked. I entered the stall, with goosebumps, wondering why I had allowed myself to be talked into such a mission. What if the pimps found out? Then they would surely kill me.

Nonetheless, I kept my promise and continued. I asked for this woman's name in particular and she was presented to me.

Once we were together, I spoke to her, 'You must leave this work and return to your family. I have come to free you.'

She said, 'No, I cannot come with you now. My life is ruined. Even if I return, nobody will marry me. Instead, my family will be ostracized by everyone. Please just tell my uncle that I have ceased to exist. That will be the best for the family. I would have been happy with an empty stomach struggling to earn honest money, but that is not possible now.'

I returned to the street and conveyed her message to her uncle. He began to sob. We had no choice but to return empty handed with our hearts full of sorrow.

Some days later, I went to see Dr Panjabrao Deshmukh and mentioned this incident. He immediately frowned. 'Nimgade, you are a young scientist now!' he exclaimed. 'Focus on your research. Don't be distracted by things that can get you killed! There is great danger there. Had you informed me, I could have arranged for a plainclothes policeman to go with you. Never again must you do this.'

The next month, during a meeting with Dr Ambedkar, the subject of bookstores came up. Dr Ambedkar mentioned that there were some good bookstores near Sadar Bazaar. I agreed, and he asked, 'When did you ever go there?'

I related to him my adventure in great detail. His response was similar to Dr Panjabrao Deshmukh's. 'The pimps would kill you if they knew you came to undo their thousand-rupee investment!'

Thus, doubly warned by two great men, I focused on my studies and partook only of "safe" social work.

Drafting the Indian Constitution

On 15 August 1947, India was granted its freedom from England. A new country, the world's largest democracy, would need a constitution that could bind together hundreds of millions of people of different castes and creeds. Prime Minister Nehru was uncertain about whether to appoint Dr Ambedkar as his law minister. For a while, the transition Indian government thought of hiring foreign constitutionalists to draft India's constitution. To Gandhi's credit, he put the needs of the nation first and he helped overcome Nehru's hesitancy by pointing out that 'We have a very good constitutionalist at home in Dr Ambedkar; why do we need to search overseas?' When the issue of the political opposition between Gandhi and Ambedkar was brought up, Gandhi explained, 'Dr Ambedkar is a true patriot; that is why he criticizes me!'

For three years in the late 1940s, Babasaheb had engaged in a comparative study of world constitutions as preparation for framing the Indian Constitution. The entire task of writing the Constitution had fallen on his shoulders, because all the other members of the Constitution drafting committee had dropped out because of illness or tours of duty abroad. At about the same, time Babasaheb was also working on the Hindu Code Bill, which sought sweeping reforms by banning caste-based inequalities and by providing rights for women and for other downtrodden members of India's predominantly Hindu society.

I do not know how much Babasaheb slept during that period, for he was reading through all hours of the night. Once, some American reporters asked him when would be convenient to visit him, and he told them to come whenever they pleased. They visited him at midnight and found him still working in his study. Astonished, they asked him, 'We approached Nehru and

Gandhi, but they were asleep; why are you still working so late?'

'They are lucky as leaders because their followers are awake,' Dr Ambedkar replied, 'I have to keep awake, because my oppressed people are still sleeping.' Sometimes at night Babasaheb was engrossed in his reading to the point of being lost to the world. Once, during this time period I quietly appeared in his study and touched his feet. He said, 'Tommy, don't do that!'

I was startled. But so was Babasaheb, when he looked up and saw me. It turned out he had mistaken me for his dog!

When his Constitution was finally ratified on 26 January 1950, the Maharashtrian community feted Babasaheb in New Delhi. There, Kakasaheb Gadgil, a minister said, 'In India, the Taj Mahal is beautiful; but even more beautiful is our new Constitution which was framed by the most learned Maharashtrian Dr Ambedkar.'

Babasaheb noted with satisfaction that the government, which had once viewed him as a traitor, had now started to embrace him. Still, the recognition due him was slow in coming from the Indian establishment. He obtained an honorary degree in law (LL.D.) in 1952 from his alma mater Columbia University, before being similarly honored domestically for his contribution to constitutional studies. In fact, at celebrations in Delhi for Babasaheb's honorary degree from Columbia I spoke to the audience, 'This is a great honor to our country and at the same time this is a great kick to Babasaheb's critics and opponents.' At this moment, Babasaheb said, 'Please don't use such harsh words!'

I smiled and explained, 'When I say "kick" it refers to Babasaheb's method: K stands for knowledge, I stands for Intelligence, C stands for Character, and K stands for Karuna—compassion. Babasaheb smiled back at me, a little more satisfied.

AFTER HIS LABORS on the Constitution and the Hindu Code Bill, I saw that Babasaheb seemed to have slowed down, and increasingly relied on a walking stick or someone's shoulder for support while walking. Once, when I found some swelling in his feet, I remarked, 'Babasaheb, just a decade ago, you walked briskly, and we could not keep up with you. Now, I do not understand why you have slowed.'

He sighed and said, 'My health was solid as a rock. But during the framing of the Constitution I went against nature. Sometimes I would sit for 20 out of 24 hours each day. It is no wonder I have lost the strength of my legs. But I do not want to brood about this, because my father taught me to do good work and then move on.'

Sometimes he would ask about my academic progress. I would tell him that I was being slowed down by my work duties. He replied once, 'You may be slow, but you must make progress day by day. You should be like the man entering deep waters, who proceeds slowly and ultimately reaches the other shore, not like the man who dashes in and drowns.'

Babasaheb's diabetes worsened and his feet were always sore. We would sometimes sit by him and massage his legs. If his wife Savita Ambedkar walked by, she would scold us, saying, 'Right now his legs are sore, but if the diabetes worsens, then his hands will also be affected. Will you then rub his hands and ruin them for further work?'

Our hands would drop away but as soon as she left, we would resume our massage. I think Babasaheb must have found relief with these massages because he himself never turned our hands away. And, of course, for us, we thought ourselves most fortunate to help serve him in our own small way.

AFTER HAVING SEEN how hard Babasaheb had labored over the Constitution, I was surprised to read that in a recent speech he had said, 'Sometimes I feel like I should burn the Constitution that I have written.' I requested him to explain this remark in one of our group discourses on Babasaheb's bungalow lawn. He said, 'Politicians are not following the Constitution. For instance, Morarji Desai was defeated in elections, but still a post was created for him through someone's resignation and ultimately he became Chief Minister.'

Babasaheb's face would become red when he talked about the politicians who could barely even understand parliamentary law. 'I am not afraid of anyone,' he said. 'In parliament, if someone needs scolding to straighten them up then I am not afraid to do so. But sometimes I wish I could enter parliament with a weapon and knock some sense into some of our parliament members!'

Conservative forces opposed provisions of the Hindu Code Bill that provided for safety valves for women through divorce and women's inheritance of property, not to mention rights for other depressed members of society. Nehru feared that passing the Hindu Code Bill at this point would ruin the Congress party's chances for re-election and withdrew support. It was no wonder that Dr Ambedkar was becoming increasingly frustrated and felt betrayed. Ultimately, in disgust, he resigned from his post as Law Minister. Although the Hindu Code Bill did not pass in its entirety, over the years virtually all of its provisions were passed one by one.

In retirement, Babasaheb had more time, but had health problems including diabetes, muscle pains, and dimming vision. Once, in 1953, when he was in his sickbed, I paid a visit, announcing myself to his assistant as a student from Bombay. Babasaheb, upon seeing me said jokingly, '*Arrey,* I was expecting someone from Bombay, but you are from Delhi! Only because they announced that someone had come from faraway Bombay did I allow this visit!'

'I was missing your company!' I explained. 'Furthermore, even though I am from Delhi, I am a Maharashtrian first!'

I took his hand and put it to my chest. His hand felt hot. 'I have been suffering from pneumonia for the past two weeks,' Babasaheb said. 'I cannot concentrate on my work.' Babasaheb let me remain by his side for a half-hour during which he asked about my research and then told me about his latest manuscript.

Despite his health problems, Babasaheb pressed forward with his writings on social reforms and religion. In these late years, Babasaheb once confided several more worries to me. He said, 'I am older now, and can barely do anything more than provide advice. And you will be astounded to know that I have debts to clear—some 2,200,000 rupees.' This was an amount beyond my imagination (recall that my salary was 240 rupees a month at this time).

Founding the Siddhartha College at Bombay, the Milind College at Aurangabad, and running in elections had proved very expensive for him. I am sure Babasaheb also spent a fortune on books. (The Milind College librarian once told me how Babasaheb spotted a beautiful scroll of the Koran with gold lettering at the house of a Muslim landlord. Babasaheb fell in love with it and ended up paying 8,000 rupees for it.) Furthermore, Babasaheb refused to exploit any of his high positions for personal gains. In fact, a friend of mine overheard Babasaheb's outraged response when someone proposed appointing his son as the manager of a housing project in Delhi: 'Because I am minister you want to appoint him!' Babasaheb shouted. 'But you should not appoint my son—he is not qualified! It is not in my blood to take undue advantage of anyone.' Thereupon, Babasaheb even asked his son to move to Bombay to reduce similar temptations on part of other sycophants.

'When my health improves,' Babasaheb confided to me, 'I shall have to ramp up my private law practice to pay off these debts. Despite these troubles, one must remain steadfast as a mountain.'

Dr Ambedkar explains life

I once asked, 'Babasaheb, you are often alone, and your opponents are numerous. Are you not afraid sometimes to face them?'

Despite being of scientific temperament, Babasaheb admitted, I have two superstitions: the first is that the spirits of my parents hover near by and would save me from any calamity. The second is that the Lord Buddha would save me.' He even admitted that 'my faith leads me to consider the Buddha as my God. Without faith, how can a human find the right path? A person without the path would just stumble around in the dark.'

Once I asked about the book he was working on, *The Buddha and His Dhamma*. Babasaheb said this was one of his most important works. He had been working on it for many years, and he had instructed his wife where to find the manuscript in case he should perish in something like a plane crash. In fact, with this in mind, he worked very hard to get this manuscript finished before leaving on a trip to the USA.

Babasaheb explained how he grew closer to Buddhism with time. 'I grew up being quite well acquainted with Indian religious lore,' he said one evening on his verandah to several of us students. 'My father was a devout Hindu and even made us memorize religious passages. I was supersaturated with religious epics. He wanted my focus to remain on the spiritual and even forbade his friends from feting me for being the first Scheduled Caste member to matriculate from high school. Nonetheless, my father's friends celebrated the occasion and Mr Keluskar, a brahmin, presented me with his own book on Gautama Buddha. That opened my eyes to Buddhism, and I have read voraciously on the topic ever since. Whatever I have achieved, I owe to the

Buddha. I find thorough equality and superb humanism in Buddhism. The literature of Buddhism is as vast as the ocean. Therefore I wanted to write something that provides ordinary people access to this literature.

'In the whole world, there are just a few founders of major religions: Jesus Christ, the Prophet Mohammed, Abraham, Mahavira, the Buddha, and, according to the Hindus, Rama and Krishna. Many of these leaders played the role of "postman" bearing the message of God and sometimes claiming to be related to God. How can one expect equality for all under this type of a religious icon?

'Although the Buddha was no ordinary man, he claimed only to be a man. Followers of many of the major religions have been embroiled in wars for centuries and millennia. The Buddha, however, focused on reducing wars and struggle, and for a thousand years in India under Buddhism, there were no wars to speak of. Even though Buddhism has waned in India, it has waxed elsewhere in Asia, including in China, Japan, Tibet, Manchuria, Burma, Ceylon, and Thailand.'

In his strong voice, Babasaheb then narrated to us the life story of the Buddha:

> The Buddha was born a prince, but left behind his palace and all its accompanying pleasures including his devoted, charming queen. One might ask what else a rich prince might need in this world. But Gautama had realized that the world is full of sorrow. He retreated into the forest, eating only one berry a day, and meditating for days on end. In due course he became weak and thin. As his body sank in health, he thought, 'I left my kingdom to find out how humans can become happy, and to lessen the misery of the masses. Will this sort of *tapasya* (religious austerity) serve me? Or shall I perish in vain first? I do not want to die like this.'
>
> He thought further and concluded that 'Nothing but the mind can provide a solution to my quest. If I want to use my mind properly, I must stay healthy. Only a strong and healthy body can provide the basis for the mind. Therefore I must leave this long meditation and extreme fasting, and I

> must now eat something.' His fellow ascetics were upset at the Buddha for abandoning their path. But he had concluded that he needed to follow his own path of scientific inquiry.

'The Buddha was a scientist,' said Babasaheb, 'and he never made claims beyond the data at hand. Therefore, he never made claims such as "the world was created in so many days." Instead, he humbly claimed, "I have nothing to say about who has created the world." In fact, the Buddha did not concern himself with questions of whether there is a soul or a god. There is no space for anything unscientific in Buddhism. In fact, I challenge any scientist to disprove the doctrine of the Lord Buddha. If they can, I will eat my hat!' Babasaheb was fond of pointing out that the findings of modern physicists were more in line with the Buddhistic view of the transient nature of life than with the more classical philosophical thinking about the world and its atomic structure being immutable and indestructible.

Dr Ambedkar's views on superstitious thinking spilled over once into a parliamentary debate. Once, in these august chambers, one Member of Parliament angrily shouted to Dr Ambedkar, 'God save your soul!' To this, Babasaheb replied, 'Let me save you some trouble. Like the Buddha I do not believe in God, nor do I believe in soul!'

'What the Buddha concerned himself with instead,' said Babasaheb to us students at his verandah, 'was human suffering. If a man has an arrow lodged in his body, one should concentrate first on saving his life and removing the arrow, not on asking how the arrow got there.'

I once asked Babasaheb about how Buddhists prayed. He replied, 'There is no prayer in the sense of asking for boons from God, instead we chant to affirm our taking refuge in the teachings of the Buddha.'

Dr Ambedkar explained further, 'Two things are essential for religion: wisdom and compassion. The Buddhist treatise *Lohik Sutta* explains things very nicely. This treatise derives from a conversation the Buddha had with one of his converts who initially opposed him, a brahmin named Lohik, who asked, 'Tell me what you mean by wisdom. How can we give it to everyone?' The Buddha replied, 'My dear Lohik, knowledge is not a monopoly of any particular caste. It is as essential to living as food. It should be transmitted to everyone regardless of caste or creed. But knowledge is like a sword that can be used for good or for evil. It can save or it can kill. To best use knowledge, one must have character.'

Babasaheb was not fond of unscientific Hindu orthodoxies. He would say things like, 'A religion that relies on distinctions between humans—how can that be considered a good religion? Consider the point that Krishna himself takes credit in the Bhagavadgita for creating the four varnas, the categories subdivided into many castes and subcastes.'

Babasaheb also felt that Gandhi lacked a full understanding of the concept of ahimsa, nonviolence. The Buddha himself had preached more fully about ahimsa. Once, a general named Sinha came to the Buddha and said, 'Oh, Lord! My mind is greatly troubled. I command a mighty army, and we are sworn to protect our land; and yet I believe firmly in the principle of ahimsa. If a neighboring nation attacks us, what is the right course of action?'

To this, the Buddha replied, 'You are doing no wrong in punishing the offender; you are putting Law into effect. But first try peaceful methods. If the offender is not convinced by the preaching of the Good, then you must act to support the rule of justice; Good must not be sacrificed to Evil. Good is so small in the world, and Evil so great, that you must safeguard the Good by whatever means at your disposal.'

Babasaheb's interpretation of the Buddhistic view of ahimsa is illustrated by how his blood would boil when he heard about the mistreatment of our Scheduled Caste women by upper-caste men. Once, he said, 'Had I been younger, I would have shot the miscreants with a gun!' On another similar occasion, he scolded some men who came to tell him about being victims of atrocities against Scheduled Caste people. He said, 'You cowardly rascals! Why did you not mete out justice yourselves, instead of coming running to me first? *Darogey to marogey!* (The coward gets killed!) Why is it that the goat gets sacrificed and not the lion? I exhort you to become lions!'

ON 18 DECEMBER 1953, I sat nervously on Babasaheb's lawn awaiting his return from a walk. In my hand was a printed wedding invitation that had been sent to me from Nagpur. How would Babasaheb react to my upcoming marriage? On a previous occasion, when his eyes were tired and he had just put in some soothing eye drops, I had taken the opportunity of asking for his opinion about marriage.

He had said with irritation, 'Why are you in such a rush to get married! Overseas, they take their time.'

'Well,' I said, 'in our society, we believe that the parents do not get salvation or relief until they get a grandson.'

'What stupid ideas you are carrying in your head! You must knock down those silly ideas. I don't like such foolish talk. In the West there are so many unmarried people living fulfilled lives.'

When Babasaheb calmed down, I told him about how my family had found a good and educated girl for me to marry.

'Still I think you should not marry now,' he said. 'If you want to gain something in life, you should accomplish that first. Go to foreign countries for your higher education, settle down well in life, and then think about marriage.'

I added, 'But I already have employment, Baba.'

'Is this small job what you call your employment?' he boomed. 'No, no, set your sights higher. I won't advise you to marry at this stage. But since you are already engaged, there is no way out. If she is a wise girl, she will wait for two more years.'

With these words etched in my mind, I was afraid to even present him the invitation.

About four in the evening, Babasaheb returned from his walk, and appeared in a jovial mood. He picked up my invitation and read it. Then he turned to me and said with a smile, 'You have brought me your wedding invitation, now you must sit with me and have tea.' When the tea and biscuits arrived, he said, 'I have diabetes, so you must eat my share!'

I was so hungry from my long wait on his lawn that I ate all the biscuits.

Finally, I asked, 'Baba, will you please write a message of good will for my wedding.'

'*Arrey*,' he apologized, 'my hand is aching so much.'

'Baba,' I persisted, 'you also write with your left hand; that would be fine also.'

'Even my left hand has been aching. The last three days I had to give up writing entirely. That's why I went out for a long drive and walk today.'

Finally, inspiration struck Babasaheb. He said, 'Go to my study, and there you will find a Marathi version of Emperor Ashoka's edicts concerning Buddhism. Please consider these my good wishes, which you can read out to everyone. Please give one copy to the bride's family and keep the other for yourself. In the near future, we will all embrace Buddhism. But we must prepare for that now.'

My mind overflowed with joy with Babasaheb's words. Happily I bore these messages with me, knowing that I had Babasaheb's blessings. And these were the edicts of Emperor Ashoka, as carved on a rock some 2,200 years ago.

> The beloved and respected Emperor Ashoka desires that everywhere in the kingdom people should always follow the Dhamma to gain control of the senses and maintain pure thoughts. Remain well mannered with servants, provide service to parents from the bottom of your hearts, have respect for all living beings, and always speak the truth. Seek to inculcate these qualities. Similarly, students should respect their teachers and keep friendly relations with relatives and friends. These are the virtues which have been passed on since time immemorial. Follow these rules for a long and useful life.

> Emperor Ashoka desires that all the people in his empire live in happiness and interact with each other in peace and amity. Do not kill. All great religions should teach tolerance and purity of mind. Everyone should contribute to the common good according to their means. Even the poor, who

do not have means to donate, can also practice tolerance, good character, gratefulness, and faith. However, all good deeds are in vain if performed without faith and purity of mind. There is no greater gift than Faith. Therefore, abide by the Dhamma.

'देवानाम् प्रिय' प्रियदर्शी राजाची इच्छा आहे कीं त्याच्या साम्राज्यांत सर्व पंथांच्या लोकांनीं गुण्यागोविंदानें नांदावें. कारण कोठलाही पंथ झाला तरी तो संयम आणि मनाची शुद्धता हवी, असेंच सांगतो.

निरनिराळ्या पंथांचे लोक आपल्या हातून पुण्य घडावें या हेतूनें आपल्या कुवती-प्रमाणें हरतऱ्हेचीं लहानमोठीं धर्मकृत्यें करीत असतात. पण लक्षांत ठेवा कीं हीं कृत्यें करीत असतां माणसाच्या ठायीं संयम नसेल, त्याचें मन शुद्ध नसेल, त्याच्यांत कृतज्ञता व श्रध्दा नसेल, तर त्याचीं सारीं कृत्यें-मग तीं कितीही मोठीं असलीं तरी-कुचकामाची ठरतील.

'देवानाम् प्रिय' प्रियदर्शी राजाची आज्ञा-

मातापित्यांची मनःपूर्वक सेवा करा. सर्व जिवमात्रांविषयीं मनांत आदर बाळगा. नेहमीं सत्य तेंच बोला.

धर्माला अत्यावश्यक असलेल्या ह्या गुणांचें संवर्धन करा.

तसेंच शिष्यानें गुरूला मान दिला पाहिजे आणि आपल्या आप्तेष्टांशीं प्रेमळ वर्तन ठेविलें पाहिजे. हे वागणुकीचे नियम अनादि कालापासून चालत आलेले आहेत. प्रत्येकानें तसें वागलें पाहिजे. तशा वागण्यानें तुम्ही दीर्घायुषी व्हाल.

Babasaheb's message for my wedding—the Marathi version of Ashoka's Edicts.

PART V

TYING THE KNOT

The wedding

I returned home to Umrer mid-December, full of anticipation for my wedding, the prelude to the next chapter in my life. I found my family hut unrecognizable thanks to several additions. A beautiful festive tent covered the courtyard. Several ceremonies took place there, featuring singing by village woman and even a village band. The mang people, who had a special place in their heart for me, since I had persuaded the mahar community to allow them to draw water from our community well, played sacred music on drums and stringed instruments.

On the wedding day, 27 December 1953, the groom's procession went by train to Nagpur. I was wearing a new beaded cap, a white shirt and gold-threaded white dhoti with a jacket. This was the first time in my life I recall wearing new clothes from head to toe. At Nagpur, I sat in a decorated rented car with several family members. Behind trailed a procession of 50 rickshaws with guests and relatives. We arrived to the music of a band and fireworks. Apparently, my brother Ankush had made these arrangements. When I worriedly asked him about the costs, he said, 'This is not the time to be thinking of such things; be happy, this is the time for celebration!'

At 6 p.m. our wedding ceremony was performed in the festive tent. I tied a *mangalsutra*, an auspicious beaded necklace worn by married Maharashtrian women, around Kamal's neck and placed a red sindoor mark in the parting of her hair. Now her name was changed from Kamal to Hira. Hira was now my wife, my partner in life's ups and downs. Over 5,000 people had come to the wedding, and nearly 2,000 stayed for food. Many of these guests were people I had met in the course of my social reform work in the villages. The Nagpur Scheduled Caste Federation was holding its annual meeting, and many of the delegates also

Hira, the city girl, strikes a pose while visiting my village.

came for the wedding.

I was very happy and proud that my new father-in-law, an educated professional, treated my father, an illiterate villager, with the utmost respect. The next day, my parents told me to take Hira to our familial village of Sathgaon so she could pay respects to our village elders and local gods. Unfortunately, we missed the last bus, because we were trying to say our farewells to everyone.

Then I saw an empty truck about to depart the city. Hesitatingly, I asked Hira, 'Should we go in the truck? It will be the fastest way there.'

Hira looked taken aback, but then she nodded in assent, and after paying the truck driver a small fee, we climbed in the back. So here we were, riding in the back of a truck used for hauling bricks and sand. Most other newlyweds go to Kashmir or other Himalayan resorts for their honeymoon, traveling in trains or even planes.

The dust from the road flew up over us, and a half-hour later, we transferred to a bullock cart for the last leg of the journey. By 10 p.m., we were at Sathgaon. Hira was bone-tired at the journey's end. We enjoyed our visit to my birth village, with Hira making a very favorable impression on everyone.

The next day we returned to Umrer. Even the beautiful Gana, the higher-caste woman with whom I had a long "love affair," was taken by Hira. Gana was now happily married with two children. She placed a tilak upon Hira's forehead. I had earlier told Hira about everything that had transpired – or should I say, not transpired – between Gana and me. They eventually became good friends.

One evening, we went to meet friends, and then we decided to go to a popular movie featuring Dilip Kumar at the new "talkies" (cinema hall) in Umrer. It was midnight by the time we reached home. The whole village was asleep. We thought we could sneak in quietly, without waking anyone. But there was Father outside in the courtyard, waiting up for us. I was afraid that he would be angry at us for being out so late. 'Ah, Children, where have you been on this chilly night?' he asked in an affectionate tone. He was warming up some water outside over a wood fire. 'Come wash your limbs in warm water. You will feel better.'

Seeing his thoughtfulness, Hira's heart melted. She knew then that she was entering a family filled with love.

Hira in front of our village house in Urmer. At 5'2", she is the tallest woman here. My mother is to Hira's right.

A new life for Hira

Hira stayed on in Nagpur to finish her college exams while I returned to work in New Delhi. But my heart remained with her. I wrote often, but because of exams she could not always reply. My friends congratulated me, but they also teased me because I could not have my new wife with me in Delhi. I was still staying in Bhure's room at the hostel. One cold night, he shook me awake. 'Guru! It is me, Bhure here! Me, Bhure! Not your wife!' Apparently, in my sleep, I had come over to his bed with a blanket in hand, babbling that she must be feeling cold and that I would put another blanket over her. I was very embarrassed, and it gave my friends new ammunition for teasing me.

In April, I went back to Nagpur to get Hira and bring her to New Delhi. The physical and psychological magnitude of her relocation to Delhi was illustrated by an incident at the Nagpur train station. With tears in his eyes, Hira's father took me aside as he gently asked me, 'Will there be rice in Delhi for my daughter to eat?' North India, after all, was India's wheat belt! I reassured him there would be plenty of rice for her. My mother and my ten-year-old sister Tara traveled with us. Hira cried as she watched her hometown railway platform recede as the train pulled away from the Nagpur station. Delhi was an unimaginable distance away, and she had never really been anywhere outside of Nagpur. The thirty-hour train ride, with just benches to sit on and no sleeping berths, must have been interminable for her.

At Delhi station, she was surprised when, instead of hiring coolies, I carried all the luggage myself, as was my habit. We took a horse-drawn carriage to our small apartment on the institute grounds. I had rented one and a half rooms (with the closed-off verandah being the half-room).

The next day, I was back at work. At lunchtime, I bicycled

back to the apartment with great anticipation for my first meal cooked by my wife. This time it was delicious—with the right amount of salt. She sat nearby, serving my meal with great care and tenderness. I ate with gusto, and kept asking for more. Eventually, though, from the kitchen, I heard the scraping of a spoon against the pot, signifying that there was no more food. By her standards, Hira had cooked a large amount, enough for the four of us, but to her horror, I had eaten it all, and I was still hungry! My mother consoled her, and she had to cook another batch, but after that, she never made the same mistake.

Our landlords were brahmins. I never concealed our identity as being from the Scheduled Caste. They said, 'That is no problem as long as you cook only vegetarian food.' But they did ask for ten more rupees from us above the prevailing rate; perhaps that was the price for belonging to the Scheduled Castes.

I took Hira for several rides after work on the bicycle to introduce her to Delhi. There were few buses serving our area at that time, and I was a strong cyclist. On one trip, we got stranded by India Gate with a punctured tire, and had to walk about ten miles to get home. This was no burden for me, but it was quite rough for Hira. She was very tired, but somehow retained her spirits. My mother gave me quite an earful that evening for making my new wife walk such a distance!

On one trip, we visited the nearby village of Naraina, where I introduced her to some of my north Indian village friends. A large number of neighborhood children often gather to gawk at visitors. At one hut, I asked the woman there, 'Whose children are these?' Following the north Indian tradition, she said, 'These are all your children.'

A chill entered Hira's demeanor that evening, and I could not tell why. She rebuked any attempts towards conversation. At home, finally, she stirred up the courage to say, 'You have so many children already; how dare you marry me in such a casual manner!' She broke down and cried. It took me quite a long time to explain about the children; the local tradition of hospitality calls for hosts to ascribe all their belongings, including their children, to the guest, for the guest is equated with God. At long last she became convinced and a smile returned to her face.

WHEN NEWS REACHED us that Hira had passed her exams, we passed out sweets to everyone to celebrate. Her father had promised to pay for her bachelor's degree but we agreed that I would shoulder expenses for any further education. A few weeks later, we went on a pilgrimage tour to several Hindu shrines at Haridwar and Rishikesh, on the foothills of the Himalayas.

One day, back in Delhi, we had returned from our usual evening bicycling. We were eating dinner when suddenly Hira ran out to the sandy courtyard and I heard some retching sounds. I was scared, and so was Hira. But my mother remained calm. The next evening, the very same thing happened again. The landlady, who was nearby, started to laugh. I was perplexed. Then the landlady stopped laughing and announced, "Congratulations, you are going to be parents!"

My heart overflowed with joy.

But the question now arose of whether Hira could continue

her education in Nagpur. We debated many possibilities of how this could work out. At one point, my mother even suggested dropping the whole idea of further education. Of course, that was out of the question. Eventually, she ended up leaving Delhi to spend two years in Nagpur. At the Delhi Railway Station, I tried cheering her up with a Sanskrit verse:

> *Sukhartinaha kuto vidya kuto vidyarthina sukham*
> *Sukharti va tyajat vidya vidyarthiva tyajat sukham.*
>
> (One who seeks knowledge, will find no pleasure / One who seeks pleasure, will find no knowledge.)

Family and Dr Ambedkar

Classical India's foremost poet, Kalidasa, had written a famous poem about how a deity separated from his wife would send love messages to her using the medium of clouds. I empathized with that deity. At the same time, I felt that we human beings were more fortunate, being able to send messages long distance, even overseas, through the postal service. I found myself alone in Delhi for several long months at a stretch, and my mind was always with Hira and my family. I would teach, do research, and then return to my empty home. To save money, I cooked at home myself.

The thought of going overseas for higher education had started to creep into my mind after one of my colleagues, Yawalkar, had gone to America for his Ph.D. Instead of returning to my empty home each night, I started spending evenings in the library researching the prospects for obtaining a Ph.D. in the US. After much inquiry I found out that the University of Wisconsin had the best agricultural school for my purposes. I wrote to the head of the department there, Dr Attoe, and was pleased to learn that they did indeed have educational opportunities for foreign students along with scholarships and part-time jobs.

On the social front, my solitude was broken by two developments. The first was the surprise opportunity to return to Nagpur during the Diwali holidays with a good friend, Wanjare, (a Scheduled Caste member whom I helped secure admission to IARI). I appeared without warning at the Sontakke family doorstep. We had several pleasant days together. On my return trip, I took along Uncle Patwar, thinking it would be a wonderful occasion for him to see the capital. He proved a remarkable chef. But the days were long and lonely for him, because he could not speak Hindi. This was yet another reminder that I was a "pioneer" of sorts from far away, carving out a place for myself and my fellow Maharashtrians in the remote city of Delhi.

On 18 February 1955, I received a congratulatory telegram informing me that I was now the father of a boy. I named him Bhimrao, after Dr Ambedkar's first name. We were all overjoyed and I distributed sweets and gave a party for some colleagues.

Soon I got a letter from Hira asking about when I was coming to see our child. Now, reality dawned upon me. I cursed myself for my impetuous Diwali visit to Nagpur, for now I had no money left for another journey. Every month I had been sending money to my parents to help relieve their debt incurred by my marriage.

By April I had amassed enough money for the trip home. Fortunately, Hira had been able to pass another year of college on the strength of her good ongoing performance and without even having to appear for the final exam.

My first view of the baby Bhim provided much joy. We then went to my village to display our son and also to marry off my sister Pushpa. The joy of the marriage was tempered somewhat by the incurring of additional family debt.

But fortunately, the joy of new life in my family eased my mental burden to a great extent. We enjoyed the return to Delhi as a family, and even made a stop at the Taj Mahal.

THE INTRODUCTION of my son to Babasaheb was not as idyllic. Hira and I brought our son to Babasaheb's house where we laid him at the great man's feet. Babasaheb stared at the baby and then said, 'You just got married and now you bear your child like a trophy that you have won. Now what will happen to your future education? You have fallen into the same trap as everyone else from our community. You study just a little, get a small job, and then settle down. Don't you know how long it takes to rear a child? You have to spend all day with the baby, you have to play with the baby in the morning, then rush to work, then rush back and again attend to the baby. How will our community ever progress if you tie down your hands like that? Is this all that your education has led up to? How will that help our society?'

I waited until he calmed and then said softly, 'Babasaheb, I am naming this child Bhimrao.'

Babasaheb paused. 'You can name your child whatever you want. But with so little education what will you make of your child? What good is a name by itself? There is a girl somewhere out there named Laxmi (after the Hindu goddess of wealth), but she washes pots and pans; there's a Subash Chandra Hair Cutting Salon somewhere out there (named after a famous Indian freedom fighter), there's even a Shivaji brand bidi out there (named after the maratha king).'

At this moment I earnestly promised Babasaheb, 'I will always try to obtain further education. It is my highest aim in life now. I named my son Bhimrao so that until my death I will always have your name on my tongue.'

'Overseas, people will be ready for their children with clothes and sweaters even before birth. Here, because of poverty, we cannot take care of our children even after birth. Let me share my own experience. I have myself suffered many years in poverty. Even after returning from overseas with a legal degree, I had difficulty practicing law because of caste discrimination. Because of my financial struggles I used to eat just broken rice and grew weak. One of my own children died of illness. I was too weak to even bury him. All that I had to wear were my suits brought from overseas, and those were woolen (and too hot for India). My legal practice slowly improved but then fate struck another blow: my wife Rama became grievously ill. The doctor warned that if she had another child she would surely die. To keep her alive, then, we maintained celibacy.'

Babasaheb became lost in his reminiscences. 'She was so frail. I did everything in my power to save her; we used all sorts of pills and injections. I spared no efforts. Yet she slipped away from this earth. She left me.' His voice caught, and then a tear fell from his eye. He cried almost like a child. At this sight, everyone in the room started crying. I had never seen even a tear from him before.

The man who fought like a lion with political opponents to protect his oppressed people was now silently human... helpless as he remembered his late wife. He had expressed his feelings for her publicly before through dedicating one of his books thus: 'To the sweetest memory of dear Ramu. For nobility of her mind, purity of her character, and forbearance and courage which she has shown along with me in those days of friendlessness and solitude.'

I was astounded now in our private setting as I looked upon Babasaheb and realized the deep love he must have had for her. With heavy hearts we returned home.

Caste out

Once, a girl named Santosh from the sweeper caste, who washed our latrine and swept our courtyard, asked Hira for some paper to serve as a makeshift plate to use for her lunch. I asked Hira to lend her one of our plates. Seeing this, our landlady became upset, and scolded Hira. 'You cannot behave like this while staying in our house!'

I said to her, 'Mataji, your dog gets to go anywhere outside and then roam in your own house freely, even on your bed and on your lap. Are these cleaning ladies any worse than this dog? They are also human. The same blood that courses through your veins courses through theirs. We clean only our own house; but they clean everyone else's house. So they are better than us because they serve everyone. The poet and saint Kabir once said:

> *Hum bhi bhangi, tum bhi bhangi; sabh hai bhangi ka pasara*
> *Kahata Kabira, suna bhai sadhu; kaun hai bhangi sai nyara*
>
> (We are bhangi, you are a bhangi, everybody is a bhangi/ Says Kabir, who is not a bhangi?)

'Mataji, you read these holy books, you engage in prayers, and still you are narrow-minded.'

When the landlord came home, he took the side of his wife. He shouted angrily at us. Hira cautioned me not to provoke him further since we were outsiders here. I turned to Hira and said, 'But I told them from the very beginning who we were; that we belong to the Scheduled Castes. It was only greed that allowed them to rent to us. The result of our brewing differences is now apparent. Sharma has told us now to leave.'

We also decided not to live there, but now where could we go on such short notice? To make things worse, Bhimrao was ill. We had left the light on all night long, tending to him.

The next day, Sharma said, 'You seem to leave the lights on overnight. You should quickly vacate our premises.'

I understood that this was the result of yesterday's quarrel. Angrily I paid our account. I told Hira, 'Let us take all our possessions out into the common courtyard under the big jamun tree. Then we will find another place to live.

WE MUST HAVE been a ridiculous sight, our family now sitting on cots with all our worldly possessions under the shade of the jamun tree in full sight of the entire neighborhood. A Bengali brahmin neighbor, Bhattacharjee, saw us and said, 'Your child is ill. You cannot leave him outdoors. You come to my place and I will immediately vacate a room for you.

The Bhattacharjees were a loving couple who looked upon Hira as a younger sister. They had two children, Khokan and Buru, who enjoyed playing with Bhimrao. Mr Bhattacharjee was a well-read man, and we would talk about a variety of topics. I would often tell him about Dr Ambedkar.

The astonishing thing was that even after we had moved out, our old landlord's family continued borrowing a variety of things ranging from scissors to postcards to soap. Slowly we became irritated by their ways, and we resisted lending them things.

Eventually, Hira had to return to Nagpur to continue her education. I was alone once more. But now I had a new family, the Bhattacharjees. I would spend long hours with them, conversing in the mornings or evenings.

Losing *Sadhu-boa*

'Father was ailing,' wrote Ankush with great urgency. I sent money to help with his care. The family wanted him transferred to Nagpur Medical College, but he declined, stating, 'Whatever should happen, let it happen here.' But his condition worsened, and finally, on 23 July 1955 he was sent by ambulance to Nagpur. As soon as I heard about this news by telegram, I dropped everything and took the evening train to Nagpur. But it was too late; he had expired in the ambulance right upon arrival at the Nagpur hospital. The same ambulance now returned to Umrer bearing his body.

Everyone's heart was filled with grief. Even Hira, who had known him for such a short time, was crying inconsolably. For my brothers and sisters and me, our shelter against the rain and the elements had been taken away; we were exposed and gravely weakened without his presence. I could not sleep, for perhaps the first time in my life. We numbly went through the motions, but life no longer appeared to have any meaning.

The entire town seemed to have turned out for the funeral procession, and people jostled with each other just to have the privilege to serve as pallbearers. A man named Jokhar from the lowliest caste of the bhangis asked me if he could also provide a shoulder for bearing my father. One of my relatives was horrified, but I told him, 'Whoever has tears in his eyes is our relative. Father did not care for distinctions between people, so why would he care even now, after death?' People of all castes and creeds saluted his body with folded hands and tears.

Truly, Father had earned the title of *Sadhu-boa*. He was buried on government land, with the officials' permission, which was easily forthcoming. Later, we built a small memorial to Father at his burial site.

I feel that I could not serve my father as much as I would have liked to. He had borne a life of trials and tribulations with grace and dignity. I had hoped to take care of him after my education had ended. But alas, I did not have the chance.

Despite my weakened state – indeed, I felt very much like an orphan – I was now the head of the family.

At my father's samadhi, final resting place, at the edge of the village where he was revered as a village saint. 'Whoever has tears in his eyes is our relative.'

PART VI

A NEW WORLD

No end to knowledge

When I returned to Delhi, it was only through the condolences of my friends and the support of the Bhattacharjee family that I survived. There was only one ray of hope for me: my family, my new son. During the winter holiday, I returned to Maharashtra, and when I beheld my son and wife, hope blossomed once more in my heart.

There were also distractions that seemed to seek me out. Later in that winter of 1955, when I took advantage of my flexible research assistantship schedule to go to Palam airport to see the visiting Soviet leaders, Bulganin and Kruschev. This was a moment of unprecedented excitement for India, because no leader of any superpower had ever visited our young nation. A thick crowd of over a hundred thousand had gathered. In fact, the police watched helplessly as people spilled onto the tarmac, even edging out VIPs such as Indian statesman Krishna Menon.

In the hustle and bustle, I noticed that Prime Minister Nehru's daughter Indira was also separated from her father and his security guard. I had gotten to know Indira through my membership in her Bharat Sewak Samaj (India Service Society). Indira was a lovely young woman, and it seemed that she would soon be jostled by a crowd of louts. The security guards milled around the Prime Minister, unaware of her dilemma. I pushed my way through the crowd. When I came to Indira, I shouted, '*Behenji*, I am here to protect you. Do not worry.' I put an arm around her and then hectored the immediate crowd to make way. I pushed a path through the crowd until I reunited her with the security forces. To her credit, Indira did not register any fear throughout this episode. She thanked me as she disappeared into the phalanx of the guards.

WHEN SPRING CAME, I was happy. Hira was sitting for her final exams for her B.A. degree. After this, she would be able to join me in Delhi. But destiny held another twist in the road. In February, Hira wrote me that she was having vomiting spells again. She was thin and frail to begin with, so how could she prepare for her exam now?

Hira was able to sit for several of her exams but then deteriorated in health and could not appear for her last exam. I was angry with myself that I had let her down. I was also ashamed, and for this reason, did not even visit Nagpur. How could I face the Sontakke family? In the summer, Hira returned to Delhi. But taking care of our child and tending to guests left her insufficient time to even consider re-taking her exams.

While the prospects sank for Hira's education, my hopes rose for my own chances to go to America to further mine. I secured admission for a Ph.D. at the University of Wisconsin, and even an assistantship. But I did not have funding for oversees travel. I wrote to numerous foundations and charities, but to no avail. Fate, however, appears to have a sense of humor, because after virtually giving up on going to the USA, a visiting friend happened to leave behind a newspaper from his hometown of Jhansi. Out of curiosity, I picked it up and stumbled across a small article stating that a professor from Agra had gotten a scholarship for traveling to the USA from the Rockefeller Foundation. Hope was restored!

I applied for a travel grant to the Rockefeller Foundation, and eventually an interview was set up for me with their representative Dr Chandler, who would be visiting Delhi soon after. Now, with the upcoming interview with Dr Chandler, my aspirations no longer seemed like a pipe dream. Hira could not believe that I would even dare think of studying overseas when my financial position was already so tenuous.

Hira began worrying now that she would be stranded in Maharashtra while I would be far away in America. The thought must have crossed her mind, in keeping with local prejudices, that perhaps a single man in a different land might succumb to the charms of an alien woman. Thus, the night before my big interview, while I prepared for it, Hira stayed awake pondering the growing family's future. It was a time of some friction between us. At one point, I even suggested that she could stay with my family for a few years until my return. But, of course, that was not an easy proposition to swallow.

The next day, Dr Chandler appeared in the agricultural institute at the appointed time. About six feet tall, Dr Chandler was a scholarly and energetic gentleman with a pleasant face. Almost immediately, however, with a piercing expression he questioned me closely about my research, scientific papers, thesis, certificates, and marks. Then he asked if he could meet my guide, Dr Raychaudhari. But Dr Raychaudhari had already left for lunch at home. With an hour to kill, I suggested to Dr Chandler that he come to my house.

So we proceeded in his car to my humble quarters. The whole neighborhood looked curiously as this foreign man and I emerged from the car. Hira appeared at the door bleary eyed with a broom in hand. When Dr Chandler reached out a hand to her, she dropped the broom and folded her hands in namaste. Our guest took her right hand and said, 'This is how we shake hands in America!' Then, with a gentle tone, he began questioning her closely.

Hira answered in halting English. Finally, his questions ended, and he smiled, saying, 'Mr Nimgade, I am satisfied with your interview.' I did not know whether he referred to my interview or Hira's interview.

Then on the wall he saw a photo of Dr Ambedkar.

'Sir,' I said, 'This is Dr Ambedkar's photograph. He framed the Indian Constitution and inspired my own struggle for education. Sir, I was about 14 years when I started my schooling. Until then I was tending to the cows in my village of Sathgaon. When I started my village school, because of my untouchable status, I was forbidden to even enter the classroom or "pollute" any other student with my touch.'

Dr Chandler said, 'Mr Nimgade, you applied for a 3000-rupee

travel grant, but I thought over your case and admire your courage. You have nothing but a small room and a small rack of books. But you have a burning desire, high ambition, and courage. I shall strongly recommend your case for the travel fellowship, and also for an additional $250 per month. Your wife is also educated, and I also wish that she join you. I will recommend a family allowance of $150 per month for her, too. The Rockefeller Foundation will be glad to help such a suitable and deserving family. I wish you best of luck!'

I was overcome with happiness, and in my vision Dr Chandler appeared like a God. I related to him a story about a villager who went in the forest to fetch firewood but dropped his axe in the water. An angel rose up out of the water bearing a silver axe, and asked, 'Is this your axe?' The villager said, 'No, mine is just a simple iron axe.' The angel dived into the water and emerged with a gold axe, asking, 'Is this your axe?' The villager again replied, 'No, mine is just a simple iron axe.' The angel dived into the water again and emerged with the original iron axe. The villager was now overcome with joy as he claimed his own axe. Impressed by his humbleness and honesty, the angel presented him with all the axes.

Dr Chandler laughed wholeheartedly.

After he left to meet with Dr Raychaudhari, I took a spoon of sugar and placed it in Hira's mouth. 'This is to sweeten your mouth,' I joked, since we Indians often celebrate good news with sweets. She smiled and said, 'You are something: first you make me cry and then you make me laugh!'

I HAD TO borrow money from a large number of friends to buy the tickets for my two children. In a notebook, I entered the names of these friends and the sums, even if it was just five rupees. One friend even lent me a hundred rupees, a princely sum back then.

Only one obstacle now remained in my path: obtaining a study leave from the institute. Unfortunately, the wheels of bureaucracy moved slowly, and weeks passed without any action. Finally, in desperation, I brought this up with Babasaheb

B. R. AMBEDKAR,
M.A., Ph.D., D.Sc., LL.D., D.Litt., Barrister-at-Law,
Member, Council of States.

26, ALIPORE ROAD,
CIVIL LINE,
DELHI.

Dated the 9th September 1956:

TO WHOM IT MAY CONCERN
-.-.-.-.-.-.-.-.-.-.-.-.-.-.

This is to certify that I know Mr. Namdeo Marotrao Nimgade, B.Sc., (Agri), Assoc. I.A.R.I. personally. He comes from a respectable Scheduled Caste (Mahar) family of Madhya Pradesh. He has pleasing manners and bears a good moral character.

I wish him all success.

B R Ambedkar

(B.R. Ambedkar)

Dr B.R. Ambedkar's letter of endorsement written a few weeks before he led a mass conversion to Buddhism in Nagpur.

on one of my many visits to his house. He looked at me with astonishment and said, 'You come here so many times, and you never mentioned this problem! So many people come here just to ask for favors and then never reappear.'

Mrs Ambedkar, who was present, said, 'He is a nice boy, a good student.'

I said, 'Babasaheb, your time is taken up by the needs of the nation and our community. I did not feel right stealing away your precious time.'

Babasaheb immediately picked up the telephone to speak with Panjabrao Deshmukh, the Agriculture Minister. Dr Deshmukh said, 'I know that boy Nimgade quite well, but he never mentioned the problem to me. I would have fixed it earlier had he mentioned it.'

Babasaheb was beaming at me. Emboldened by this and with Mrs Ambedkar's vote of approval, I asked humbly if Babasaheb would consider writing a character certificate for me.

He laughed, '*Arrey*, I never write character certificates for anyone, because they say that everyone's character changes in six months!'

Ultimately, with the help of his secretary, we drafted a character reference that stated: 'This is to certify that I know Mr Namdeo Maratrao Nimgade, B.Sc., (Agri), Assoc. I.A.R.I. personally. He comes from a respectable Scheduled Caste (Mahar) family of Madhya Pradesh. He has pleasing manners and bears a good moral character. I wish him all success.'

'I will not die a Hindu!'

True to his nature, Babasaheb did not officially convert to Buddhism until he felt fully prepared. This meant taking time to research and write a definitive text on Buddhism for his followers, *The Buddha and His Dhamma*. Babasaheb wanted his followers to understand that conversion was not a strange and convoluted process, but a very natural thing; after all, what could be more natural than welcoming back Buddhism into the land where it had originated and flourished for a thousand years?

Babasaheb also viewed conversion as not just a religious, but also as a political transition. I heard him explain this in a speech a few months earlier: 'I am getting old and need the help of young persons who will look after my work. Unfortunately, I am like the central pole of a circus; if I fall the whole tent will fall. It is difficult to find a replacement, but I have now found an alternative: I have decided to embrace Buddhism so that the coming generations will be safe and can proceed further.'

There was much truth to Babasaheb's circus tent pole analogy, because many of his well-intentioned followers often disagreed vehemently about tactics and the future paths for the Ambedkar movement. The choice of where the initial conversion ceremony should take place may appear trivial to outsiders, but many factions had developed, championing one city or another within Maharashtra for hosting this honor. Ultimately, it would come down to a choice between Bombay, where Babasaheb lived, and Nagpur, for which a social activist named Wamanrao Godbole had argued on historical grounds. (Apparently a tooth of the Buddha was somewhere in Nagpur.)

In August 1956, in the daytime, I paid what I thought would be a routine visit to Babasaheb. Dressed in his informal garb,

Babasaheb was working intensively in his study. He appeared deeply disturbed about something. I slowly asked, 'Babasaheb, you look worried. Are you not feeling well?' Then Babasaheb said to me, 'Yesterday I had an accident. I now worry about what would have happened to the public vow I had made not to die as a Hindu.'

'Oh, what happened yesterday?' I asked.

'I had gone on a book-buying excursion. On the return trip, during the heavy monsoon downpour the road became slippery. The car lost control and would have fallen into a big ditch. My driver managed to steer us out of trouble and regain control. I thanked the driver and also presented him with some money.'

I, too, felt relieved that our savior was saved.

'I have decided to convert very soon to Buddhism,' Babasaheb continued. 'I informed Godbole from your city of Nagpur to arrange for the conversion ceremony. Many people do not want Godbole to handle the conversion,' Babasaheb admitted.

'Godbole is a very good social worker,' I said, fully aware that people often misunderstood his brahmin-sounding name as a strike against him. 'I consider him to work in the interest of the community.' Babasaheb appeared reassured by my words in support of Godbole.

'Sir,' I said too confidently, 'wherever and whenever you have this conversion ceremony, I will surely come!'

Babasaheb laughed and shook his head. '*Arrey,* don't make rash promises. You have your research and family commitments to worry about. Do not worry, because there will be many conversion ceremonies throughout India, including in Delhi. You will have your chance.'

ON 14 OCTOBER 1956, Dr Ambedkar, along with a half-million of his followers, converted to Buddhism in Nagpur. I was burning with desire to join this new mass of liberated Indians. But I could not leave my family in New Delhi. Just a week earlier, Hira had delivered a baby girl, whom we named Rekha. She was just a little under five pounds, and the doctor appeared gravely concerned about her condition. Hira, too, appeared weakened. They ended up staying a fortnight in the hospital before Hira grew tired of the hospital. Against medical advice, she and Rekha joined me at home. Fortunately, my mother had arrived in Delhi to help. Hira flourished with the cooking and care.

A few months later, on 6 December 1956, I went to a bookstore to purchase Dr Ambedkar's latest book. The bookseller said, 'The author of the book you seek has passed away. I heard it on the morning news.' I replied, 'That cannot be! Perhaps that was some other Baba you were talking of.' I cycled furiously to Babasaheb's bungalow.

Several people had gathered there with hung heads and teary eyes. Realization of his passing dawned on me gradually. The crowd thickened and soon the lawns overflowed with mourners. Everyone was lost in their own thoughts. I entered the bungalow and found Babasaheb's lifeless form surrounded by our Prime Minister Nehru and many high-ranking leaders. Tears were in all of their eyes. I could not bear the sight anymore. I returned to the lawn and cried. I thought, 'I have seen so many facets of Babasaheb, now I have seen a facet I never thought I would see.'

Babasaheb's followers arranged to take his body to Bombay for his final resting place. His body was placed on a truck in a sandalwood casket and was soon covered with garlands of every color. Along the route to the airport, thousands of followers had gathered despite the chilling cold to salute him and chant:

Babasaheb amar hai!
Jab tak suraj, chand rahega,
Baba tera naam rahega!

(Babasaheb is immortal / His name will remain
As long as the sun and the moon shine.)

I wanted to go to Bombay, but could not because of my family. As I reflected on the significance of his life so many thoughts came to me. Here was a man who lifted us up—dalits, women, and other oppressed people. Here was the man who gave our new nation its Constitution. Here was the prophet who resurrected the ancient faith of Buddhism in India. And the impact of his life rippled beyond India, by awakening a deeper interest in the faith in the surrounding Buddhist nations.

The timing of Babasaheb's death was prophetic. He had once said, 'I was born a Hindu, I was raised a Hindu, but I will not die a Hindu!' Less than two months before his death, he had fulfilled this wish by converting to Buddhism.

The certificate I obtained from Babasaheb took on even more significance, as I realized that that had been my last meeting with him. Even to this day, when I see the certificate, I think back to the joy he radiated at that last meeting. That certificate is the most priceless treasure of my life.

I HAD A very hard time the next few days shaving, bathing, or eating. I moved like a numbed person. My landlord, Mr Bhattacharjee, took me aside and said, 'Death is a part of life. You must face up to it and not flee from it.' His advice helped me recover from my stupor. On 12 December 1956, I took my family with me to Ambedkar Bhavan for a condolence meeting and a viewing of Babasaheb's ashes. People stood up, but could not speak—so deep ran their emotions.

When it came to my turn, I too was choked up, but finally managed to recite the following Sanskrit words:

> *Yasya priyajanaha smarayante saha na gataha.*
>
> (Those who are deeply adored should not be considered as departed.)

I suggested that we create a statue in Delhi to honor the memory of Babasaheb. I stated I was willing to give a whole month's salary for this. Everyone liked the idea, and donations started to pour in.

Eventually, a statue of Dr Ambedkar was created in time for commemorating Babasaheb's birthday the following April at Ambedkar Bhavan. Dadasaheb Gaikwad, now the most prominent leader of the Scheduled Castes, led the commemoration. Gaikwad was a magnificent orator, with a fine command of Marathi, although he had attended school only up to eighth grade. He had a deep voice and the matching build of a former wrestler and swimmer. He had been with Babasaheb since the very beginning, from the struggles in the 1930s to enter Hindu temples as untouchables, and other activist causes. Gaikwad was now an elected Member of Parliament, and we turned to him for leadership.

The following day, several visitors from this function stopped by our house. Hira would cook lunch for one party on a coal burner and by the time the guests ate, another batch of visitors would arrive. She ended up cooking lunch for four batches of guests! Yet, she did not have enough food for herself in the end. Poor baby Rekha was wailing, since she had gone without her milk as well. Hira had truly sacrificed so much to make these visitors feel at home.

I did not feel like remaining any more in Delhi, so I threw myself into preparing for my trip to the USA—taking care of passports, travel vaccines, tickets and such. Once again, Dr Raychaudhari came to my aid, by helping cover for a shortfall in funds by personally guaranteeing that I would return once my Ph.D. was over. If I did not, then he was liable to the Indian Government for 28,000 rupees. To send me off, my Delhi Scheduled Caste friends arranged a farewell function for me on the lawns of Dadasaheb Gaikwad's bungalow. Dr Panjabrao Deshmukh presided over the festivities and N. Shivraj, a Member of Parliament (and former mayor of Madras) said, 'In education our community is lagging behind. For instance, look at the airplane that will take Nimgade overseas. The airplane will be filled with people from other communities going abroad for education and training, but Namdeo will be the only one from our community!'

To the New World

Five hours to pack and get ready to fly to America! It was 20 September 1957, and I had just received the authorization for study leave. Already, we had had to change our flight plans three times because of bureaucratic delays. Fortunately, we did not have many possessions to burden us, and we packed quickly. How would we eat in a strange country? We had heard that Indian spices were not available there, so Hira sent me to the bazaar to buy some powdered spices to last several months. Mr Bhattacharjee's family very kindly cooked dinner for us and helped us pack and arrange for a taxi to the airport.

The baby, Rekha, had started teething; already weak and underweight, she was now crying and vomiting. Hira held Rekha in her arms and tried to soothe her, but she herself was weeping quietly, dabbing at her eyes with a corner of her saree. She was afraid of flying in an airplane for the first time in her life and traveling with two small children to a strange land so far away. Concerned neighbors crowded around us, to help us and wish us well, and some suggested we delay our trip again till Rekha's health improved. But the university term at Wisconsin had already begun a week prior, and I was worried about missing any more class time. I joked, 'Whatever happens, happens. If she gets worse on the plane, we will just toss her out the window!'

Hearing this, Hira clutched the baby tightly and began to sob. My joke was not helping things at all. We climbed into the taxi amidst a crowd of neighbors and friends calling out their farewells. At the airport, relatives and friends surrounded us. I was surprised to see Dr Cummings, the Rockefeller Foundation Field Director, who had started many agricultural universities in India, had arrived with his wife to see us off. I was holding

Rekha, and just as he approached, she chose this inopportune moment to vomit on me. But he and his wife were very understanding. They praised my boldness in seeking further education overseas, and the kindly Mr Cummings put her hand on the back of the weeping Hira to console her.

Once we were seated in the airplane, my mind turned to Rekha. Fortunately, her condition did not deteriorate further. In New York City, we checked in at a hotel and promptly fell asleep because of jet lag. When we awoke it was midnight. Room service had shut down. Therefore, despite having dollars in my pockets we had to remain hungry. The next morning, when we rummaged in a suitcase, a cloud of powdered spices rose. Apparently, some of our hastily packed paper spice bags had burst open. It was difficult to breathe, especially with the hot chili pepper powder in the air. Our eyes watered and we started sneezing.

In this confusion, the housekeeping staff must have knocked, but we did not answer. The door opened and the maid stepped in. She got a deep nose full of the growing cloud of spices, and she shrieked and ran out. It took us a half a day to clean out our clothes. Our children were crying, as they had not been fed since the airplane trip.

I went to the Rockefeller Foundation headquarters and met with Dr Wernimont, my official advisor there. Then we took in some of the tourist sights. We were impressed by the skyscrapers, neon lights, and broad avenues. People stared with curiosity at Hira's flowing saree, for there were very few Indians around at that time. I was ecstatic, because I was now in the city where Dr Babasaheb Ambedkar had studied at Columbia University.

A FEW DAYS later, our plane touched down at the small Madison, Wisconsin airport, about a thousand miles to the west. Dr O.J. Attoe, the head of the Soil Science Department at the University of Wisconsin, had arrived himself to greet us. To our astonishment, once he shook our hands, he picked up our two suitcases and strode towards his car. In India, a man of such prominent position would never have done such a thing for a new student. This was an eye-opening glimpse of the egalitarianism in this new land. He dropped us off at the Madison Hotel, where he had thoughtfully made reservations for us.

He also helped us search for a place to live. Ten days later, we moved into an apartment at 505 West Dayton Street. Ready or not, we were now immersed in a new culture in a new country.

Warmth in a freezing land

I started attending my classes, where sometimes I found it difficult to follow the American English pronunciation of my professors. The class work was detailed, and difficult. I had never studied this hard before in my life. I would leave home at 7 a.m. and return at midnight, after a day spent attending classes, then going to the laboratory, and then studying at the library until it closed.

I would only really get to see my wife and children on Sundays. Hira's life was empty since she could not stand the bland food, and she had no adults to talk with in the daytime. Even in the streets she never saw any people walking, since everyone was in their cars. And then winter started. The birds left and the snow came.

Hira was feeling increasingly isolated and frustrated. The worst task for her was filling the coal-burning furnace in the dark basement daily. Our apartment used two tons of coal per month! We had no radio, no television, and no telephone, so her English communication skills were still primitive. But she could read newspapers. And now, unfortunately, she was reading the lurid headlines about Ed Gein, the infamous Wisconsin psychopath, who robbed graves, murdered women, cooked and ate their flesh, and made furniture out of his victims' skin. He lived in a small town within an hour of Madison. She now feared very much going into the dark basement by herself, and so the family would shiver in the cold when the furnace would go out. Not long thereafter, a house on our block caught on fire and exploded. Luckily, the fire was put out before it spread to our place.

Now, on top of everything, Hira was feeling sick to her stomach, and she started vomiting. There was another baby on the way. How could she give birth in this strange, cold, and frightening land, far from her mother and female relatives to help her? I tried to comfort her, saying that we would see people in the streets once winter ended and when the new baby arrived she could be happily busy. But she still saw the path ahead as a difficult ordeal.

And then, in the deep of winter, the thermostat malfunctioned, and we were plunged into the cold of the frozen tundra. I tried, but I could not figure out how to turn the heat back on. 'I want to return to India with the children,' said Hira, shivering. 'I cannot bear to stay in this place any longer.'

IT WAS SUNDAY, and so we could not do much about the heat. We put on layers of clothing and we still felt cold. Then there came a knock on the door. My fellow student, Gordon Wells, and his wife, had come to take us with them to their church for Sunday services. They looked at us with concern. Luckily, he was mechanically gifted, so he figured out the problem and fixed the thermostat, and we all went to church; he assured us that the apartment would be warm when we got back. Hira confided to Mrs Wells that she was unhappy and wanted to go back to India. The Wells' consoled her, and the next day returned with winter clothing for her and the children.

I was interested in other religions so I took advantage of the opportunity to learn about Christianity while I was in the USA. I went to church with many of my friends and colleagues. In India, inequality based on caste is ordained by the Hindu religion, and I was curious to see how other societies and other religions deal with human interrelationships. When Dr Babasaheb Ambedkar had left India to study abroad, he had felt a refreshing freedom from the strictures of caste, and this is what I found as well.

We visited the church of my major professor, Dr Attoe. Here we met Dr and Mrs Pickett, who befriended us and became a sort of second family. Mrs Pickett visited our apartment and created a list of items we needed for living in the USA. Our children called them Pickett Daddy and Pickett Mommy. Gradually, we made more American friends. The children found playmates with the neighboring family, the Stitgens.

We were now prepared for the Midwest winter. I would go to school covered from head to toe. The children frolicked in the snow and threw snowballs. With Christmas came the lights and colors that seemed to ward off the cold. Mrs Pickett would sometimes drive Hira and the children to the shopping malls, where the children got to meet and play with Santa Claus and admire the decorated shop windows.

We spent our first Thanksgiving, and all subsequent Thanksgivings, with the family of Dr Hole, another of my professors. His children played with our children, who by now were becoming fluent in English.

By the time spring came, Hira was much happier. She no longer brought up the subject of returning home to India. We moved into a slightly smaller apartment within walking distance to downtown and the university. Our family could walk to the beautiful Student Union overlooking Lake Mendota, and see many films and cultural events. This apartment had an automatic furnace, so Hira was pleased. We had also met some Indian families in this university town; in fact, in the apartment below us there was another Indian family, with whom we became quite close. The only downside now was missing out on family events back in India, such as the marriage of Hira's sister Meenakshi to a community activist, Vasant Moon.

One evening in mid-June, Hira said to me that she felt a stirring in her abdomen and that she thought the new baby was coming. I was very tired from my work, however, and I mumbled, 'Let me sleep just a little more. The baby will not come today, I predict, based on the experience with our first two.' I slept deeply until close to midnight. Hira and I headed off to the hospital, leaving the children Bhim and Rekha in the care of a close friend, Nilkant Bhure. This is the same Bhure in whose room I had stayed rent-free as a student at the Indian Agricultural Research Institute hostel for two years. Now he was a fellow student, and once again he had come to my assistance when my need was great.

In the hospital, another expectant mother, Mrs Becker, shared a room with Hira. Her daughter Cindy was born the same day as our son Ashok. The two new mothers stayed in the hospital for three days, as was customary in that era, and they grew to be close friends. The Picketts were away on vacation, but they still managed to mail us a parcel of baby clothes.

At the hospital, I told the obstetrician that I would have to pay his fees later, as I had left my money at home. Dr Collins, to my surprise, pulled out some bills from his own pocket. He had misunderstood me and thought I was entirely destitute. I was touched by his humanity and concern for his patients. We became close friends with his family. The Collins' did not have children of their own, and Mrs Collins once said, 'My husband has delivered thousands of babies, but he has not given me even one!'

I said to her, 'Please consider my children to be yours!'

With the help of friends and well-wishers, we survived the difficult period of the arrival of our third child. And with hard work, I was getting straight As. Based on this performance, the Rockefeller Foundation extended my scholarship. I was overjoyed. I sent money that I had saved back to India to pay off my debts. Ankush, my brother, took care of disbursing the money.

The Indian government also extended my work leave, but only for the purpose of obtaining an M.Sc. degree. My institute also cabled me stating that I had to return to India, otherwise government action would be taken against me. I was upset because I had wanted to stay longer and obtain a Ph.D. Keeping a level mind, I wrote back that I needed more time.

Appeals to stay

In 1960, when I found out that a delegation of Thai Buddhist monks was staying at the Madison Hotel, I immediately called them and arranged a meeting. In their saffron robes they exuded an air of peace and harmony, even in this strange modern setting.

I told them of my long-cherished dream of converting to Buddhism. I had missed the official ceremony in Nagpur where Dr Ambedkar had led nearly half a million people to join the Buddhist fold. They agreed to help, and thus it was, that thousands of miles from India, in a hotel room in the American Midwest, one Indian family converted to Buddhism under the guidance of monks from Thailand.

THEY SAY THAT troubles come in a group. Back in Nagpur, the newly converted Buddhists began trying to gain control over a sacred spot of land, now known as Dikshabhoomi, where Babasaheb and his followers had converted to Buddhism. R.R. Patel and Sakharam Meshram from Nagpur asked me to write to officials from several Buddhist nations to exert pressure upon the Indian government. With great difficulty I found the time to write several letters. But one officious Ceylon bureaucrat wrote to my advisors at Wisconsin stating that a foreign student named Namdeo Nimgade was attempting to agitate and launch a religious movement. This was a period of conservatism in America, in which university students were supposed to avoid engaging in social activism.

Not too long after, I was summoned to see the Dean of Foreign Students at the University of Wisconsin, to answer these charges. I spent some restless nights as I anticipated this meeting.

At my study in our apartment in Madison, Wisconsin.

To make matters worse, my advisor Dr Attoe had also come to know about this affair. He was extremely strict with his students regarding academics. In the matter of discipline he was like my grandmother Saguna! Already he had some misgivings about me: during the 1960 elections I had gone to see both presidential candidates Richard Nixon and John F. Kennedy when they came through Wisconsin for their election campaigns. On both occasions I had advanced through the crowds to shake hands with the candidate. I suspect that Dr Attoe knew about this, because I ended up on the local television news!

Dr Attoe summoned me to his office, and coming straight to the point said, 'I think you should be leaving after your M.Sc. First of all, your Rockefeller scholarship has terminated. Second, I think your attention to academics is waning. Your grades in mathematics and physics are slipping.' I left his office with great worry weighing on my mind. I would have to justify my continuing in the Ph.D. program with him, but first I had to deal with my meeting with Dr Milligan.

'SIR, TODAY, I consider myself the luckiest of students!' I was seated in the office of the Advisor of Foreign Students, Dr Milligan.

'And why?' he asked me. My words clearly caught him off guard.

'Because there are now hundreds of foreign students here in your great university; but how many of them can say that they have gotten to see the Dean himself?'

He smiled. The ice had been broken. I had been dreading this moment for some days, and had prayed for the right words to come to me. Dean Milligan now repeated the charges leveled against me and asked for an explanation.

'If you search my home,' I said in a low voice, 'you will not find a shred of evidence that I am conducting any anti-national activities.' Pressing my point I continued: 'I was not a traitor to my country and I was doing no harm to Ceylon. Those who want to do something good for society are often the ones criticized unjustly. Did Jesus Christ deserve the charges brought against him?'

Dr Milligan, a thoughtful scholar, listened closely to me and nodded. I explained further to him about how a great Indian leader, Dr Bhimrao Ambedkar, had worked to remove the blot of untouchability in India and had inspired my quest for higher education. I told him of the struggles I had gone through so far and of my determination to continue on the path of higher education.

At length, Dr Milligan leaned back and said, 'You are a good student. I am convinced that you are doing the right thing. I will write to the Ceylon officials explaining that you are doing no wrong.'

NOW I HAD to make a final attempt to win over Dr Attoe. I made an appointment with him but could only obtain fifteen minutes. How could I explain to him in such a short time? I would have to choose every word carefully. I did not know where to start my plea. Finally, when the appointment started I talked about the oppressed rural community that I came from, and how I had struggled against caste discrimination to obtain my education. If I did not finish my Ph.D., it would be a setback not just for me personally, but also for my community. Younger students in my community would then view a Ph.D. from overseas as an insurmountable obstacle. Furthermore, other castes would cast aspersions on our character and mental abilities.

When I looked up at the clock, I was astonished to see that a half-hour had passed. Dr Attoe had also become engrossed in my story. Finally, he said, 'Now that I understand your background and your determination in overcoming your obstacles I agree that you should continue with your Ph.D. studies. But, unfortunately, we cannot grant you financial aid.'

I was so overjoyed to be able to continue my studies that I did not worry about the lack of financial aid. I shook his hands and assured him that I would not disappoint him. Had this been a meeting in India, I would surely have touched his feet in respect.

No turning back

In six months, I'd used up my savings from my first two years. Then, I found a part-time job that involved soil testing for the state laboratory. This involved grinding numerous soil samples. The dust would get into my nose and mouth. I was so tired between work and research that on reaching home, I would sink into the bathtub and sometimes fall asleep there. A worried Hira would often have to knock on the door to wake me for dinner.

Several friends would give me fresh vegetables from their gardens. I also took part in some experiments in the Food and Nutrition Department, which involved eating special diets. At least I was now getting food for free! For a while even Hira was thinking of getting a job, but as it turned out her visitor visa did not allow this. We stumbled across the idea of a home babysitting service. Hira started taking care of several children from the neighborhood. Our children enjoyed this opportunity to be with other children.

A half-year later Dr Attoe arranged a lab job for me that paid $150 a month. Our financial troubles were lessening. In a year or two, our children Bhim and Rekha started attending public school and became introduced to the American education system.

One of our children's friends was a girl named Joanna, who loved being at our apartment so much that she would feign sleep when her mother called for her. Her mother was a single parent, and Joanna admitted to us once that, 'I don't like going home, because my mother is more interested in being with other men than with me.' We thus became introduced to another facet of life in the USA. She became like a fourth child for us until her mother re-married and they moved away.

Once in a while I would have to leave my work in order to take a sick child to the doctor. It was harder for Hira to do this, because she would have had to take all three children with her. Rekha came down with impetigo, a skin condition. The doctor's bill was $200. I was crushed, for it was more than my monthly salary. When I went to pay Dr Talbot, he said, 'Don't worry, I have already got the payment.' I was mystified. Then he informed me that our friend Mrs Pickett had already paid the bill!

Then, Dr Talbot said, 'Please stand up straight now.' I stood up and he looked me over. He said, 'You are the same size as me. Come to my home, and we can pick out some suits for you.' He gave me five suits, all in excellent condition.

Another friend named Mrs Carter, a nurse, would visit our home to help with washing Rekha's skin to treat her impetigo. Our landlord, Mr Brown, a very decent and kind gentleman, also came to our help. He was a high school principal and would often visit us to give the children toys and books. When he came to know about our precarious financial condition he lowered our rent, and he would bring us fresh produce from his kitchen garden.

Most of my fellow students in agriculture were male. For my Ph.D. I had to study two foreign languages, and in those classes there were some female students. One day in a bookstore, I ran into a very pleasant girl from my French class, Jeanette Robbin. She was also far from her home in Washington, D.C., so I invited her to come to our house for lunch. She appeared hesitant until I explained that in India, since we did not have the convenience of telephones, we maintained an open-door policy.

When we arrived at the apartment door, Hira greeted Jeanette politely, but then looked at me with some anger and irritation. Jeanette Robbin, after all, was very pretty, and I suppose when a husband comes home with a beautiful woman it can set the grounds for an argument. But as with all other guests, I took the opportunity to talk about Babasaheb Ambedkar. She was very interested and took home some books about him to read.

This was the beginning of her interest in Babasaheb, and with my encouragement, Robbin decided to write her Masters thesis in political science on the Ambedkar movement. Her thesis was so well-written that, with the assistance of my brother-in-law Vasant Moon, it was published as a book in 1964 in India as *Dr Ambedkar and his Movement.*

Although I was successful in continuing my social reform work, my academic life was starting to suffer. Between financial troubles and taking care of the children I got some poor grades in Physics. I had underestimated the difficulties involved, and for a while I almost thought of leaving the Ph.D. program.

BUT NOW, IT was Hira who said to me, 'We cannot turn back now. What will people back in India say if you fail in your attempts at a Ph.D. here? They might blame you, or even your family for having distracted you. And you will live the rest of your life repenting your failure.' As added inducement she said, 'If you finish your Ph.D. here, I will finish the remainder of my B.A. degree studies back in Delhi.'

There is a saying in Hindi: *Dhiraj, dharma, mitra, or nari; Apat kaley parkhiye chari.* (Times of trouble will test these four things: Courage, faith, friends, and spouse.) I have indeed been most fortunate in having Hira as my wife as she helped me face so many challenges over the years. On weekends, Hira would join me in my laboratory to help with tasks such as labeling test tubes, mixing soil samples, and cleaning, weighing and measuring. She would also copy in her beautiful handwriting entire books from libraries complete with detailed charts of biochemical pathways, as in those days we did not have photocopiers.

Hira and the children also became cultural ambassadors. They would answer hundreds of questions such as, 'Why do your women wear saris? Don't they get in the way of your work? How long are the saris? Why do you wear the red dots on the forehead? How do you date?' Their astonishment knew no limit when we mentioned that Hira and I did not know each other before marriage. They looked at us as though we had landed from another planet.

A fifteen-year old American girl said, 'I would rather die than marry a complete stranger!'

Once I helped an elderly woman in our neighborhood cross the street. She introduced herself as Mrs Novicks. It turns out that she lived right across the street from us and had seen our three children playing in front of the apartment. Thereafter she would keep a watchful eye on our children as closely as any of our village grandmothers. On frigid Wisconsin winter mornings she would call out to prevent me from leaving the apartment if I did not have my muffler and warm hat. The children would go to her place to play with puzzles and sit in her lap listening to her read stories.

We met another lifelong friend through my friend Bhure. He had brought a guest to an Indian Association Diwali festival, Vera Myer, a lively and fashionable divorcée, with glasses and gray hair pulled up in a bun. She must have been around 60 years old. I shook her hand, and then pulled my shy children out from hiding behind their mother. 'Come on, come and say hello to Grandma Myer!'

She greeted them, and then turned to me coldly. It turned out that I had said the wrong thing. Taking me aside, she said in irritation, 'Why do you call me Grandma? Do I look that old? I don't even have children of my own, let alone grandchildren!'

I was contrite. The culture was different here. 'In India, we use terms implying a family relationship even for people not related to us. Since I thought you might be of my parents' generation, you would be like a grandmother to my children. But now I understand my mistake. To make amends, I will consider you as my wife's younger sister. The sounds of Hira and Vera, after all, go well together.'

Vera's anger melted and she clapped with joy. From then on, we were the closest of friends. She would never forget the birthdays of our children and brought them many presents. She would always take the side of Hira in any argument. On one memorable occasion when I grew a mustache, Vera and her friends attacked me thus, 'Why are you growing a miserable wormy-looking mustache? It makes you look middle-aged. And next to you, your wife looks positively under-aged. You make a comic couple now. If you don't take that thing off, my friends and I will forcibly do so!'

I had no choice but to remove my mustache. To this day, except for one or two lapses, I have not had a moustache.

Once, while walking on campus, I struck up a conversation with a history professor named Salter. He accepted my impromptu invitation to visit my apartment, and then invited us later to his place. He and his wife encouraged our children in their love of reading, giving them many books that became their favorites. Several Madison area friends, including the Thayer, Winans, and Eberhart families would invite us for dinners including celebrations for our children's birthdays. They would come and pick us up in their car to go to their house. They would invite many other international students to some of their dinners. The Mitchell family, in particular, made us part of their family. We truly felt that Americans were the most welcoming people on earth.

My interaction with them truly made me feel empathetic towards any foreigner that I would later encounter in India. I could feel the pain of anyone's separation from their homeland

and family, sometimes without news from home. I would therefore bring any foreigner from any corner of the globe back home with me to help lessen their homesickness, even if for just a short while. Later, we were fortunate in turn to host Bob, Bill, and Steve Mitchell as well as the Winans when they visited Delhi.

Once, I saw some Indonesian students looking downcast. They admitted to feeling homesick and not able to put their heart in their studies. I brought them home in time for dinner. Indian food is somewhat similar to Indonesian food, so they enjoyed it very much. They stayed late playing with the children, and at the end of the evening their spirits had lifted.

One upper-caste colleague named W.B. Rahudkar was so touched upon hearing my experiences that he wrote up my life story and sent it in to the prestigious *Kirloskar* magazine in India, where it was published in July 1961. This story made me very well known in Maharashtra even while I was still in the USA.

Dr Nimgade and Dr King

My guide Dr Attoe very ably led me through the process of writing my thesis. Near the end of the process, I had to prepare for my final comprehensive exam. For several months my life revolved around the library, where I spent every moment reading and studying, night and day. On 30 March 1962, I sat in a room with five of the top agriculture professors in the world – Drs Smith, Attoe, Torrie, Murdock, and Corey – as they grilled me for three straight hours on virtually any topic in agricultural science. Fortunately, I was very well prepared and could answer every question. Each one of them passed me.

It was my greatest joy to walk out of the room knowing I had succeeded. In fact, my feet almost did not touch the floor. My four years of preparation had borne fruit.

HOURS LATER, I wandered into the Student Union for the first time in weeks, and stumbled upon a notice that the Reverend Martin Luther King was speaking on campus. Although I did not have a ticket, I went anyway, and pleaded to be let in. 'I have passed my exams and will soon be leaving this country. I will never have the opportunity to hear Dr King again.'

They heard my plea, and I entered the hall. I was thrilled to see the leader of the oppressed African American population in person. At one point he chose to remark on India's caste problems, and it was evident to me that he was sadly misinformed. Dr King said:

> I was able to stay at the house of Prime Minister Nehru. Nehru said to me, 'Dr King, we have totally eliminated untouchability. If you were to go to any corner of India you would not be able to find even five people who admit to following untouchability! We have really lifted up our

> country.' This type of abolishment of oppression is what we need in America. We must follow the Indian example.

At the question-and-answer session I raised my hand but was not called upon. The moderator declared the session ended, saying that Dr King must now be tired.

I kept my hand up and stated:

> I do not have a question, since Dr King is above question. But I have a comment. Our Prime Minister is blessed to be able to invite to India many leaders and rulers. But with Dr King we truly have a king of kings visiting.

There was much applause at this point.

> The true credit for abolishing untouchability in India goes to Dr Ambedkar, who was inspired in his studies in the USA at Columbia University by the example of Thomas Jefferson and Booker T. Washington. Therefore, the real credit goes to the USA. When I grew up in India as an untouchable, I had to stand outside the window of my classroom. When I passed my exams I could not even touch the feet of my teacher to pay my respects because of his concerns about being polluted by my touch. I gained several degrees in India and made it here to Wisconsin for my studies. Today, I passed my comprehensive exams. Soon I will leave with my Ph.D. and return to India. I will face several troubles there. Perhaps the washer/man will not wash my clothes, the barber will not shave me... But still, I shall return to serve my country and humanity. In fact, when Dr Ambedkar returned to India and wrote its Constitution he was rewarded with honorary degrees; but these were only from universities outside India, such as Columbia University. Had he been of a high caste, he would have been showered with honorary degrees within India. In my country, as in yours, discrimination has not gone away, and discrimination will not vanish overnight.
>
> It is our duty, without rancor or bitterness, to remove discrimination. It does not matter what is the color of a person... what counts is what is inside. The color of skin does not alter the color of one's blood. We must follow the example of Martin Luther King. He went to India to learn. But in my

> opinion, Dr King ended up going to India to teach. He is the one who reminded Indians how to use nonviolence. Indians have forgotten about Gandhi's philosophy of nonviolence. Dr King is the living example of using nonviolence to bring dignity and rights to those who have been long oppressed, and therefore he is the ideal human.

After speaking I sat down. But the applause started and continued for quite a while. I had not intended to speak so much about the black spot on India's history. But upon hearing the mistruths of Nehru I was moved to make my comments.

When I got home, Hira was very pleased to hear about my passing the comprehensive exams. That evening we also got many phone calls from African Americans who had heard my comments to Dr King.

Unfortunately, I could not stay in Madison to receive my diploma in the formal graduation ceremony, since I had to return to India by a certain date and I wanted to allow enough time for some travel in Europe. But for the sake of photographs, I rented an academic graduation robe and cap. One of our friends, Mrs Carter, invited a reporter from the *Wisconsin State Journal* to witness this.

That Sunday, when I unfolded the *Wisconsin State Journal* I was startled to find my picture on the front page of the paper. The headline read, "Untouchable Gains Ph.D." In the days to follow, as we packed our belongings, we received a shower of phone calls. Many of our dear friends

'Untouchable' Gains Ph.D.

Indian's Struggle Worth Effort

By MARCIA CROWLEY
(State Journal Staff Writer)

The young Indian boy was given permission to attend school on one condition — he was not to enter the school building.

For N. M. Nimgade of New Delhi was one of India's untouchables, the lowest level in the country's caste system.

So Nimgade, desperately hungry for education, stood outside the school and received his elementary school training by listening to the teachers as they taught the children of the upper classes.

With his black hair now streaked with gray, Nimgade reached his goal Mar. 31 when he received his Ph.D. degree in soils from the University of Wisconsin.

He returns to India today with his handsome wife and three children. He returns to a promising and challenging career with the Indian government.

His story is one of almost unbelievable determination and hardship. So it is small wonder that a stranger should feel the glow of pride as Nimgade mentions his doctor's degree.

As a member of a poverty-stricken untouchable family, he was not allowed to touch anyone from the upper classes, and he was unable to attain an education.

Nimgade isn't sure when he was born, the month, date, or year, since that was never recorded. He thinks he was born about 1921.

First Work

He began to work in the fields when he was about 8 so that there would be another wage earner in the family. When he was 16, he was given a monthly job at which he worked every day. He was paid a monthly wage of 4 cents worth of sorghum grain.

Wanting their son to be able to at least write his name, Nimgade's parents obtained permission for him to 'attend school' by standing outside the building, in a neighboring village 3 miles away, to which he walked each day.

"I consider myself lucky to be given permission to do that," he said, explaining that few untouchables did even that.

He Went On

After four years of the school, Nimgade's parents thought he had enough and it was time to engage in the fields. But he wanted to go on — and so did.

From there he went to a county school in which he was allowed to sit with other students, for the school was run by missionaries. During this period he lived with his younger brother and sister, cared for them, and did the household chores. He also worked part time bringing grass to the market

Turn to Page 2, Col. 1

Indian 'Untouchable' Gains Life Goal With UW Degree

Continued from Page 1

where it was sold for cattle food.

With all his outside work and responsibilities, the 18-year-old youth still was the top student in his class.

He achieved what few untouchables do in 1943 when he was graduated from high school. Then he wanted to go to the college of agriculture.

16-Mile Walk

"My parents were against it again, saying how very costly it would be and how could I go? I received a scholarship, but the amount was not enough," Nimgade said.

"I wanted to live in a dormitory with other students. But I was not allowed. I had to live in a hostel with other untouchables," he added. "From the hostel, I walked 16 miles a day to get my college education."

To get more money, he tutored other students in his home.

Social 'Crime'

Nimgade was arrested during this time for stepping inside a temple. He had committed no crime, but his social status made his action unlawful.

As punishment for his "crime," he had to report to court frequently for four years and prove he had not gotten into trouble again. It meant cutting many classes, but he continued his education.

"I felt wonderful, just wonderful, when I received my B.S. degree in 1949. My parents thought I had enough but I wanted to go on."

Nimgade attended the Indian Agricultural Research Institute after that where kind professors helped him out with material items such as clothing. He obtained his master's degree in 1951, and the next year got a job as a research assistant at the institute to earn money to come to the United States and work for a doctor's degree.

Measure of Fame

When he was about 32 years old, his anxious parents selected a wife for him—whom he met for the first time at his wedding!

His determination for an education and his fight to get it were described in an Indian magazine, and word spread throughout the country. His wedding was attended by 10,000 well-wishers, professors and untouchables alike.

For about nine years, he tried to get into the United States; but he had no money and received no scholarship. A Rockefeller Foundation interviewer heard of him and went to see him in India.

Nimgade asked for a total of $400. The foundation, impressed, offered him $350 a month and passage for his wife.

American Aid

"I couldn't believe my ears when he told me. I thought he was kidding. I only wanted $400."

Nimgade was accepted at the University of Wisconsin soils department which he wanted to attend because of his respect for Dr. Emil Truog whom he calls "the greatest living soil scientist in the United States."

The foundation scholarship was for one year and was extended for another on the recommendation of the university professors. But Nimgade wanted to attend another two years and receive his doctor's degree.

He Saved

So, he spent about $200 a month on his family and saved the other $150 for his education.

Since he started his learning so late in life, Nimgade wants his children to start while they are very young. And the quest for education seems to run in the whole family.

His eldest son, Bhimraco, 7, was anxious to learn how to read when he was 4. His father taught him, in part, by pointing out words in The Wisconsin State Journal. By the time he was 4½, Bhimraco could read the paper's masthead and countless other words.

Gifted Child

Bhimraco was pronounced a gifted child after testing at the university and was placed in a gifted child's class at Washington school. The school's officials have told the Nimgades the boy's intelligence is equal to a fourth grader's.

Where Bhimraco is a serious boy who stands straight and proud pretty Rekaha, 5, is a bouncy little girl who is anxious to take her blonde birthday doll with her to India. Ashok, who will be 4 in June, is a handsome fellow with brown eyes so huge they seem to swallow you.

American life already has an influence on the youngsters. As the reporter prepared to leave, Bhimraco, in a clear, proud voice, recited the entire Gettysburg address.

came to visit us for the last time. We could barely pry our son Ashok from our friend Mrs Replinger's loving hands as she held him with tears in her eyes.

Thus, as we returned to our homeland, we were filled with much sadness to leave behind the foreigners who had welcomed us wholeheartedly, had helped us in many ways, and had bestowed their love upon us. I had felt free of the curse of untouchability here. It was a point of amusement, in fact, that Americans used the term "untouchable" interchangeably with the term "brahmin" (as in "Boston Brahmin")!

EVENING ECHO

CORK WEDNESDAY, APRIL 25, 1962 PRICE: TWOPEN[illegible]

BECAUSE of their father's determination to shatter unjust tradition, these three little Indian children, seen here with their parents, face a bright, full future.

With the father, Dr. Namdeo Nimgade, and his wife, Hira, they are in Dublin for a week to "see one of the world's greatest democracies" and to permit their father study the soil-testing schemes in the country.

Dr. Nimgade was born in the "untouchables" class of the rigid Indian caste system and was at first denied even the right to education but was allowed attend school — by sitting outside the walls and listening to the class inside.

Dr. Namdeo Nimgade, with his wife Hira and children Bhimrao, Rekha and Ashok, when they disembarked from the U.S. Lines S.S. America at Cobh to-day.

My story intrigued an Irish newspaper.

Journey home

'Why must you go? Just turn around and return with us to your home in Madison.'

It was with excitement mingled with great sadness that on 9 April 1962, we boarded a Greyhound bus. Many well-wishers had accompanied us to the bus station and pleaded with us to remain in Wisconsin. Our eyes welled up with tears as we waved goodbye to our dear friends from America's heartland. As the bus pulled away, I wondered if we would ever see them again.

Over the past several years our family had never even left Wisconsin because of my intense studies. Now my travel plan was to see as much of the world as we could on the way back, as who knew when such an opportunity would come again? To do this we would have to travel as cheaply as possible, and all this with three small children and a great deal of luggage. We would travel nearly a thousand miles across the USA to New York City by bus; then take a passenger ship to Ireland; then tour Europe by train; and then take a passenger ship from Italy to Bombay; and finally take the train to New Delhi to take up my job with the Indian Agricultural Research Institute again.

I had a great love of books and learning. So it was difficult for me to choose which books to leave and which ones to pack. I mailed some books to India, to my brother Ankush in Nagpur. But still I had 22 steamer trunks, full of mostly books, to take with us. I shipped them to New York City, in the care of the Rockefeller Foundation, and I made plans to have them on the passenger ship with us to Europe, then I would send them on ahead to our port of embarkation in Italy. The pile of trunks made a small mountain that the children enjoyed climbing on until Hira or I would stop them.

It was a three-hour trip to our first stop, Chicago. We spent a day or two there, and the city surprised us with its size. It had large office buildings and museums. At night there were hundreds of thousands of lights across the skyline. It was a beautiful sight.

Our next stop was Niagara Falls, which stunned the imagination with its unending roaring fury. The river took its precipitous and thundering plunge over the edge, never resting for a moment, churning the swirling water to a milky froth. We watched with amazement until we were soaked by the spray. We walked along the Niagara Falls to the Canadian border where the immigration officials stopped us. To our horror, our three-year old boy Ashok was no longer with us. He had skipped ahead in the crowd and vanished into the Canadian side.

The officers, however, would not let me cross to find him. I panicked, thinking about how Ashok would feel when he realized we were no longer with him. 'Sirs,' I pleaded, 'kindly let me proceed into your section so that I can find my boy. As soon as I find him I will return.' But the officers were adamant. I started sweating, wondering what to do. Fortunately, Ashok had turned around once he realized he was alone in the crowd, and he came back to us; and the first catastrophe of our trip was averted.

On 13 April, we reached the capital, Washington D.C., where my friend from French class at Wisconsin, Jeanette Robbin, had arranged for us to stay with friends at the apartment of the Chetty family. She had a small party planned the next day, to celebrate Ambedkar Jayanti, the birthday of Dr Ambedkar. We enjoyed the sights of Washington D.C., including the beautiful Japanese cherry blossoms and the Mall, and the memorial monuments to Jefferson, Lincoln, and Washington. It was a great thrill for me to see the grandeur of the monuments to the founding principles of the United States, of freedom and equality, as these ideals had inspired Dr Ambedkar in framing the Constitution of India.

A few days later, we reached our point of embarkation, New York City. We took the lift up to the top of the Empire State Building, the tallest building in the world at that time. From 101 stories up, people on the ground appeared like ants. We enjoyed gazing out at the horizon for hours, feeling the temperature drop every time a cloud would pass overhead, and enjoying that we were so high up that some of the clouds even passed below us.

Another wonder was the Statue of Liberty in the harbor. We climbed up inside, and marveled at the sight of the waves all around us from our commanding height.

That evening we chanced upon a hotel with several workers from India, and we chatted with them. We even found an Indian restaurant – there were not many in those days – and the Indian meal brought the remembrance of our homeland to us.

WE HAD TOLD the children that we would be traveling over the ocean in a big boat. They were excited. They must have pictured something like a large rowboat. At the dock, we boarded the passenger steamship for the voyage to Europe, the *SS America*, using a covered walkway. The ship was immense, with large dining halls, nurseries, and libraries. In fact, Ashok was upset and screamed, 'You lied to me! You said we would be in a ship, but instead we are in an ordinary building!' Only after I showed him the water over the boat's edge did he believe us and celebrated his understanding with a little dance.

On 25 April 1962, after about a week at sea, we reached the shores of Ireland. Our one contact there had arranged for an Irish journalist to meet us. The next day, to my surprise, a picture of our family was in the newspaper. We stayed in charming Irish inns as we traveled the country. At one place, Chubby Checker's popular song "Let's Twist Again" was playing on the jukebox in the dining room. All three of our children ran to the floor and started dancing the Twist. The inn guests were so delighted that when the music ended someone put more coins in the jukebox. People reloaded the jukebox several times while our dancing children entertained the crowd.

In England, we stayed in London with the Dorlikar family. I recall being stunned by the brilliance of the Koh-i-noor diamond, on display in the Tower of London; this famous diamond was originally from India. Using London as a base, I visited many fine universities such as Oxford and Cambridge.

Once we reached Paris, we came upon language barriers. It had been one thing to learn academic French involving science, but when it came to navigating the streets of France, I was at a total loss. Fortunately, I was able to call a French colleague from the University of Wisconsin who was now in Paris. Upon receiving my desperate phone call, she immediately came to join us at the train station and helped us arrange accommodations and tours. In Paris we marveled at the 300-meter-high Eiffel tower, which was the tallest building in the world until 1930. At night, Hira took care of the children, while I toured the city.

The rest of our tour included stops in Luxembourg and then Switzerland, where we enjoyed the mountains and alpine meadows. I was impressed by the neatness and cleanliness of the streets that contrasted so much with the dust and chaos of India. We picnicked whenever possible to save funds. On one occasion a Swiss family offered our children food. But because of the language barrier, we did not accept. The family persevered, contradicting the stereotype of the Swiss as being aloof; they tore off pieces of the bread and ate it themselves as though to show us the food was safe. When our children accepted their offerings there was much joy on both sides of the language divide.

In Frankfurt, we had problems verifying our hotel reservations and were stuck at the train station. Fortunately, there was a refugee camp for people fleeing East Germany at the train station and they were willing to extend hospitability to Hira and the children. I, however, was stuck without accommodations. Hira did not want me to tramp around the city, especially at night, so she kept my shoes, jacket, and wallet with her. However, that did not deter me. I somehow took the "Frankfurt by Night" tour.

IN ITALY WE were fortunate to view the works of Leonardo da Vinci, Michelangelo and many other artists. We always traveled third class, but as the weather was getting very hot, I booked a second-class train for our trip to the Vatican. However, the Italian authorities decided to change our train car to first class and they asked us to vacate our seats. I protested, saying that I had paid for these second-class tickets so the children would not suffer in the heat and crowds. We argued more and more heatedly. 'I will write a letter to the head of your country! I will complain about your shameful lack of hospitality, and I will mention your name personally!' I said. But because of the language barrier these words fell upon deaf ears.

The train car held two or three Italians who spoke English. Upon hearing my point of view, they started making inquiries. It turns out that they were pilgrims heading into Vatican City for an audience with the Pope. Inspiration struck me. I said that we were going to see the Pope as well.

Now the conductor could do nothing but leave us alone. Who was he to interfere with our meeting with the Pope! We had a very nice journey spent in the company of the pious pilgrims. They gave us cold refreshing water and treats. The women would even fan our children and play with them.

The next day, when we went to see the Pope, there were thousands of pilgrims. I had Ashok sitting on my shoulders and I was carrying Rekha in my arms. When they asked for our entry passes, I started searching all my pockets as if I had misplaced them. Seeing the predicament of this harried father, the officials were very kind in letting us proceed without entry passes. The Pope was blessing the crowd using a slender branch to wave over people. We were overjoyed when his branch actually touched us. The children were very impressed with this ritual, and for weeks afterwards they delighted in tapping each other with sticks and claiming that it was a blessing.

Our last stop was in Naples. It was a lovely town on the edge of the sea with ancient buildings and small streets. In every small alley was a church. From there we set out for India. On 31 May 1962, we boarded the *Victoria*, an Italian passenger ship, heading for Bombay.

AT THE SUEZ Canal, we stopped at Cairo. On a hot sunny day, my family decided to rest on board while I ventured onto land with some other passengers. We took a tour and rode camels. To protect my head from the fierce sun, I hit upon a novel idea. My son Ashok had been using cloth diapers, and I had not had the heart to throw them all away. After all, they were made of a nice soft white cloth and they turned out to be an excellent head covering. We saw the colossal and amazing pyramids. In my notes I have the measurements listed as 446 feet high and 740 feet long at the base. They had been built 4500 years ago with the labor of thousands and thousands of workers.

Our boat also stopped at Aden, where a lot of the passengers shopped in the bazaars. As we approached Bombay, many clever passengers approached us asking if we would help them get through customs by carrying some of their goods or even wearing some of their jewelry. But I firmly said that we did not want to become a part of their business ventures.

At Karachi, I was determined to see something of Pakistan. After all, when would I ever get the chance to visit this land? India and Pakistan regarded each other with suspicion and had even gone to war several times. Many friends had warned me about visiting Pakistan, saying that we would be cut to shreds and looted. But I had faith that people are the same everywhere. Besides, we had nothing worth looting.

I booked a taxi, telling the driver, 'We do not have much money left. Please take us wherever you can for this amount. But the one thing I want to make sure that we see Jinnah's memorial.' I explained to the driver what I understood about Islam based on what I had read. He was very pleased and drove us all around town. He even purchased our entrance tickets at museums and zoos. He fed our children candy and bought paan for us. He accepted the small amount of money I paid him – the equivalent of two dollars – with as much grace as if it were a princely sum. Unfortunately, because of the hostilities between Pakistan and India we were never able to keep in touch with this wonderful and generous Muslim who had extended the kindest of courtesies to us.

To Motherland

As we approached Bombay, a monsoon storm overtook us, and the boat heaved and tilted from one side to the other. Nausea overcame everyone. Many people vomited. All the passengers abandoned the deck and common areas. We, too, retreated to the cabin and lay weakly in bed. The loudspeaker announced that Bombay was in sight.

Hira tried to rise to gather our belongings, but she felt lightheaded and sank back into her bed. I, too, tried, but could do little better. Time passed, and then there came a knock on the door. I struggled to get up and open it, fearing that it was the officials; but to my amazement, in stepped my younger brother Ankush. To me he seemed not just a brother but a *devdoot*, a messenger of God. It turns out that all the other passengers had left the ship, and so the officials had allowed Ankush to come on board to help us. He gathered our things together and helped us down. As we looked onto the pier of Bombay, the Sanskrit phrase came to my mind:

> *Janani janmabhumishchya swargadapi gari asi.*
>
> (Mother and Motherland, these are greater than Heaven.)

At the dock, to my surprise, there were a dozen relatives, with tears of joy in their eyes. While Hira and I rushed forward to greet them, our children hid behind us, wondering who these strangers were. As soon as we touched them and embraced them, and our elders gave us their blessings, our minds were filled with bliss. That day was one of the most blessed days in my life. Our entire party stayed at the spacious house of Shankarao Sontakke, Hira's cousin. He was head of the Bombay airport traffic control. For three days we went sightseeing in the bustling city of Bombay. But a lot of our time was spent fielding questions about America.

On 17 June, we headed for Nagpur. Although it was Ashok's birthday, we were so tired that we could not do much more to celebrate than say 'Happy Birthday!'

In Nagpur, we were very happy to reconnect with old friends and well-wishers. For two weeks there were numerous feasts, receptions and festivities for me in Nagpur, Umrer, Sathgaon, and other villages. I gave speeches about my experiences, about the USA, and about the American style of education. I acknowledged that all credit for my accomplishments was due to Babasaheb Ambedkar. Through these talks people could vicariously experience the wonders of the New World.

AMONG THE UPPER castes back then, women lagged in education and often clung to old traditions such as caste discrimination. In Nagpur, before eating at someone's house, my children would go to wash their hands, when from the window I could sometimes hear the women's voices saying, 'Oh, stop those children before they touch the water vessels.' I was stunned. We had traveled through many foreign lands and had been met with so much kindness. I had almost forgotten about the miseries of untouchability. Here, in our homeland, we were still treated like untouchable mahars. On one occasion, a street barber asked me my name and then my caste. I answered truthfully, and then he declined me service.

While we were still traveling I heard that Professor and Mrs Pickett, our beloved friends from Wisconsin, were in Calcutta, where he was a visiting professor. We went there to meet them and stayed as guests in their bungalow. For a few days we enjoyed touring Calcutta as they took us around in their rented car. When it came time for returning to Delhi, they even bought our train tickets.

At the train station, they pressed an envelope in our hands saying, 'This is a surprise—please open it later in the train.' As the train pulled out of the station we were overcome with sadness in leaving our adopted parents. Later, we opened the envelope. In the envelope was 200 rupees. The enclosed note said, 'In Delhi, please buy a kerosene stove for Hira so she does not have to work with the slow coal burning stove.' We were touched, since we truly had so little money. The kerosene stove would be a step up for us, a touch of modernity. Indian households used a single burner hand-pumped model, similar to what Americans would use as a camping stove.

Return to Delhi

When we alighted in Delhi we went straight to the apartment of our old landlord Mr Bhattacharjee. I had sent him a telegram earlier informing him that we were ready to return to our rooms, that they had set aside for us. But the telegram was lost apparently. Nonetheless, the Bhattacharjees immediately emptied the rooms for us and welcomed us warmly. Their children, Khokan, Buru and their new daughter Manu, loved playing with our children. But now there was a language barrier.

Once, when Manu asked Ashok to play, he put her off, saying, 'Tomorrow!' She immediately slapped him hard and Ashok cried out. It became apparent that Manu had interpreted 'tomorrow' as *tum maro* (you can slap me). After this we all burst into laughter. Nonetheless, we encouraged our children to learn Hindi after this episode.

I was so happy with my own American educational experience that I wanted my children also to attend an English medium school. With this in mind, we explored several possibilities. Professor Pickett had encouraged me to consider the American International School in New Delhi. His friend, the well-known architect Joseph Stein was drawing up plans for the school's new campus. Quite fittingly, the school mascot was the tiger. At the admission interview, Bhim made a great impression on them by answering every question. Rekha, on the other hand, had forgotten everything during our long period of travel and could not answer her questions. They admitted Bhim free of tuition, but for Rekha they charged 50 rupees per month. Because there was no school bus from our part of the city, I would take the children myself by bicycle the five miles to and then later from the school for a total of 20 miles a day.

ESPECIALLY IN THOSE days, it was difficult to obtain a science Ph.D. from an American university. I was honored to have as a classmate Iajuddin Ahmed, who came several times for dinner to our apartment in the USA. We were both students of Professor Attoe. Later Ahmed became President of Bangladesh, which reveals to some extent the high quality of our Wisconsin students. On one occasion back in India, I met the prominent statesman Jai Prakash Narain. When he found out I had a Ph.D. from Wisconsin he congratulated me. 'I went to four US universities,' he admitted, 'but I ended up with not even one degree!'

But from the initial treatment I received on my return home, my American degree hardly seemed to matter. Before leaving for the USA my salary had been 310 rupees per month. Now, after returning, for some reason it was 270. Part of this had to do with the government austerity program following the expensive Indo–Chinese war. My former guide Dr Raychaudhari had retired by now, and his replacement had thoughtlessly given away my government position to someone junior to me (a former student of mine, in fact).

I told Panjabrao Deshmukh of my troubles and he assured me that even though he was no longer Agricultural Minister he could find me a good post in our home state of Maharashtra. But I did not want to leave Delhi now that we had such a fine school for our children. For the same reason I turned down another good post in Jodhpur.

I got a temporary promotion for three months when another agricultural chemist took a leave of absence. When I reverted to my former post I admit to feeling some bitterness. In 1965, however, three years after my return to India, I did get a promotion to a junior First Class Scientist position with a somewhat higher salary. At this time Hira enrolled in a local college to finish her two remaining years of college.

We moved to a different apartment in the same block, renting rooms from the Kapoor family from Punjab. We enjoyed a wonderful relationship with them, and their two young daughters Anjali and Titoo played with our children. Their family would house-sit our children while Hira was in college. We were touched by their thoughtfulness in many things. Once, when there was a sudden rainstorm, they brought in our bedding that Hira had left out in the sun to dry.

Mr Kapoor's father, whom we respectfully referred to as Babuji, was very pious, and he would sing hymns and pray very often. On the few occasions when Hira or I would raise our voices to argue in Marathi, he would start raising his voice higher to chant the religious invocation of peace, '*Om shanti, shanti!*' We would immediately quiet down and start laughing.

Right next door we also had a Marathi brahmin family, the Baporikars, with four children. I had known Mr Baporikar from Nagpur, but I was concerned that his wife might be more conservative. When I brought this up with Mr Baporikar he laughed and assured me that caste was no issue at all. And indeed we developed a very close relationship with them, often sharing food. It was through their children that our own children learned Marathi.

We went together with the Baporikars to the annual 26th of January Republic Day parade, commemorating the adoption of India's Constitution. The parade route was down the grand boulevards of the nation's capital, passing by the monumental government buildings that the British had built during their rule. There was an impressive array of marching soldiers from every state; there were tanks and artillery, there were camels, elephants, and horses; there were troupes of dancers; and there were jet fighters shaking the ground with their roar as they flew overhead. The prime minister drove by in a motorcade. When Ashok asked me what the parade was for, I jokingly told him that all this celebration was for my birthday. Indeed, there was a one chance in 365 that I was correct, for my parents, being illiterate, had not recorded the date of my birth. Ashok was annoyed, however, that his own June birthday was not celebrated with as much gusto.

As Hira's exams drew close, I began to really appreciate the labor and contribution that women make in the household when I had to take on many of her tasks such as cooking and childcare. I would take the children out of the house so she could have some peace and quiet. But when she sat for her exam she still felt unprepared and was convinced that she would not pass. When I went to check the posted results I was very happy to see that she had. I brought sweets home from the market to celebrate. But Hira, convinced that she had not passed, thought I was playing a cruel joke. 'Why did you tease me by buying these expensive sweets?' she cried. It took some time before she could accept that I was not joking.

The Nimgade Hotel

In 1966, several Scheduled Caste groups including the Republican Party of India and the Ambedkar Study Circle raised 65,000 rupees to build a statue of Dr Ambedkar at the Parliament House. I spent a lot of time asking for contributions. At the inauguration of the statue we had thousands of people from our community on the grounds of parliament. The Indian President, Dr S. Radhakrishan, addressed the crowd. The statue shows Babasaheb in full stride, with one hand holding the Constitution that he had drafted and the other hand pointing towards parliament.

In front of the statue of Dr Ambedkar at Parliament House that I helped build.

Also in 1966, we were assigned our own quarters by the government. It was with some sorrow that we departed from our tranquil and loving neighborhood. We moved our belongings by bullock cart to the new quarters. We now had two rooms, a bathroom, a toilet, a kitchen, and a little verandah. We felt like we were moving into a palace.

Mrs Vera Meyer from Wisconsin even visited us here. We enjoyed her company for a week. I would get flowers for her daily from our office gardener. One day, I handed her the flowers and she kissed my cheek. The kabbadi wallah, the itinerant buyer of scrap paper and cloth for recycling and refuse, happened to be passing by on his rounds at that very moment. He hurried off to pass on his juicy bit of gossip: 'This Nimgade-sahib is keeping two wives under the same roof, one of them being a white woman.' When news reached us we all had a good laugh.

We also had a steady stream of visitors from all over India. I would often help visiting students coming to seek admission. I would sometimes even have to buy train tickets for them, even though it might entail dipping into my family funds or even borrowing from friends. I knew what struggles students of our downtrodden castes had to overcome. Mr Bhattacharjee once joked, 'Your place is a restaurant, information center, and lodging house, all in one!

On one occasion I came home and the door was opened by a strange man in his undershirt, with shaving cream on part of his face and a razor in his hand. Irritably, he said, 'Dr Nimgade is not here right now. Perhaps you can go away and return later.' And he started closing the door on me.

But I was not about to stand for this; I pushed the door and I came in. This could very well have been an innocent episode, but as it turns out, he was a fellow of questionable character. He claimed that his wallet had been stolen at the train station and that when he wandered around Delhi someone had told him to turn to me for help.

But this was a different story from what he had told Hira earlier; he had claimed that he was an old family friend of mine. I said that we should report his stolen wallet to the police and he became visibly nervous, muttering some excuse like, 'The police would not be likely to be much help.' It took some tact and the help of friends to convince him to leave. I even gave him money to take the next bus out of town. After this, Hira and I decided we would have to be far more circumspect with our guests.

One guest from Maharashtra, Krishna Zodape, however, made it to my doorstep bearing his five-year-old son. He had had a fierce fight with his wife in the village and boarded the train to Delhi, knowing only my name. He did not even have my address, but by making enquiries at the train station and at the office of the Home Minister, who hailed from Maharashtra, he finally tracked me down. Unlike other guests, who came to New Delhi for the purpose of bettering themselves, for job interviews or for community work, he had come only because of a family quarrel.

For a month he and his son stayed with us. The air would be strong with the smoke of his bidis and the shrieks of his son. He even talked about finding a job in Delhi and living with us. At this point, Hira insisted that I have a long talk with him. I said that by now his wife's anger must have subsided, and that it was likely they could reconcile. Furthermore, by occupying space in our home, he was denying others the benefits of our hospitality and was thus blocking my ability to serve our community.

These words had a positive effect, and he took up residence elsewhere in Delhi and started selling vegetables. He married a local north Indian woman. Once during the winter he brought her and her children to visit us. Hira and the children were away visiting Nagpur at the time. This woman asked for some warm clothes for her children. I gave her several of the sweaters that Hira had knitted for our children. Later I learned that shortly thereafter, this woman left Zodape. After some two years in Delhi, Zodape returned to his home and went back to his original wife.

In my discussion with Zodape, I had also mentioned that we needed the space for occasional foreign visitors. In fact, the very next week after he reluctantly left, we had the great pleasure of receiving Pickett Daddy. We would listen to his stories and jokes. We would all sleep outdoors in the backyard in cots with mosquito nets. I awoke one morning to the sound of clapping from Pickett Daddy's tent. I wondered if he had adopted the Indian tradition of morning bhajan, which involved chanting and clapping. But as it turns out, he was merely fighting off mosquitoes that had managed to get inside the netting.

This ended up being our last visit with him, because a few

months later he passed away peacefully in Madison. We all wept when we heard the news, for he was truly like my second father. We maintained a long-term correspondence with Mrs Pickett to help her through her years of widowhood until her passing away in the 1980s.

Later, we were fortunate to host other Madison friends when they visited Delhi. Dr and Mrs Winans came and stayed with us. From the Mitchell family, several of their boys came through New Delhi on their globe-spanning travels during their college years. Steve Mitchell came when we were gone on travels of our own, but we had left word with our neighbors, and they took him in for several days; and a few years later, Bob and Bill Mitchell came and stayed with us.

We were also fortunate to host Dr Eleanor Zelliot, who was one of the first scholars to study the Ambedkar movement, and the effects of the conversion to Buddhism on the dalits. She also worked with dalit literature, translating texts from the Marathi. In 1964, when she came to Delhi for research, I took her around the city and to neighboring villages to talk to social workers. She spoke fluent Marathi, but not Hindi, the prevailing language of the Delhi region. I arranged a Dr Ambedkar Study Circle at the Ambedkar Bhavan when she visited, and we met with Bhagwan Das, a chronicler of the dalit movement, who had just put together the first of his four-volume *Thus Spoke Ambedkar* series. At a celebration of Ambedkar Jayanti years later at Columbia University, Eleanor Zelliot would remark that, 'Nimgade is the second mahar after Dr Ambedkar to get his Ph.D. from the USA.'

WHEN ASHOK STARTED going to school, it became difficult to bicycle with all three children, so I sent them by public bus. The erratic bus schedules combined with the crowded conditions proved cumbersome, so I then sent them by auto-rickshaw, even though this further added to our financial burdens. Later, a teacher in their school, Mrs Vachher, who lived nearby, kindly offered to take our children along with hers in their family car to and from school together.

Ashok was a picky eater when growing up, and once I found that he had thrown his school tiffin away in the toilet. I was so overcome with anger, because of my childhood spent in famine, that for a day we did not cook any food, to let our children experience hunger. The next morning Ashok was starving and asked for forgiveness. I told him that at his age I was often working the fields on an empty stomach. I suggested that he do penance and touch the feet of his mother, the provider of care and food in the house.

The children learned this lesson well. Years later, when they studied in the USA, they wrote back about how saddened they were to see so much food in the dining halls often going to waste. To this day, whenever they eat they avoid wasting food, remembering my childhood poverty.

Ashok would often lose or break things, like his lunchbox or his glasses, or scuff his shoes and tear his socks. One morning when I was helping him tie his shoes to get ready for school, I became enraged because he was not cooperating. While lifting my hand to slap him, the front leg of the stool I was sitting on lifted off the ground. The fearful but quick-thinking Ashok quickly pushed the leg up and I ended up landing on my back. Scared, Ashok ran outside and took refuge behind his mother.

I approached, full of wrath. Hira now turned upon me, saying, 'You take care of everyone one else who is in need, but you often neglect our own children. You even give away the sweaters that I had to hand-knit for them. If I die you won't be able to protect my children or care for them. The only thing you will be able to do is bring them to my samadhi (my gravestone).'

I replied, 'What samadhi? Instead of building a samadhi for you, I shall use the money to acquire a new wife!'

'That is your plan? Then I refuse to die!' replied Hira hotly. 'I will never die and I will never give you a chance to get a new wife!'

At this point we had to stop arguing and start laughing with each other. To this day, whenever we recall this episode, we always end up laughing. Truly, the strains that society had placed upon my family were great; but with the grace of God I was blessed with such a wonderful wife and family. In this manner we struggled together, sometimes fighting and quarreling, but always making up, and sharing the ups and downs of life.

'An Untouchable has won world status'

In 1968, I was invited to present a paper based on my research at the International Science Congress in Adelaide, Australia. Caste politics and bureaucracy continued to dog me as my boss wanted to go to Australia in my place. I had to go to the head of the institute, M.S. Swaminathan, a wonderfully open-minded world-class scientist who was a leader in India's Green Revolution, and explain my case.

But even after I was chosen, arranging for the visa proved difficult. All three other scientists were chosen very quickly, obtained their visas and left the country on time. With bureaucratic dawdling over my case, it was only through the intervention of a Member of Parliament, Arjun Shripal Kasture, that in the nick of time I gained the passport and visa. Other hurdles also came my way in gaining permission from the Reserve Bank of India and obtaining a release of funds from the Agriculture Ministry. By the time these hurdles were overcome, however, no seats were left on the airplane.

In desperation, I called the Minister of Aviation, Dr Karan Singh, and explained the difficulties I faced as a Scheduled Caste scientist. He graciously arranged for a seat, and I was able to join the Science Congress two days later in Adelaide.

When I met the conference organizer, I was full of fears about having been so late. My fears were by no means alleviated when he greeted me with the words, 'You have come to die.'

'No, no,' I protested, 'I will be going back to India to live my life, but I have come for the conference to present my paper.'

'Ah,' he said, 'But I see that you have come to die!'

Finally we realized that his Australian accent had misled me. He was only observing that 'you have come *today*.'

In the fields of the Indian Agricultural Research Institute, Delhi.

I SPENT THE next few days in the library to refine my presentation and catch up on reading the latest scientific literature.

When it came time to present my talk, I started with a remembrance of Dr Ambedkar, explaining briefly how his efforts had made possible my presentation. My own style of talking is different from that of other scientists. When I explain things, I sprinkle in stories and humor and also speak from the heart. My talk was very well received and mine was chosen as one of the six best conference papers.

The next day, which was also 15 August, India's Independence Day, the leading Adelaide newspaper, the *Adelaide Advertiser*, carried an article declaring 'An Untouchable has Won World Status.' This led to more interviews from the press including a television interview.

Dr Kanwar, the Deputy Director General of the Indian Council of Agricultural Research, telephoned me at my hotel saying that the Indian government would not be happy that I was giving all these interviews to the Australian press. I explained that I was only trying to spread good will for our country, not trying to besmirch it.

In the meantime I mailed a copy of the newspaper article to Dr M.S. Swaminathan, the head of our institute in New Delhi, who appeared delighted. I also sent a copy to Prime Minister Indira Gandhi.

At a reception with the South Australia Premier, Dr Hall, when I got a chance to shake hands with him, I mentioned my desire to see how farming is done in Australia. He assured me that he would make this happen. On 17 August he picked me up in his official car and took me to tour his own family farm where I got to meet his parents and even have a meal with them.

I was overcome by the warmth of the Australians, which reminded me of my time in Wisconsin. The Shearer family, the Cooper family, and Reverend Coventry all invited me into their homes to stay with them. I truly appreciated this as it allowed me to stretch my meager travel funds, which allowed me to travel through the Philippines and Hong Kong on my return home. I was sad that our schedules did not allow me to meet with Dr Chandler, who was now stationed in the Philippines. It was through his kindness, after all, that the Rockefeller Foundation had arranged for my US education and my subsequent scientific triumphs.

MY BOSS, HOWEVER, sought revenge for my trip to Australia by allowing the funding for my post, which came through the US government PL480 program, to expire.

I had to explain my case personally to the Prime Minister, Indira Gandhi. I explained that this funding expiration likely came about from my talking so freely with the Australian press. I asked her, 'Have I done any wrong by talking with the Australian newspapers?' She smiled and recollected reading the Australian article about me. She said, 'No. In this manner you have shown that we do have democracy in our country.'

My boss, fortunately for me, was promoted elsewhere. In his place came the sensitive Dr Ramamurthy. He knew about the discrimination that I had faced and immediately promoted me on an ad hoc basis as a Senior Class I Officer. But a year later, when it came time for interviews for permanent status, Dr Kanwar, of the Ministry of Agriculture, who had questioned my contacts with the press in Australia, exacted his revenge. He gave the job to a freshly minted Ph.D. candidate who was far junior to me, and I reverted to my prior post.

Fortunately, the forward thinking Director-General Dr Pal advanced me to a new post as Senior Class I Scientist. This, however, was in the agronomy division, in a somewhat different field. My chief here was Dr Bains, a Sikh scientist of the highest moral character. I very much enjoyed working with him.

I used my promotion to help Scheduled Caste students with certificates or letters of recommendation. I wanted to remove any bureaucratic hurdles in their way. Many of these former students have now gained prominent positions and are posted all over India. Wherever I travel, I often visit them and they invite me to stay with them.

A few months later, the institute director Dr Swaminathan sent a jeep to my home to summon me to his office. When I arrived he said, 'Dr Nimgade, I want to make you the hostel warden at the institute. I believe that you will be the best choice for this since you have such a wonderful relationship with the students.'

With so much trust placed in my hands, how could I refuse? But I worried about how I could take care of the 400 male and 50 female students. Furthermore, the prior few hostel wardens had had a rather bitter relationship with the students that had ended in their resignations. I asked Hira for her advice and she said, 'What is there to fear? This post calls for sensitivity to the needs of students, helping them through periods of difficulty and providing them advice. You have already been doing these tasks out of the goodness of your heart. Everything will work out.'

After that I would spend time after work making the rounds of the three hostels on my bicycle, asking students how they were doing. Sometimes I would have to arrange for transporting sick students to the city hospital. Once, while arranging for furnishing the new hostel, I had difficulty convincing the contractor to provide high quality furniture. He kept shrewdly trying to pass on inferior quality furniture, which I repeatedly refused. Finally, he appeared one day at my house and asked me what type of commission I was getting. This, no doubt, was prelude to a bribe. But I told him firmly that my only commission consisted of seeing the happiness of the students in having good furnishings.

I arranged for things such as better accommodations for married students, a Scheduled Caste/Scheduled Tribe scholarship and seat reservation, informal interview-coaching programs, and travel allowances for visiting academic candidates. Although I was a popular hostel warden, I stepped down after four years. For all my work, I did get a nominal increase in salary, but I donated this to the national defense fund. The job also provided a phone line at my residence. But this proved a double-edged sword, since not too many people had phones at that time, and we ended up with many neighbors knocking at our door day and night to use the phone.

I also established a Scheduled Caste and Scheduled Tribes Welfare Association at IARI. People selected me to serve as president, and I continued as president until my retirement. We would help investigate incidents such as job suspensions, and would sometimes meet with the supervisors. Our meetings were held anywhere from under a tree to my own living room. As our membership grew, we would meet in auditorium halls.

For the Buddhists among us, we set up the Siddhartha Welfare Centre. I was chosen to serve as president for this as well. Each Ambedkar and Buddha Jayanti we would celebrate together. Eventually, we set up centers in major cities such Bombay, Pune, Nagpur, Indore, Patna, and Bhopal. We also helped with converting people from the downtrodden castes to Buddhism and we tried to provide any form of assistance we could. We would set up essay contests, debates and art exhibitions; and also cultural, sports, and educational programs. Hira would often win sports competitions for women in her group such as races and musical chairs. I, on the other hand, would often finish towards the end. We would also serve as watchdogs, to ensure that government funds allocated toward the wellbeing of our people were not diverted into the pockets of politicians. Often we would bring reports of atrocities committed on our people in the villages to the attention of prominent politicians. I served as elected president for 20 years and Hira served as vice-president for two.

In November 1969, I took Hira to Indira Gandhi's bungalow for her birthday celebrations. Hira never had believed the story of my rescuing the young Indira at the airport, so this was my chance to show her. At this stage, Indira had been Prime Minister for about five years and was quite popular. The signature silver streak in her hair was just starting to show. A few thousand well-wishers had gathered with flowers and garlands. As Hira and I drew closer, Indira spotted me and waved me closer. 'Bhai-sahib, come!' I drew forward and said, 'Madame, please meet my wife.' Hira stepped forward and shyly said, 'Happy Birthday!'

Indira graciously replied, 'Oh, Bhabiji, please have some sweets.' She picked up a sweet from a plate and placed it in Hira's folded hands.

WHEN DR BAINS passed away quite suddenly, a scientist who hailed from Maharashtra became my new supervisor. Although we shared the same home state, he did everything to make my and everyone else's life miserable. I later found out that he had turned his own wife and children out of his house. Truly, there is a correlation between discrimination and other forms of injustice.

At the last moment the new boss canceled a tour to Bangalore that I had worked on for several months. Then Dr Swaminathan asked me to serve as his emissary to the National Integration Society meeting in Calcutta since he could not go himself. When I showed Dr Swaminathan's letter to my boss his countenance clouded, like that of a hunter who sees his prey escape.

At the conference, many of the younger Bengali organizers were in an unsettled state of mind and were unwilling to listen to non-Bengali speakers. I was warned about this before I stepped to the podium. This is what I said:

> Dear friends, twenty-five years ago I was young and dashing like you. In 1946 during the state elections, riots broke out at Nagpur and bullets were fired at the mob. I was canvassing there for a candidate from my community. My friend Ramdas Dongre was killed by a bullet. But I missed death. Therefore I am alive and standing here in front of you to share my views. I personally thank you kindhearted Bengali people who elected Dr Ambedkar to the Constitutional Assembly. Therefore he had the opportunity to frame one of the finest constitutions in the world. The Bengalis thus provided the best example of cooperation between different states, thus paving the way to national integration. We should forget all of our differences and work whole-heartedly together for the progress of our Motherland.

The short speech was well received. The Bengali hosts, in particular, were very pleased. This helped reset the tone for the conference.

IN THE EARLY 1970s, the Ford Foundation set up the Water Technology Center at IARI, and I was posted there.

Dr Vinod Shah was an agricultural scientist from a higher caste. He came from a rich family and he had been promoted above me. But he was a victim of politics and bureaucracy, and he committed suicide because of blocked promotions. This led to a big outcry and the establishment of a commission of inquiry headed by the retired Chief Justice of India. In the course of reviewing the materials and interviewing numerous scientists, he also interviewed me. Justice Gajendragadkar said, 'Dr Nimgade, I see that several times your juniors were given promotions, while your claims were neglected. You had every reason to commit suicide, but I find that you are quite calm and composed. How can that be?'

I replied, 'I feel that life is a gift from our parents. It should not be destroyed. I was born in a poor untouchable family in a remote village. I cannot afford the luxury of committing suicide. I must face the world, struggle hard, and educate my children better than myself. I was inspired by Dr Babasaheb Ambedkar.'

Justice Gajendragadkar was very pleased by my words. He had known Dr Ambedkar very well himself.

MY THREE CHILDREN graduated as either first or second in their classes in the American International School. All three of them gave graduation addresses and thus made a clean sweep. Our Nimgade name became very well known in the American International School. Each of our three children ended up leaving us to go to the USA for college. In those days it was very unusual for anyone to go to the USA for education, let alone for undergraduate studies. Our neighborhood was proud and happy for our children. We had to rent a bus to accommodate well-wishers who wanted to see each of our children off to the airport.

Our oldest son, Bhim, went to the University of Wisconsin where I had spent so many years of hard work and made many friends. He stayed with our dear friends, the Mitchell family, in his first year of college, becoming a full brother to their children Barbara, Gene, Tom, Steve, Bob, and Bill.

Rekha was very small and thin when she graduated at the age of sixteen. The airport officials almost did not let her into the USA because she lacked a piece of paper explaining that her living expenses would be covered by Harvard University. She had to firmly and politely insist that Harvard had not admitted her with free tuition, room and board, only to neglect her personal expenses. Upon her arrival in Boston, her host family, the Krags of Lexington, Massachusetts, were outstanding and extremely helpful throughout her whole college experience.

Rekha's presumed frailty and youth actually proved a blessing in disguise, because something in her brought many people forward to help her. The admissions officer at Harvard, Vicki Smith, arranged for her own sisters – Deyne, Sandy, and Wendy

– and her parents, Howard and Betsy, to keep an eye on Rekha, and thus she had a new family in the West. Sandy, who was married to an Indian gentleman, Ranganath Nayak, a well-known engineer and Indian business executive, provided a bridge between India and the USA that eased her transition. Eventually, Rekha would get married in the house of Deyne and Richard Meadow.

As it turns out, all three of our children gained admission to the prestigeous Harvard University, and we received many people from this institution in our own home. One of them was a gentleman from Taiwan, Samson Tu. He would stand in the kitchen taking detailed notes about recipes while Hira cooked.

One rainy day in the monsoon season we heard a knocking at the door. We opened it to find a Caucasian girl of about 20, and she kneeled down to touch my feet in the traditional Indian gesture of respect for elders. I was astonished. As it turns out, she was my daughter Rekha's roommate in college, Elizabeth Toll. She and Rekha had become like sisters, and she had assimilated much information about our Indian ways and civilization. Rekha had written us to inform us about her coming, but the mail was slow, and only two days later did we receive the letter of introduction.

In the meantime we had firmly bonded. Elizabeth referred to us as Uncle and Aunty and looked upon Ashok as the brother she never had. She and Ashok one day decided to play a joke on my aged mother, who was staying with us for a long visit. Ashok put his large orange kurta on my very short mother, and it reached down to her shins. Next Elizabeth put her green hat on my mother's head. The effect was most comical, and we referred to her as the "human carrot." She laughed heartily too, as she posed for several pictures in the garden.

IN THE TWO weeks she was with us, Elizabeth would occasionally massage my feet, as I was ill at the time. A few days before Elizabeth visited us, while in the fields of my institute, I had experienced some chest pain. The doctor informed me that I had hypertension. I immediately underwent a course of bed rest and no salt. But then I developed intransigent hiccups. I could not eat or sleep as the hiccups continued day and night. Finally, the doctor questioned me closely and after finding out that I had eliminated salt he gave me drops of iodine. The hiccups went away.

The good thing was that I now lost some weight. Since that time I have maintained this lower weight and I go for morning walks regularly. I have returned to my interests in herbal medicines, building on what I had learned during my growing up in the village.

My walking has slowed down with time, but in 2003, when we visited the USA, my son Ashok, who is a physician in Boston, insisted that we walk as much as we could. Hira and I would go for short walks, but in the month we were there our walks grew longer and longer, partly because of my habit of talking with everyone. In our last week, we had gone so far that we forgot our way back. For some two hours we walked around, up and down the hilly area, looking for his place. Ashok used this story to set an example to his overweight patients. He was very pleased when a patient came to his office sweating profusely, explaining that he had decided to jog to the clinic because of my example.

The status of health in India has changed very much since my childhood. When I was a boy, many children died in infancy, including my own sister Rukmini's children, and three of my wife Hira's siblings. With increasing wealth and lifespans we Indians and other citizens of the world are plagued with diabetes, asthma, and hypertension. We need to learn to deal with these new problems. The path of Buddhism fits beautifully to help people by cultivating peacefulness of the mind and by paying attention to the breath through Vipassana meditation. I find myself returning to the simple diet of my early days in the village, and in that respect I have come full circle.

WHEN THE LAST of our three children left the nest, we felt very lonely in the house. My mother was still visiting us and she would always remember the children. Hira had difficulty with her housework. She would barely be able to make food. By this time my hunger was increasing, now that I was recovering from my ailment. So I said to her, 'You may feel bad, but the rest of us are starving!' After that things started normalizing slowly. Hira and I developed new interests, attending more functions in Delhi, such as events at the Indian International Centre. We also went to every international Buddhist event that took place in Delhi including visits of the Dalai Lama and other Buddhist leaders.

One day, during lunchtime at work, I started chatting with a young man named Rambhaj from Haryana who had just come from the villages. I invited him to eat at our home. He declined politely, saying that it might not be appropriate for him to eat at the house of a senior officer. I told him these distinctions did not matter, and then I inquired whether there were any issues involving caste that might prevent him from eating with me, a dalit. Rambhaj's eyes brightened and he informed me that he was also from the Scheduled Castes. At my home he saw pictures of Dr Ambedkar and the Buddha. He inquired about these personages and I told him their story. Rambhaj was so inspired that thereafter he would read any relevant material I could find in Hindi for him. He struck me as being very intelligent despite only having a middle school education. Upon my encouragement, he enrolled in correspondence courses and finished school and college. I tutored him in several subjects along the way.

Today he is a technical assistant in the Indian Agricultural Research Institute. Through hard work he has now enjoyed the fruits of education such as a nice home and a car. He spends much time helping convert other people to Buddhism and often hosts Buddhists at his home. His children are continuing with the odyssey of further education and were married in the Buddhist tradition.

I encouraged other students in a similar fashion. One memorable student was Banwari Lal Suman, who started as a technical assistant. Hira and I encouraged him to get his B.Sc.

and eventually a Ph.D. His wife also gained a Ph.D. At their wedding I conducted the Buddhist marriage ceremony. Because his mother had just had a cataract operation, Hira stood in her place. Banwari was moved to remark, 'When I was born, I had just one mother; but now Mrs Nimgade has stood in the role of mother at my wedding, and I am blessed with two mothers.'

In May 1977, we celebrated the wedding of Hira's youngest brother, Yuvraj, in Nagpur. My mother decided to use this as an opportunity to return to our home village. Now our home in Delhi felt entirely empty.

We decided to travel as much as possible to weddings or other functions. On the 25th anniversary of our wedding the following year, we made a grand tour of south India, touching all the corners of our great country. I will always remember one of our journeys: in February 1984, in Bombay, at a cultural night in honor of Dr Ambedkar, a few writers and scientists from our community were feted. I was one of the notable members of our community selected for this honor.

IN THE FOLLOWING years, our children have visited us several times and we have also been able to return to the USA. Once, when my son Ashok visited Delhi, we took our neighbor's young son Akshay to the Delhi Zoo, which is housed behind the ancient walls of the Old Fort. While Ashok was taking photographs I absent-mindedly put his blazer jacket on the grass by a tiger's cage. The tiger sauntered toward the jacket and then relieved its bladder, spraying the jacket while my son watched horrified. I quickly pointed out the upside, 'Just think, Ashok. You will be the only person in America whose jacket is blessed with tiger urine!'

On one trip to Madison, we were pleased to see that the field of Buddhist studies was flourishing at the University of Wisconsin. We arrived during a world Buddhist conference. A Tibetan Buddhist spiritual and learning center called Deer Park was established outside of Madison in the beautiful countryside. The Dalai Lama had also come for ceremonies at Deer Park. Our son Bhim visited India as part of an international science delegation for studying the monsoons. This involved him flying in a research plane over the ocean and over the monsoon clouds.

I was also pleased to have a reunion in Toronto, Canada, with Yogesh Varhade, an intelligent man from our community for whom I had earlier written sixteen letters of recommendation. Now he had completed his studies in engineering and was a successful businessman. He had started an international group called VISION—Volunteers in Service of India's Oppressed and Neglected.

During one of our visits to the USA in 1981, we tried to meet with the Indian ambassador to the USA, K.R. Narayanan, who was also from the Scheduled Castes. We spoke on the phone. I said, 'Thanks to the grace and the hard work of Dr Ambedkar I could become a scientist and you could become an ambassador.' We recalled how, years earlier, in New Delhi, when he had been appointed ambassador, our Scheduled Caste Association, of which I was president, had feted him on the occasion. He invited us to dine with him, but we could not because of our schedules. Years later, in 1997, to our great pride, he rose to become the President of India.

A second generation Buddhist wedding

On 31 March 1985, my mother, who was weakening, finally passed. We quickly made plans to go to Nagpur, but unfortunately could not even make it to the last rites. To this day, I feel very bad that I could not perform the duties of the oldest son. Her lifetime had spanned so many changes, from a primitive village with no light or running water to a period when men had walked on the moon. Her love was the center of my life and brings to mind the Marathi verse:

> *Swami teenhe jagga cha; Ai bina bhikari.*
>
> (Even the Lord of the three realms, bereft of a mother is a beggar.)

One month later, in April 1985, I retired from the Indian Agricultural Research Institute after thirty three years of service. Several farewell parties were held for me. At the Water Technology Center, everyone from the director to the sweepers held a big celebration and presented me with a large clock. The Scheduled Castes and Scheduled Tribes Welfare Association also held a similar program and gave me a beautiful bronze statue of the Buddha. Other festivities were held in different offices where I had served.

The first morning of my retirement I slept in late and then read the newspaper. I felt no need to rush. I started talking to Hira about my thoughts and experiences. After about two hours of listening patiently, she politely said, 'You have retired, but I have not. I still have my daily household tasks.'

Embarrassed, I said, 'Then let me come to the kitchen, and I will cook alongside you.' I took a knife and started chopping vegetables. Hira joked, 'If you keep this up, soon I shall be the one retiring!' We started laughing together, and she became the only woman in our generation to have her husband alongside her in the kitchen.

I was still able to help our community in retirement. I encouraged Mr Kasture, Member of Parliament, to build a memorial to Babasaheb Ambedkar at his birthplace. When Mr Kasture asked for my advice on someone to edit the unpublished papers of Dr Ambedkar, I suggested Vasantrao Moon. I told him, 'I am not proposing Mr Moon because he is my brother-in-law, but rather because I have gotten to know him very well and am aware of his wide-ranging interests and capabilities. He will be able to accomplish this ambitious task.' Indeed, Mr Moon proved worthy of this great labor, producing some seventeen thick volumes.

Fortunately, Hira and I had already built up a foundation of activity and travel to keep us busy after my retirement. I visited my native Sathgaon village several times and was pleased to see the progress being made by our people. Now there were statues and paintings of the Buddha and Dr Ambedkar as well as the flag of the Panchsheel (the fivefold Buddhist vows) in several corners of the village. Now the villagers had some electricity and running water.

IN 1987, REKHA visited India to seek our permission to marry. She had met a gentleman named Krishna Doraiswamy (Chandru), a tall scientist and management professional with whom she had met and developed a friendship. His family was Tamil brahmin, but they were progressive and did not observe caste restrictions. He met all of the criteria one would want in a spouse and son-in-law: scholarly, kind, thoughtful, and more. Caste never entered into their decision to marry each other.

For the next several months, my mind was filled with preparations for Rekha's wedding. About a week before the big event, I was walking with a stack of invitation cards to distribute, with my mind far away, when I felt a violent impact on my leg and all the cards flew out of my hands. My last words as I fell dazed in the dust were, 'My daughter's wedding...!'

I felt a great pain in my knee, and I struggled to get up, but my leg did not seem to work. A man on a scooter had just hit me. Fortunately, the driver was a good man and, instead of driving away, he came to my assistance. The police arrived and asked if I wanted to register a case. I was afraid that a police case might interfere with my travel plans, so I said, 'No. This was my fault, I was negligent. I am an old man who was lost in thought.'

My kneecap was dislocated, and had shifted to the side, but summoning what determination I could, I pulled it back to its original track. I also refused a trip to the hospital since I feared they might put my leg in a cast and thus limit my mobility.

I ended up riding back home on the back seat of the scooter. I even gave him a wedding invitation. I was trying to hide my

Ashok, Rekha, Krishna, Bhim, Meenakshi Moon, Hira and I on the occasion of Rekha's wedding. Meenakshi Moon, Hira's sister, has written several books in Marathi about the contribution women have made to the Ambedkarite movement; a few years before her death in 2004, Meenakshi had launched a Marathi magazine Amhi Maitrani (We are Girlfriends) *to provide a platform to the voices and struggles of Ambedkarite women.*

wound from Hira, lest she forbid me from traveling to attend Rekha's wedding. I went next door to our neighbors and close friends the Marwah family, and took Dr Marwah into my confidence. He was a fellow agricultural scientist, a doctor of entomology, and his standard treatment for any crying child, whether from a tantrum or a scraped knee or a spanking from a parent, was to first exclaim, 'Go drink a glass of cold water!' Then he would examine the child and prescribe treatment, even giving pills and medicines of which he somehow had a store. Thus, an entomologist served as my children's pediatrician.

Dr Marwah's boy, Nishu, and our children would roam freely through our adjoining apartments making little distinction between the two. Now Dr Marwah helped me with herbal remedies and massage. Eventually, though, Hira saw me limping and intermittently clutching my knee. In any case, my leg was swelling now. For the next several days I lay down with my leg elevated. Fortunately, I was able to travel, though I did have to use a cane.

Hira and I garland each other on the fiftieth anniversary of our wedding as our children look on.

Rekha and Chandru got married Buddhist style at the beautiful home of Rekha's adopted family, Richard and Deyne Meadow, at Canton, just near Boston. They, along with Richard's parents, Henry and Mary, had arranged for a beautiful tent with nice food and drinks, with flowers flown in from Hawaii. Our friend, Yogesh Varhade, drove from Toronto with his family, bringing with him a Sri Lankan Buddhist monk from the Buddhist temple of Toronto to preside over the ceremonies. Deyne Meadow's parents, Howard and Betsy Tompkins were very helpful in writing a pamphlet for guests that explained the wedding rituals and ceremonies. Even so, the arrangement must have appeared confusing to some visitors.

Rekha was in a sari, Chandru in a kurta-pyjama, and the monk, Bhante Punnaji, in his saffron robes with a shaven head. All four of Rekha's adopted American sisters – Vicki, Deyne, Sandy, and Wendy – were resplendent in colorful saris. One of the guests, Robert Gordon was dressed in formal Scottish attire, with a kilt. Our monk was much impressed with Mr Gordon's booming voice and imposing presence, and commandeered to stand at the entrance to the Unitarian church and direct the guests. A Muslim friend of Rekha's had arrived just in time for the reception and had missed the wedding ceremony. He joined the reception line and joyfully embraced the bride, but when he turned to congratulate the groom, whom he had never met, he somehow got disoriented and reached his hand out to congratulate the monk! Fortunately, the quick thinking Chandru thrust his hand out to shake his and thus defused any embarrassment.

Chandru's mother made a lovely toast (using a soft drink in a champagne glass). For my toast, I said 'I am moved by seeing the grand wedding ceremony and reception. We parents have given birth to dear Rekha, but she has been raised by her American sisters, family, and friends like the Meadows, Tompkins, Mitchells, Tolls, Klionskys... May the teachings of the Lord Buddha and Dr Ambedkar guide this couple through a happy and prosperous marriage.'

While Rekha and Chandru honeymooned in Europe, Hira and

I went on our own second honeymoon. Rekha and Chandru would eventually have two wonderful children who bear the Buddhist names of Karuna and Rahul. At the invitation of the social activist Barbara Joshi, I participated in a conference sponsored by Amnesty International and spoke about the oppression of the dalits in India. Accompanying us was Hira's sister, Meenakshi Moon, who would become a prominent writer about the dalit women's movement. We were able to attend the graduation ceremony of our son Ashok from MIT I was also pleased to see the large and beautiful Peace Pagoda built by Japanese Buddhist monks in Massachusetts.

HIRA AND I celebrated our golden wedding jubilee in 2003 during a visit to the USA. Several families hailing from different

During the golden jubilee celebration of Babasaheb's conversion at Nagpur in October 2006, Dr Christopher Queen from Harvard University visited our family. Ashok is seated as Hira holds our wedding portrait.

parts of India and of varying heritages attended the event. The cake was decorated with our wedding photograph, and it brought back memories of our fifty years together. The laughter and shouts of the young children playing around the tables filled me with gratitude that these children would grow up without the borders of caste or creed to separate them from one another.

But for less fortunate children in rural and even urban regions within India's borders, the struggle against caste discrimination will go on for decades to come, as evidenced by ongoing reports of heinous crimes and atrocities still being committed in the name of caste. It took centuries in the USA to fight race discrimination, and, despite numerous triumphs, the struggle still continues.

The Buddha and Dr Ambedkar, and other luminaries such as Kabir, Christ, and Mahatma Jotiba Phule, over the centuries have offered us solutions, and we would do well to remember their teachings. Dr Ambedkar was unique in embodying the multiple facets of his genius to use political, legal, social, and religious structures to fight the evils of discrimination based on caste, gender, and other divisions.

As I look back on my life, I see how Dr Ambedkar's example has guided me. He exhorted people to advance themselves, and to pull their whole community forward. I have been helped by many good people, from my humble village to people all over the world, as I advanced. I had to work hard to make my career in agriculture. And then I helped other students to come up. I have worked for social reform and I have also tried to help others in person, mentoring them and telling them of my struggles and how I was able to overcome them.

It was with a feeling of great gratitude for his contributions and inspiration, that in October 2006, I attended the 50th anniversary of Babasaheb's mass conversion to Buddhism at Nagpur, at the sacred grounds of Dikshabhoomi. Hundreds of thousands of people attended this event, not only from nearby villages, but from every corner of India and even the world. The national press downplayed the event, but that did not deter scholars from Japan, Europe and America – such as Dr Christopher Queen of Harvard – from attending. Visitors alighted at Nagpur's beautifully renovated airport, now renamed 'Dr Babasaheb Ambedkar Airport.'

At Dikshabhoomi I walked with family members inside the grand stupa and circled around the central sanctum where the ashes of Babasaheb are interred. I had massaged his limbs and I had guarded him from the crowds when he was alive. Now his physical body was gone, with just dust and ashes left within the stupa. But the Constitution that he gave India remains, to wisely guide the destiny of over a billion people in the world's largest democracy. For myself, I heard once more his booming voice, chiding and hectoring me in the caring manner of my elders, sometimes even praising me like a proud father, his strong spirit always illuminating and inspiring me.

At the Dikhshbhoomi on the fiftieth anniversary of Babasaheb Ambedkar's mass conversion to Buddhism in Nagpur with Hira and Ashok.

A village boy returns home

I returned many times to my ancestral home, each time providing a precious opportunity to recollect those old times of poverty, hard work, and frequent and arbitrary humiliation. Shortly after my retirement in October of 1998, my wife Hira and I went to Umrer where we also visited Tara, whom I had been so smitten with in my youth. I presented her with a copy of my autobiography in Marathi. She was very happy, and held my hand in the presence of my wife, saying, 'Namdeo, I have always loved you, and I always will.' She turned to my wife and said, 'You are the most fortunate woman.' My wife Hira and I both felt that this was the finest expression of pure human affection.

In the intervening years, Tara had married a railway ticket checker. They had three daughters. But about five years after the marriage, tragedy struck. While working, Tara's husband took a misstep and fell from the moving train and was killed. One of her daughters married a millionaire's son; his family was opposed to the union, because they preferred a wealthier daughter-in-law. But love prevailed. This son-in-law was very pleasant and we got along quite well. He informed me that Tara had told him of our love for each other in our youth.

Once, after I had earned my Ph.D., I returned to Umrer for a visit, and came across Chimurkar, my old school classmate and class monitor. Back then, he had once been harsh and impatient with me, even to the point of urinating on me to show his superiority.

'Nama Bhao,' he spoke quietly to me now. 'I have remained here in this small area all my life. But you have traveled the world!'

I replied, 'It was your sprinkling of holy water that provided the determination to make this all possible!' We shared a good laugh together.

Another story illustrates the turning wheel of time, which lets nothing stand still, sometimes shaking the fortunate and the powerful from their lofty positions, while the poor and oppressed rise. In 1962, after I had earned my Ph.D., I went to visit friends and relatives in Umrer. Shortly after getting off the bus that brought me there, I noticed a poor man in tattered, dirty clothes, dragging one foot as he approached me. His hair was disheveled and his beard was ragged. Who knows how many days had passed since he had a bath?

'Sir, please give me some money,' he implored. 'I have had nothing to eat for a few days.'

On hearing his voice, I stopped and looked at him closely, and with surprise, I recognized him as Neelkanth Rao Mutthe, the proud father who had fed thousands of guests at a grand wedding for his daughter—the same wedding where I had tasted the discarded patals of food with my cousin Phajit. How could this same man now be holding out his hands to beg for a few coins? Where did his wealth and happiness disappear, where was his large and extended family? How true was the devotional poet Sant Kabir's saying, *'Issa tana dhana kee kaun badhayi? Dekhata naina mitti milai.'* (Why be proud of your beauty and wealth? Even as you look, they mix with the dust and vanish.)

I felt compassion for him. Even though I was not rich, I felt that I was fortunate to have the wealth of education. I took him to a nearby roadside restaurant and let him eat his fill. I contemplated how time and circumstances could change and reduce a person to nothing. In Sanskrit we have a saying, *'Kalaya tasmaya namaha.'* (We bow down to Time.)

On one occasion in 1968, I was being driven in a friend's car in the neighboring village marketplace in Maharashtra. Automobiles were still rare, and an evident sign of wealth. From the car window, I spied in the crowd an elderly barefoot man in ragged clothes. I recognized him as my old teacher who had beaten me back in my school days so long ago. I asked the driver to stop, and I called out to my teacher, 'Oh, Guruji. It is I, Namdeo.' Recognition flashed in his eyes, giving way to a look of embarrassment.

I stepped out of the car and said, 'Now that we are an independent nation and untouchability is a crime, we are allowed to touch each other. I have for so many years wanted to thank you for giving me the gift of learning. Therefore, Guruji, I am now determined to show you the reverence due to our teachers.' I bowed down and touched his feet in respect. He made no move to step aside, and, instead, put his hand on me. As he reached to help me up to my feet I saw his eyes welling with tears.

Despite all the foregoing about the reversals of fortune, my thoughts are weighed down by this topic. I worked diligently towards success, at great cost to me and later to my family as well—years of degrading humiliation I could have done without. With limited food and denial of opportunities I saw sister after sister succumb to illness and constant stress. Would more relatives, friends, and others sharing our lot have lived longer and healthier lives had they been able to eat and live with more security and quality? Despite the remarkable progress India has been making as an economic and intellectual powerhouse, the struggle goes on for countless millions still in the grip of poverty.

My wonderful identity card

During an excursion in recent years that Hira and I made to Bombay, I took a side trip alone to India's Bhabha Atomic Research Centre. This was a high security facility with armed guards. Although I had arranged for this trip as a visiting scientist, and my name was printed on the visitors list, I had forgotten to bring any identification card with me. The guard tried to help me, and soon we were grasping at straws: any ration card, any letter of introduction? The guard even tried calling a fellow scientist who knew me, but that scientist was in a meeting.

Then, inspiration struck me. I said excitedly, 'Sir, I have a permanent identity card, which is always with me. I have never lost it and it has never left me. Such an effective and most faithful form of identity is in my possession. Let us see if it serves your purpose.'

'Then produce that wonderful identity card,' said the guard skeptically.

I raised my right hand in the air and pulled up my shirtsleeve. There on my forearm was the now blurred tattoo from my childhood in the village. Next to the figure of a Hindu god was my name, "Namdeo Maratrao Nimgade."

The guard was astonished. 'Sir,' he said. 'You are evidently a highly educated scientist, but yet you have this tattoo—the mark of a lowly village beginning! How can that be?'

I related to him my story in a few minutes, essentially a synopsis of this book, about how a poor and illiterate untouchable could leave the bonds and shackles of poverty and discrimination by following the path of Dr Babasaheb Ambedkar. *Tathagat. Jai Bhim*!

The tattoo I got as a child, now blurred. The unlettered tattoo artist's payment came in the form of two handfuls of dry chilies.

Further Readings

Ambedkar, B.R. *Dr. Babasaheb Ambedkar: Writings and Speeches*. Edited by Vasant Moon. Bombay: Education Department, Government of Maharashtra, 1979– . Twenty-three volumes have been published till 2010.

Ambedkar, B.R. *Buddha and His Dhamma,* Nagpur: Buddha Bhoomi Publication, 1997.

Ambedkar, B. R. *The Essential Writings of B. R. Ambedkar* (Ed. Valerian Rodrigues). New Delhi: Oxford University Press, 2002.

Das, Bhagwan. *Revival of Buddhism in India and role of Dr. Babasaheb B.R. Ambedkar*. Lucknow: Dalit Today Prakashan, 1998.

Keer, Dhananjay. *Dr. Ambedkar: Life and Mission*. Bombay: Popular Prakashan, 1954.

Moon, Vasant. *Growing up Untouchable in India: A Dalit Autobiography*. Translated from the Marathi by Gail Omvedt. New Delhi: Vistaar Publications, 2002.

Omvedt, Gail. *Dalits and the Democratic Movement in Colonial India*. New Delhi: Sage Publications, 1994.

Queen, Christopher S. and Sallie B. King, editors. *Engaged Buddhism: Buddhism Liberation Movements in Asia*. Albany: State University of New York Press, 1996.

Robbin, Jeanette. *Dr. Ambedkar and His Movement*. India. Hyderabad: Dr. Ambedkar Publications Society, 1964.

Sangharakshita. *Ambedkar and Buddhism*. Glasgow: Windhorse Publications, 2006.

Zelliot, Eleanor. *From Untouchable to Dalit: Essays on the Ambedkar Movement*. New Delhi: Manohar, 1992.

Zelliot, Eleanor. *Untouchable Saints: An Indian Phenomenon*. Edited with Rohini Mokashi-Punekar. New Delhi: Manohar, 2005.